THE BIG BREAK

ALSO BY STEPHEN DANDO-COLLINS

Operation Chowhound
Legions of Rome

THE BIG BREAK

THE GREATEST AMERICAN
WWII POW ESCAPE STORY NEVER TOLD

STEPHEN DANDO-COLLINS

ST. MARTIN'S PRESS ⚏ NEW YORK

www.stmartins.com

Design by Kelly Too

Maps by Jeffrey L. Ward

Cataloging-in-Publication Data is available at the Library of Congress.

ISBN 9781250087560 (hardcover)

ISBN 9781250087577 (e-book)

Our books may be purchased in bulk for promotional, educational, or business use. Please contact your local bookseller or the Macmillan Corporate and Premium Sales Department at 1-800-221-7945, extension 5442, or by e-mail at MacmillanSpecialMarkets@macmillan.com.

First Edition: January 2017

10 9 8 7 6 5 4 3 2 1

CONTENTS

ACKNOWLEDGMENTS

Many people around the world have contributed to this book's creation. Not least my New York City literary agent, Richard Curtis; my supportive publisher at St. Martin's Press, Karen Wolny; and Karen's assistant, Laura Apperson.

In Poland, I am especially grateful to Mariusz Winiecki, who was born in Szubin and is a passionate researcher of Oflag XXI-B and Oflag 64 history and author of *The Oflag 64 Record* blog. Thank you, also, to German historian Peter Domes, who was born just outside Hammelburg, for detailed information about Task Force Baum from the German perspective.

In the United States, I received enormous help from relatives of Schubin prisoners, starting with Elodie Caldwell, daughter of Reid Ellsworth, who also helped in the illustration search and facilitated my contact with many other members of the Oflag 64 Association. Among those members, I want particularly to thank Marjory Holder, daughter of H. Randolph "Boomer" Holder; Ed Ward, Jr., son of Ed Ward; Brian Rose, grandson of Robert J. Rose; Mary Shular Hopper, daughter of William A. Shular, Jr.; Linda Krueger, daughter of

Alfred C. Nelson; and Mary Meacham, daughter of Merle A. Meacham, for sharing their relatives' memories and mementos.

My sincere thanks, also, go to the very helpful Fania Khan Mohammad of the International Council of the Red Cross, Geneva, Switzerland; Allie Baker of the Ernest Hemingway Project; and Laurie Austin at the John F. Kennedy Presidential Library and Museum, Boston.

Finally, and most importantly, thank you to my dear wife, Louise, my ever-supportive partner in life's adventures.

AUTHOR'S NOTE

Schubin or Szubin?

To Poles, the town where the POW camp known as Stalag XXI-B, then Oflag XXI-B and later Oflag 64, was located, was—and is—known as Szubin. For two centuries, Germans called it Schubin, a name also used by American and British prisoners incarcerated there. In this work, because they were the form used during World War II by POWs, German styles and terms are used.

Likewise, the camp at Sagan (today's Żagań) in Silesia, location of the famous Great Escape, was written as Stalag Luft 3 by German authorities, not Stalag Luft III, the style later adopted in the books of Paul Brickhill, author of *The Great Escape*, and others. Brickhill actually wrote it as Stalag Luft 3 in his early writings, with the change to Roman numerals imposed by his British editors in the 1950s.

GLOSSARY

Abort—German for latrine or lavatory.

Abwehr—German military intelligence.

ADC—aide-de-camp. Junior officer serving as personal assistant to a general staff officer.

Altburgund—German name for Schubin from 1941. The name never caught on, with Germans in the town sticking with Schubin.

Amerikaner—German for American.

Amerikanski—Polish and Russian for American.

Appell—German for roll call.

Appellgrund—parade ground in a camp, where *Appell* was held.

Asselin—code name for escape tunnel at Oflag XXI-B Schubin dug from main *Abort*. Named after Canadian POW Eddy Asselin, who master-minded it.

Aussie (Ozzie)—Australian.

Big S—British code name for head of security on POW camp escape committee.

Big X—British code name for head of POW camp escape committee.

Bulletin, The—daily handwritten American newssheet at Oflag 64.

burp gun—American slang for a submachine gun.

Circuit, the—exercise track around the inside of POW camp wire. Also, *The Circuit*, name of Stalag Luft 3 South Compound newsletter.

CO—commanding officer.

cookhouse tunnel—escape tunnel at Oflag XXI-B Schubin.

Cooler—British and American slang for separate solitary confinement jail in POW camps.

CPM—Captured Personnel and Materiel branch of US Military Intelligence.

ESCOM—USAAF Eastern Command, based at airfields in Russia during 1944–1945.

Ferret—British and American slang for specialist German POW camp guard whose job was to unearth escape activities and contraband. At Oflag 64, the Ferret was the American nickname for the German sergeant who was the camp's chief ferret.

Flak—German for antiaircraft gun/s or fire. Abbreviation of *Fliegerabwehrkanonen*.

Fudge—high-energy POW escape food, in cake form.

G-2—American military intelligence.

Generalmajor—German major general.

Geneva Convention—Third Geneva Convention of 1929. International agreement on the conduct of war, in particular covering the treatment of prisoners of war.

Gestapo—Geheime Staatspolizei, German secret police.

Goo—high-energy POW escape food, in cake form.

goon—British and American slang for German POW camp guard.

goon box—British and American slang for German sentry box.

goon tower—British and American slang for German guard tower.

greatcoat—long, thick military overcoat.

Great Escape, the—Stalag Luft 3 escape by 76 Allied POWs from 13 countries in March 1944. Three reached Britain; the rest were recaptured. Fifty were subsequently executed by the Gestapo. The escape's name came from the international bestselling book by the Australian author and former POW Paul Brickhill, who participated in the escape's preparations. Brickhill wrote the story five different ways before the book finally was published in 1950. It became a one-off NBC TV drama in 1951 featuring Rod Steiger; the most famous adaptation of Brickhill's book is John Sturges' 1963 Hollywood movie version.

Hanomag—lightly armored German halftrack truck.

Hauptmann—German captain.

Hetzer—German 75 mm tank destroyer.

honey wagon—POW slang for vehicle used to remove sewage pumped from camp latrines.

Hundeführer—German dog handler.

Item, The—monthly American camp newspaper at Oflag 64.

Jerry—British and American slang for a German.

Klim—tinned powdered milk received by American and British POWs in Red Cross food parcels. Empty Klim cans were used in escape apparatus, and for stage equipment in Oflag 64's Little Theater.

Kommandant—German commandant.

Kommandantur—German command center at POW camp, outside the prisoner compound.

Kraut—American slang for a German.

kriegie—American and British slang for POWs in German camps. Abbreviation of German *Kriegsgefangener*. Also sometimes written "kriegy."

kriegieitis—American POW term for the chronic depression that seized some prisoners.

Kriegie Kollege—American school for inmates of Oflag 64, operated by inmates. Also called the Altburgund Academy by some kriegies.

Kriegsgefangener—German for prisoner of war.

Kripo—*Kriminalpolizei*. German criminal police.

Lager—German for camp.

Lageroffizier—German officer of the day in POW camps.

Lazarett—German military hospital.

Leutnant—German lieutenant.

Limey—American slang for a British serviceman.

Little Theater—theater created in a barrack block at Oflag 64 by American inmates.

Luftwaffe—German Air Force.

machine pistol—submachine gun with a pistol grip.

mess—dining area in a military camp.

MI9—British WWII security bureau responsible for aiding POW escapees and obtaining information from or via POWs. Part of same military intelligence agency as the more famous MI5 and MI6.

Mixture, the—high-energy POW escape food, in cake form.

MO—medical officer.

M3—American light tank. Known as the Stuart in British and Australian armies, which also used it.

NCO—noncommissioned officer.

NKVD—Peoples' Commissariat for Internal Affairs. Russian state security agency. Forerunner of KGB.

Oberfeldwebel—German master sergeant.

Oberleutnant—German first lieutenant.

Oberst—German colonel.

Oberstleutnant—German lieutenant colonel.

Offizierslager—German for officers' camp.

Oflag—*Offizierslager*.

Oflag 6-B—Allied officer POW camp at Warburg, Germany, 1941–1945.

Oflag 64—American officer POW camp at Schubin, Poland, 1943–1945.

Oflag VII-A/Z—Allied officer POW camp at Rotenburg, Germany, 1943–1945.

Oflag XIII-B—American and Serbian officer POW camp at Hammelburg, Bavaria, 1943–1945.

Oflag XXI-B—British and American officer POW camp at Schubin, Poland, 1942–1943.

OSS—Office of Strategic Services. US spy agency, forerunner of Central Intelligence Agency (CIA).

Personalkarte—German record card for POWs.

POW—prisoner of war.

RAF—Royal Air Force. British air force.

RAMPs—Returned Allied Military Personnel.

recon—reconnaissance.

rugger—rugby football.

Russkies—American slang for Russians.

SAO—senior American officer.

SBO—senior British officer.

Schmeisser—Allied nickname for German MP38 and MP40 submachine gun/machine pistol.

Schubinite—the author's term for a Schubin POW or former Schubin POW.

security committee—at Oflag 64, the American POW escape committee.

Sherman—American M4 medium tank.

6×6—six-wheel, 2.5 ton, American-built Studebaker truck.

SOE—Special Operations Executive. British intelligence and sabotage agency that operated agents behind enemy lines.

Sonderführer—special appointed Nazi rank; not an enlisted man, but not an officer either.

Spandau—Allied name for German MG42 machine gun.

SPG—self-propelled gun.

SS—Schutzstaffel, "defense force," Nazi German special corps. Originally Adolf Hitler's bodyguard. Later encompassed all Nazi security agencies and police.

Stalag—abbreviation of *Stammlager*. German POW camp, usually only for enlisted men, but for all ranks at Luftwaffe-controlled camps.

Stalag Luft 3—air force POW camp at Sagan, Silesia. Sometimes incorrectly written as Stalag Luft III.

Stalag XIII-B—POW camp for enlisted men at Hammelburg, Bavaria. On the northern side of Oflag XIII-B.

Stalag XXI-D—POW camp for enlisted men at Posen, Poland.

stooge—British and American slang for a POW on lookout duty to prevent German discovery of escape activities or material.

Strasse—German for street.

S-2—intelligence officer on US Army headquarters staff. At Oflag 64, the title of head of the escape committee.

tanker—tank crew member.

Task Force Baum—US Third Army task force sent by General George S. Patton to rescue Schubin POWs from Oflag XIII-B at Hammelburg.

Unteroffizier—German corporal.

USAAF—United States Army Air Force.

VE Day—Victory in Europe Day, May 8, 1945.

Volkssturm—German home guard, made up of civilians without uniform.

Vorlager—enclosed area before the camp proper.

Waffen-SS—military wing of the SS. Fielded infantry and armored units.

Weasel—American M29 amphibious armored vehicle. Also, at Oflag 64, American nickname for the deputy ferret, a German corporal of the security detail.

Wehrmacht—German army.

XO—American executive officer, second in command.

X Organization—British code name for POW camp escape committee.

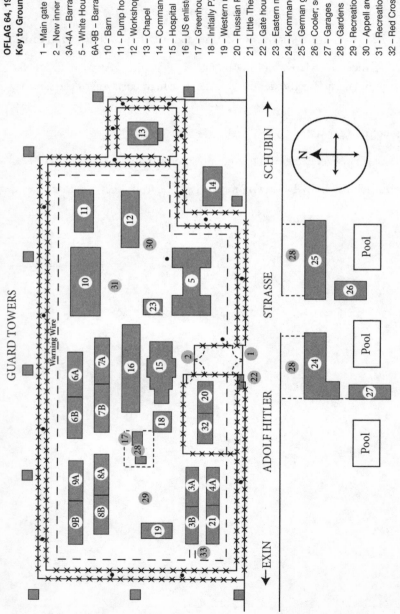

OFLAG 64, 1943-45
Key to Ground Plan

1 – Main gate
2 – New inner gate
3A-4A – Barrack blocks
5 – White House
6A-9B – Barrack blocks
10 – Barn
11 – Pump house
12 – Workshops
13 – Chapel
14 – Commandant's house
15 – Hospital
16 – US enlisted POWs (orderlies)
17 – Greenhouse
18 – Initially PX, later Kriegie Kollege and Mart
19 – Western mass Abort
20 – Russian POW barrack
21 – Little Theater
22 – Gate house
23 – Eastern mass Abort
24 – Kommandantur
25 – German guard barrack
26 – Cooler; solitary confinement cell block
27 – Garages
28 – Gardens
29 – Recreation area, softball/baseball diamond
30 – Appell area
31 – Recreation area, basketball and volleyball courts
32 – Red Cross parcel storage
33 – Cory tunnel
•– Arc light

GUARD TOWERS

Warning Wire

SCHUBIN

STRASSE

ADOLF HITLER

← EXIN

N

Pool

Pool

Pool

OFLAG 64, 1943–45

NORTHERN EUROPE, 1942-45

North Sea

DENMARK

SWEDEN

Baltic Sea

Barth

Danzig

EAST PRUSSIA

USSR

HOLLAND

Rotenburg

Stettin

to Moscow

Schubin

NAZI GERMANY

Berlin

Posen

Hohensalza

Luckenwalde

Warsaw

Rhine R.

Warburg

Sagan

Lublin

BELGIUM

Colditz

POLAND

Frankfurt

Hammelburg

LUXEMBOURG

Area of detail below

Main R.

Nuremberg

FRANCE

Prague

CZECHOSLOVAKIA

Rhine R.

Moosburg

Munich

AUSTRIA

SWITZERLAND

HUNGARY

© 2016 Jeffrey L. Ward

| 0 Miles | 200 |
| 0 Kilometers | 200 |

HAMMELBURG AREA

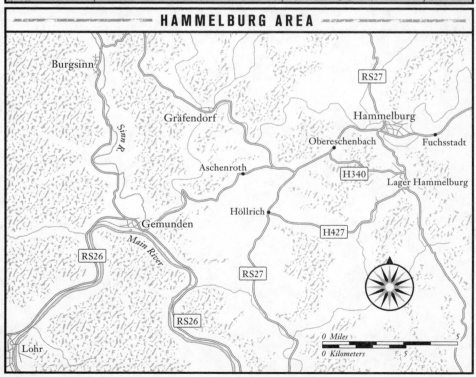

Burgsinn

RS27

Sinn R.

Gräfendorf

Hammelburg

Obereschenbach

Fuchsstadt

Aschenroth

H340

Lager Hammelburg

Höllrich

H427

Gemunden

Main River

RS26

RS27

RS26

Lohr

| 0 Miles | 5 |
| 0 Kilometers | 5 |

THE FIRST AMERICAN TO
ESCAPE FROM SCHUBIN

SKINNY, GAUNT TWENTY-FIVE-YEAR-OLD WILLIAM "BILL" ASH FROM Dallas, Texas, strolled up to the wooden shed that housed the prisoner-of-war camp's communal latrine block—the *Abort*, the Germans called it. A fellow POW lounging against the wall by the door gave Ash a nod. This guy was a "stooge," standing lookout, and the nod indicated the "all clear." With that knowledge, Ash passed through the doorway into the Abort building.

It was Wednesday, March 3, 1943, a bleak winter's day. And this toilet block was the main ablutions facility in the Wehrmacht's *Offizierslager* XXI-B prisoner-of-war camp, built on the western outskirts of the town of Schubin, Poland, or Altburgund, as the Nazis had renamed it in 1941. South of the German Baltic city of Danzig (Polish Gdańsk) and west of the Polish capital of Warsaw (Warszawa), Schubin lay near the Vistula River bend in the prewar Polish Corridor. Here, the Second World War's largest Anglo-American POW escape to date would soon go forward.

Inside the latrine building, two rows of eighteen boxed-in toilet seats extended down each wall, side by side.[1] The ancient Romans had devised this form of communal lavatory. Just as human plumbing had remained unchanged, nothing much had changed in latrine design in 2,000 years. A relatively comfortable seat, Mother Nature, gravity, and a basic sewage removal system; that's all it took. Every day, from first light, a long line of prisoners snaked away from the Abort entrance, with POWs awaiting their turn to use the toilets. Later in the morning, as now, the Abort was almost empty. Just two toilets, at the far end, were occupied as Ash walked toward them. Both occupants were "kriegies," as POWs called themselves, from *Kriegsgefangener*— German for prisoner of war. And both kriegies were expecting Ash, or "Tex," as he was known among the British.

The two men rose up. Turning to the last toilet on the left, the previous occupant reached down and lifted the round wooden seat away, revealing an opening just large enough for a man to squeeze down through. As the trio looked down into the bowels of the latrine, the revolting stink of human waste wafted up from below, hitting them in the face and filling their nostrils. It was enough to make the eyes water, the head spin, and the stomach heave. After three months of working in this gross environment, Bill Ash was still not immune to the smell. Nonetheless, in wartime, a desperate man will do things he would never even contemplate in peacetime. There was only one plus— this same revolting stink was enough to repel their German guards and disguise one of history's most disgustingly brilliant escape schemes.

With his hands on the wooden surround, Ash lifted his legs from the ground and eased them down into the hole. Letting go, he slid down through and dropped into a large underground sump, splashing into a concrete channel that carried urine and feces to an exit hole in the brick wall. Via that hole, the excrement fell into a massive sewage pit beside the sump.

With a grunt, another of the POWs dropped down to join Ash. Above, the third man replaced the toilet seat. Through the dirty window in the far wall, the stay-behind could see a POW in a brown greatcoat standing, hands deep in pockets, beside the recreation ground outside the Abort, watching others kicking a soccer ball around. If that man in the greatcoat blew his nose, the stooge in the Abort knew to warn those below that a "goon," or guard, was approaching, and all work below would cease until the goon had gone. The man in the Abort would remain on watch until the underground shift ended.

Bill Ash's companion in the sump was long-faced Quebec native Eddy Asselin. Just twenty-one, Asselin, like Ash, was painfully thin from a lack of nutritious food. The previous April, at Warburg, Asselin had been one of five men to successfully tunnel out of Oflag 6-B. All had been recaptured, with Asselin out only a few days before being caught. This time, he'd vowed, his preparations would be painstaking, and he would make a "home run" to England. The tunnel they were digging from the Abort had been code-named Asselin, after the Canadian, because this ingenious escape bid had been his idea. Participants in the escape had several nicknames for his tunnel, including Eddy's Exit and the SHJ (Shit House Job).

Ash and Asselin were two of three North Americans participating in the escape. The third was Johnny Dodge, a forty-six-year-old major from New York City and a cousin by marriage of Britain's prime minister, Winston Churchill. Most of the rest of the members of X Organization, the compound's Royal Air Force escape fraternity, were British, or from Britain's former colonies around the globe. Others were Irish, Polish, Danish, Czech. One was a German-born Jew who had changed his name to Stevens. Most had flown with the RAF. Ash and Asselin had trained with the Royal Canadian Air Force before piloting Spitfire fighters for the RAF and being shot down in combat. Since the previous October, there had also been United States Army Air Force prisoners in the camp, although they tended to keep to themselves and had little to do with Ash, Asselin and the other X Organization operatives.

Asselin now joined Ash in sliding aside a wooden cover disguising an opening burrowed into the back of the sump's brick wall. Clambering through to a chamber dug from the earth on the other side, the pair carefully replaced the dummy wall behind them. This was in case an inquisitive German plucked up the gumption to stick his head, and a flashlight, down a toilet and inspect the sump below.

Close friends Ash and Asselin were now in a cavern they'd helped hollow from the earth beside the stinking sump. In candlelight, they joined three other waiting POWs of their team who were hunched in the cramped space and began to strip down to their long johns. Including the three stooges on watch above, their group numbered eight men. This was the digging team, the first crew of the day. One man was already seated at a bellows made from old leather kit bags, ready to repeatedly push a wooden handle in and out to pump air into a low tunnel that disappeared to the west. The other three would remain at the tunnel entrance to retrieve the soil the day's dig produced and to be ready to dive into the tunnel and dig out comrades caught in a cave-in.

After their shift, the digging team would be followed by the eight-man dispersal team, which would dispose of the earth produced by the digging team, filling seven-pound jam tins and emptying them into the vast sewage pit. One POW had the unenviable job of reaching into the pit with a broom handle and stirring the earth into the lake of urine and feces. Once a week, the contents of the pit, including soil from the tunnel, were hand-pumped into a horse-drawn "honey wagon" and removed from the camp.

The honey wagon's Polish driver, Franciszek Lewandowski, was a local pig farmer who'd won the sewage removal contract from the German authorities. He used the waste as fertilizer on his farm. Just as Lewandowski was about to complain that his sewage was being adulterated by soil, a leading X Organization member had whispered in his ear and let him in on the kriegies' secret.

That X Organization representative was Józef Bryks, a live-wire young Czech who had enlisted in the RAF under the name Joe Ricks. He was one of the four tunnelers who had made the Warburg break with Eddy Asselin in 1942. Bryks' information had brought a smile to the face of the honey wagon driver. Not only did Lewandowski keep his mouth shut and cart away the soil from the tunnel, he developed a firm friendship with Bryks that was soon to pay even greater dividends for Schubin's POWs.

The third Asselin tunnel team of the day would be made up of the "engineers," men who went into the tunnel to repair and shore up the walls and ceiling in the wake of the diggers' progress, and to extend the air pipe beneath the tunnel floor, ready for the next day's digging team. That air pipe was made from used Klim powdered milk cans from Red Cross parcels, fitted end to end—the catchy brand name Klim was "milk" backward. The air now being pushed to the tunnel face by the pump came from the sump and was thick and putrid. But it contained enough oxygen to keep men in the tunnel alive.

As the pump began to wheeze, Bill Ash entered the darkened tunnel. At its deepest, it sank to seventeen feet below ground to avoid German seismic detectors buried around the camp to pick up the sounds of digging. The tunnel was two feet six inches high and the same across. Coffin-size. These dimensions were dictated by the length of three-foot bed boards taken from camp barracks to shore up tunnel walls and ceiling. Ash had personally donated every single bed board from his bunk, replacing them with a lattice of string that was concealed from prowling guards' eyes by his mattress.

On elbows and knees, pushing a flickering homemade candle ahead of him, Ash slowly worked his way along the earthen tunnel floor. The candle consisted of a bootlace wick floating in margarine in a sardine tin. It, too, stank to high heaven. Every few yards, Ash stopped to light more candles sitting on small wall ledges. Asselin came close behind, trailing a length of rope after him. All the while, the ears of the pair were pricked for sounds of moving earth above their heads that would herald an impending cave-in. This fragile tunnel, source of so much hope, was also a catalyst for nightmares in which tunnelers were buried alive.

"Each trip down it required a little more courage," Ash would later say.[2]

Once they'd crawled to a small halfway chamber, seventy-five feet into the tunnel, Asselin halted. Ash kept going, playing out another length of rope as he went. From beginning to end, it took half an hour to crawl to the tunnel face, which was now 150 feet from the entrance. According to escapers' calculations, the tunnel, growing at a rate of two to three feet a day, had passed beneath the pair of high barbed wire

fences that surrounded the camp. After that, the tunnel had begun to
angle gently upward, and, several days earlier, had arrived directly beneath their target, an irrigation ditch in a potato patch outside the wire.
The last few shifts had been digging vertically, aiming for the surface.

A wall of earth and brown and yellow clay loomed up in front of
Ash. A scoop fashioned from a Klim can lay waiting, along with a
large cloth bag, left by the last digging crew. Taking up the scoop,
Ash pulled himself to a standing position inside the shaft that rose
up toward the potato patch. With his candle to one side, he began to
hack into the earth above his head, allowing the material he freed to
fall to the shaft's floor. After digging for a while, Ash dropped to his
knees and pushed the dislodged material into the bag. Once he'd
filled the bag, he tied it to the end of the rope he'd run out behind
him, then sharply tugged the rope twice.

From the halfway chamber came an answering pair of tugs before
the bag began to trail off into the gloom as Asselin hauled it in. When
Asselin had the bag, he attached it to the rope he'd played out from the
entrance. Giving that rope two tugs, he received a reply, and the bag
slid away toward the entrance. Later, a man from the entrance cavern
would crawl to Asselin with the end of the rope, then back out again,
and Asselin would similarly deliver the end of his rope to digger Ash.

This slow, laborious method of earth removal was not as sophisti-
cated as the system of railroad tracks and trolleys that would be employed in the famous Great Escape tunnels at Stalag Luft 3 outside
Sagan a year later. But, in virtually every other way, methods employed in that later escape were pioneered here at Schubin, below
ground and above.

In preparation for the breakout, a team of POW tailors under John
Paget was secretly creating civilian clothes for escapees. This X Organization department was code-named Gieves, after Gieves Limited
of Old Bond Street in London, England's most famous military tailors, who had made the uniforms of the Duke of Wellington, Admi-
ral Nelson and Winston Churchill. The team preparing and dying
the cloth for the tailors, using blankets and old uniforms, was Pullers
of Perth, named for a Scottish dry-cleaning business. A team tasked

with creating high-energy escape food high in fat and sugar was Lyons, named for England's omnipresent Lyons' Corner House tea shops. Gammages, a London department store, gave its name to the supply department. Skilled cartographers making escape maps and forgers under Eric Shaw, who created escape documents, were Cook's Tours, a reference to the noted British travel firm Thomas Cook.

Superconfident Joe Bryks had secured a camera so that Cook's Tours could take essential ID photos of escapers for use on their forged identity papers. The path to that camera had been a dangerous one, for Bryks and others. First, Bryks had wangled his way onto a detail occasionally taken under armed escort to a Schubin produce store at 4 Hermann-Göring-Strasse, owned by German Günther Jeschke. There, the detail purchased a few "luxuries" for the kriegies, using a fund set up from the paltry sums paid to the prisoners by the German government under the Geneva Convention.

A Polish teenager named Stefania Maludzińska was serving in that produce store, and she soon fell for Joe Bryks' charms. Before long, Stefania was writing to Bryks' parents in Czechoslovakia. Joe hadn't dared write to them using the camp's mail system, as this would have alerted the Germans to his true identity and brought repercussions down on family members. Once this secret correspondence began, Bryks' parents wrote to Stefania, and she smuggled the replies to Bryks when he came into the store.

The cheeky Czech's friends in camp were soon ribbing him about his Polish "girlfriend" beyond the wire, little knowing that he was grooming Stefania for even more hazardous work. After a while, Bryks had taken the risk of confiding to Stefania that he and his comrades were planning an escape from the camp and sought her help. At Bryks' urging, Stefania asked friends working at the town hall to steal Nazi government forms, which she passed on to the Czech for copying by X Organization forgers.

Then came the most fraught task of all. Stefania acquired a small camera and film from Alfons Jachalski, formerly a teacher at the Polish boys' reform school that had occupied the camp's main buildings before the war, who was now forced by the Germans to toil on the roads. The plucky Polish girl arranged for camera and film to be smuggled into the camp by seventeen-year-old Henryk Szalczynski, a Pole who worked in the town's German bakery and delivered the kriegies' black bread ration. Szalczynski also developed the film in the kitchen and basement of his parents' tiny apartment. "Mug shots" of escapers found their way back into the camp in bread deliveries and were affixed to forged identity papers by Cook's Tours. Stefania and her helpers Jachalski and Szalczynski would have been executed had their activities been discovered by the Nazis.

Meanwhile, X Organization's security team watched over all escape activities. With the weather improving and the frozen ground thawing, seven tunnels were now being burrowed by industrious inmates. These were all team digs, as opposed to earlier solo efforts such as a tunnel dug from the vegetable garden by Tom Calnan that had collapsed onto him. Guards watched, amused, as Calnan was hauled free by comrades. He was promptly marched off to the "Cooler," the oflag's solitary confinement cellblock, which at Oflag XXI-B was behind the guard barrack, across the street from the camp. The Germans subsequently made the garden where Calnan had been tunneling off-limits to prisoners.

Now, apart from Asselin, one tunnel headed south from the senior officers' quarters. From Block 1, another headed north. Two tunnels also went north from beneath a stone washbasin and a wastewater trough in the Block 3 and 4 washhouses. Another had been started in the chapel, behind the altar. Work had also recently recommenced on a tunnel dug south from the cookhouse, which, because of groundwater flooding, had been abandoned beneath the Russian compound. Now dried out, it was the most advanced dig after Asselin.

Asselin was X Organization's gem. Not only had it gone the farthest, it stood the best chance of avoiding detection. Its starting place, the reeking communal latrine, was the last place the Germans could be expected to look for an escape tunnel entrance. Not even the Germans believed that men could be so desperate to escape that they would immerse themselves in human waste for months on end.

As Ash hacked away at the roof of the tunnel's exit shaft, he had time to think, and to wonder why he was doing this, digging in this wretched hole in the ground, breathing the foul air, and reeking of crap. Better still, what had led an American to join the Canadian air force and fly Spitfires for the British, only to be shot down by the Germans over France? Ash could only put it down to idealism mixed with a yearning for adventure. Besides, he was compulsive by nature, a jump_____nd-ask-questions-later kind of guy. It would also tran-spire t_____ulsive escaper, someone who couldn't bear being_____his numerous escape attempts had been_____nceived.

_____ Ash frequently
sp_____f far-fetched es-
ca_____ult flinging him
_____edom with wings
_____s the most planned,
_____er be involved with.
_____. The down-to-earth
_____d to concede, this tun-
_____constituted a work of

_____sible to break out of this
_____tfire pilot, Sergeant Philip
_____l escape from Schubin. Se-
_____al orderlies—"batmen," the
_____ad permitted a group of en-
_____nsferred to Schubin to be the
personal ser_____ficers. Schubin's senior British
officer, or SBO, Wing _____ Harry "Wings" Day, an old-fashioned officer in some ways, had expected these batmen to be all spit and polish, and to do as they were told. Wareing had other ideas.

In those days orderlies had occasionally been allowed out of camp, unsupervised by the Germans, to collect extra allowances of food and coal for the officers. On one such outing to collect coal, on December 16, Wareing hadn't returned. Stealing a bicycle, he'd ridden north to the Baltic port of Danzig, today's Gdańsk, where he'd stowed away on a ship bound for Halmstad in neutral Sweden. Ironically, it was a coal ship. From Sweden, Wareing had returned to England by air, and he was now lecturing aircrew on what to expect if they were shot down and captured.

The Germans had tightened camp security after that and terminated unescorted outings. But Bill Ash knew that a calculated and carefully planned mass tunnel escape like Asselin could succeed. Wings Day had himself been one of seventeen RAF prisoners to successfully tunnel out of the Dulag Luft reception and interrogation camp near Frankfurt the previous year. All those escapees had been recaptured, but that hadn't dulled their ambition to be free. And it had shown that a cunningly located tunnel could avoid detection.

Now, after digging for an hour, Ash calculated that the exit shaft had approximately two feet to go before emerging into the potato patch. To prove his theory, he poked a long stick into the earth above. For approximately two feet, he felt resistance. After that, the stick moved easily. It was time to stop work. When they came to dig that last twenty-four inches of earth away, it would be the day of the break. An X Organization meeting would decide the timing of that break. After sending his latest bag of tunnel spoil back via the agency of Eddy Asselin, the Texan slowly, wearily retreated along the tunnel on his stomach, dousing candles as he went. The poor diet in camp, which was low on protein and vegetables, meant that he was already weak. This effort underground taxed his strength all the more.

Dirty and haggard-faced, looking like refugees from the Underworld and smelling like nothing on Earth, Ash and Asselin emerged into the cavern beside the sump. Back on the surface, digging team members would wash themselves as thoroughly as possible after their shift, but the stink of the latrines would never entirely leave them. Fellow prisoners in their ninety-six-man barrack block had learned not to complain about the reeking tunnelers, knowing they were "digging for victory." Some bunkmates declared they would have a party once the tunnelers made their break—more to celebrate the departure of the stinky ones than the escapers' victory over camp security.

Diggers meanwhile did their best to keep away from guards. With little soap and no hot water for bathing, most prisoners were on the nose anyway. At the twice-a-day outdoor *Appells*, or prisoner assemblies, called for head counts by the Wehrmacht's camp security officer, Hauptmann Simms, diggers' aromas blended in with those of their neighbors as guards moved through their ranks, counting them.

Now, with a weary grin, Ash informed his colleagues in the cavern that they had just two feet to go, vertically, to reach freedom. The next dig would be the last.

■ ■ ■

"COME ON, WILLIAMS!" urged Wings Day, one of the men clustered at the end of the Abort. Day, six feet four inches tall, angular and long-faced, wore an impatient scowl. "Where the hell have you been?"

"Sorry, I've been cooking," panted thirty-one-year-old Flight Lieutenant Eric Williams, a Briton, who'd come rushing from the camp cookhouse for the 3:00 p.m. start of Asselin's engineering shift.[3]

Williams was keen to be a part of the Asselin escape, but, having arrived at the camp in late December, he'd joined the crew well into the dig, and was therefore assigned stooge duties. This afternoon, he was to be the stooge stationed inside the Abort. He watched as the other five men slipped down through the hole into the sump, then replaced the toilet seat once they'd all disappeared below. Pushing his nose up against the grimy glass of the window, he sighed as he made out the stooge in the brown greatcoat, on whom he was supposed to keep an eye open for warning signals. Williams had a feeling that he was going to miss out on this Asselin break. That was why he and his best friend, Michael Codner, had also joined the cookhouse tunnelers. At least down in that tunnel they were allowed to dig. But the cookhouse tunnel was still short of its destination. Asselin, Williams gathered, was close to its target.

From below came the faint clack and wheeze of the air pump going into action, signaling that the engineering crew was crawling into the tunnel to do their work. Unbeknown to Williams, this would be the last shift in Asselin. The engineers would shore up the section of exit shaft dug by Bill Ash that morning, repair bulging shoring along the length of the tunnel and refresh its candles, then withdraw, leaving Asselin ready for breakout day. Already bored, Williams began the wait for the shift to end.

At 4:30, the men of the final shift duly emerged from below. One of the tunnelers, Englishman Robert Kee, always felt the same when he came up from the Abort tunnel: as if he had spent the afternoon on another planet. Before long, he would visit that planet one last time.[4]

■ ■ ■

THE CAMP'S MOST conspicuous structure was a large building that had an H-shaped footprint and consisted of two main floors plus a basement and an attic. It was known as the White House—not because it resembled the executive mansion in Washington, DC, but because its exterior stucco walls were covered in whitewash. The Germans seemed to have coined the building's name. It had been built in the 1880s when the region was under Prussian rule as part of West Prussia and was initially used as the county infirmary. Before the war, when this camp had been a reform school, the White House was the institution's main dormitory building. Now it housed offices, a library and a hall used by the prisoners for theatrical shows they themselves produced. Here in the hall, in the early evening of March 3, X Organization's executive met with Asselin's main protagonists, including Asselin and Ash, and SBO Day.

There was always the fear that the "ferrets," English-speaking German guards on the prowl for suspicious activity, might have hidden themselves away to overhear meetings such as this. So stooges had cleared the hall and adjoining rooms, and one stood at every window and door to warn of the approach of Germans. In this secure environment, the breezy but efficient chief of the camp's X Organization, Lieutenant Commander Jimmy Buckley of the Royal Navy's Fleet Air Arm, aka Big X, chaired the meeting. The man behind the Asselin tunnel, Eddy Asselin, told his comrades what they all knew by now, that Asselin was ready to go. Escape clothes, maps and documents were also ready. All that was required was a date for the break.

Wings Day now spoke up, advising that, through coded messages from MI9, the British intelligence agency dedicated to helping POWs escape, he had learned that the Germans planned to soon transfer all British and American air force personnel currently at Schubin to Stalag Luft 3, Sagan. It was crucial, he said, that if Asselin was to be used, it happen very soon, before that transfer took place. To help avoid detection, the break would have to be made on a relatively moonless night. According to the meteorological experts among them, the best option was two days away, March 5, and those at the meeting unanimously agreed to break out on that night.

Next, they had to decide how many men would go out, and their identities. After some discussion it was agreed that the men making the break should be concealed down the tunnel in the early evening, immediately following the 5:00 p.m. Appell, and wait down there until lockup at 9:00 p.m. when the goons closed up the barrack blocks and the night guard came on duty. To ensure that a ferret didn't stumble on the escapers, the entry via the Abort would be sealed up once the escapers were in the tunnel. Therefore, the number of men going out would be dictated by the number of men who could survive in the tunnel until the exit was dug.

A mathematician among them calculated that twenty-three men lying head to toe along the tunnel's length and another ten crammed into the entrance cavern could survive on the available air. Several of those present voiced concerns that this was too many, that men would suffocate as they lay waiting. But the "experts" were confident there would be enough oxygen for thirty-three men for six hours, and thirty-three was the number finally agreed upon.

Eddy Asselin, as the originator of the scheme, had the right to be the first man out, and he chose Ash as his wingman. Those who had participated in digging the tunnel were chosen next, followed by leading lights in the X Organization. Johnny Dodge was one of the latter, as was X Organization's security chief, or Big S, Aiden Crawley. Among escape candidates excluded were Eric Williams and Michael Codner, latecomers who, it was agreed, should instead be put well up on the cookhouse tunnel's escape list. Wings Day now surprised his colleagues by declaring that he wished to be one of the men to go out of Asselin.

"As I'm going to be thrown in the Cooler for presiding over the escape anyway, I might as well at least give them a run for their money," Day reasoned.[5]

Some among his colleagues might have reckoned that, as SBO, it was Day's responsibility to remain behind and look after the welfare of all 600 men in his charge. But, as none of them voiced that view, and as Wings was their superior, no one opposed him. Day sealed his inclusion by volunteering to be the last man out, giving himself the least opportunity of avoiding recapture. The first few men out would have the most time in which to put distance between themselves and the camp.

It was also suggested that ten volunteers hide in the White House's attic while the break went down. Their disappearance would boost the apparent number of escapees and the Nazis' alarm. Food would be smuggled to these "ghost escapees" to allow them to hide out for as long as possible. And, to cover the mass movement of escapers to the Abort on breakout day, it was agreed that a rugby match would be organized for the late afternoon of March 5 and that it would end at twilight.

The game would be England versus Australia, always a heated contest in any sport in which the mother country and her former colony competed, made all the more heated by Australia's frequent victories. Englishmen well outnumbered Aussies in camp, but fifteen Australians would gladly kit up to go head-to-head with the "old enemy" and help cover the biggest escape yet attempted from any Anglo-American POW camp in the Reich.

With the details agreed upon, the meeting broke up, and men hurried away to make their preparations.

■ ■ ■

ON FRIDAY, MARCH 5, the guards counted the POWs as they stood in ranks on the recreation ground for Appell, then reported to squat little Hauptmann Simms that all prisoners were present. Simms, a Czech Nazi serving in the Wehrmacht, informed the British adjutant that he could dismiss the prisoners. Once they'd been dismissed, most of the 800 men flooded to the cramped recreation ground's perimeter, talking animatedly among themselves. A rugby ball was produced, and thirty players and several "officials" stripped down to shorts.

Even the camp's 130 USAAF men joined the crowd. Wings Day had asked the senior American officer (SAO), redheaded Colonel Charles "Rojo" Goodrich of the 12th Bombardment Group, a native of Augusta, Georgia, to get his men to join the RAF spectators and create as much noise and movement as possible to help cover an escape. American airmen had shown little interest in cooperating with the British and their formal X Organization structure. Several Americans had already ended up in the Cooler for ill-conceived ad hoc solo escape attempts. But Rojo Goodrich and his men had no problem with a little inter-Allied cooperation in this case, especially as it had the potential to cause the Krauts plenty of grief.

One of the USAAF men in that crowd was Bob Rivers of Santa Maria, California. He'd been piloting a Spitfire with the USAAF's 4th Fighter Squadron, 52nd Fighter Group, when he was shot down in North Africa in January 1943. Rivers had been sent to Schubin in February and, being that rarity—a downed American Spitfire pilot—had been lumped in with the RAF men even though he was USAAF.

Unlike Bill Ash, Rivers had kept to himself and had little to do with the Brits, quickly embracing fellow USAAF aircrew when they began arriving in camp—men who spoke his cultural and sporting language. Just the same, Rivers would be thrilled and proud when he learned the next day what Bill Ash and his Asselin comrades had been up to. For now, Rivers, hands thrust deep in coat pockets, would get into the mood of the rugby game, yelling support for the Aussies.

Bill Ash was at that moment mingling with the crowd, and chafing to get on with the break. This was not a time to be searched by guards. His escape clothes were concealed under a greatcoat, its pockets stuffed with four-ounce cans of "the Mixture," a high-energy escape food produced by the Lyons team based on formulas created by an English prisoner, prewar nutritionist Eric Lubbock. The Mixture came in two versions: Fudge and Goo. While it looked far from appetizing, this "cake" would sustain a man on the run for a few days. In Ash's civilianized clothes, too, were his forged German papers, an accurate map of the region produced by Cook's Tours, and a homemade escape compass.

Ash looked to the heavens. Heavy gray clouds were massing overhead, and gusts of wind blew into the camp from the west, setting the fence wire humming. German guards on duty in the goon towers on the western side of the camp had turned their backs to the wind, pulling up the collars of their greatcoats, stuffing their hands in their pockets and hunching their backs. Eric Williams, also among the rugby spectators, thought to himself that it was perfect weather for an escape; courtesy of the wind, the guards had their backs to the potato patch where Asselin would emerge.

Williams had overcome the disappointment of being excluded from Asselin's escape list and now pinned his hopes on getting out via the cookhouse tunnel within a few weeks—as long as the rumored transfer to Sagan didn't occur beforehand. In the meantime, Williams had volunteered to help the Asselin escapers aboveground. Later, he would saunter to the Abort to help close up the tunnel from the outside once all the men involved in the break had submerged.

The other escapers salted themselves among the spectators on the western edge of the recreation ground and awaited their turn to visit the latrines. Like Ash, they were clad in greatcoats covering their escape rigs. Some even toted small suitcases and haversacks to enhance their traveler status in the eyes of German police or troops who might see them on streets or trains. In the closely packed crowd, these accoutrements were invisible to the tower guards. Bill Ash purposely avoided eye contact with his fellow escapers. Instead, with a wry smile, he watched Americans in the crowd enthusiastically laying bets on who would win the rugby game.

Ash thought back to his childhood years at James Bowie School in a tough part of Dallas. Some schoolmates' favorite recreation had been forcing other kids to fight, wagering on who would win. One day, the big kids had kidnapped seven-year-old Billy Ash's best friend, George, telling Billy he had to fight George to secure his freedom.

Billy had been put in the gladiatorial ring, surrounded by yelling boys, and faced George, who'd burst into tears. On the "go," instead of fighting George, Billy had turned on the leader of the big kids, and laid him flat with a curling right to the jaw. Inspired by Billy, George had swung at another of their captors. The big kids had proceeded to pound Billy and George to a pulp, but at least the pair had had the satisfaction of defying the bullies. It was the same sort of satisfaction that Ash was deriving from participating in the Asselin escape.

At the sound of a whistle, the rugby game got under way. The ball flew downfield. Aussies and Limeys ran at each other like maniacs. The crowd roared. Eddy Asselin eased in behind Ash and tapped him gently on the shoulder. Without a word, Ash followed the Canadian as he casually made his way toward the nearby Abort. The stooge at the Abort door nodded to indicate there were no goons inside, and the pair passed in through the doorway. Volunteer X Organization helpers waited at the last toilet seat on the left, which was now lifted. As Ash and Asselin removed their greatcoats, Ash, although excited by the prospect of escape, wasn't looking forward to going down into the filth yet again.

"Let's pray this will be the last time we do this," Ash said to Asselin, who nodded, then slid down through the toilet hole to the sump below.[6]

ON THE LOOSE

ASH FOLLOWED ASSELIN DOWN INTO THE LATRINE'S STINKING SUMP. After their greatcoats were lowered to them, the pair pulled away the false side wall, then clambered into the chamber beside the sump. There, they again donned their greatcoats, as there would be no room to put them on in the tunnel. Asselin then led the way as the pair crawled into the darkness, lighting candles as they went, until they reached the uncompleted exit shaft at the tunnel's far end. There they halted, and began the long wait for 9:00 p.m., not knowing what was going on above.

Behind them, as men came to slide down into the sump, escapers began to back up. Some of those on the escape list, X Organization forgers and tailors, had never been down the tunnel before, and they came with bulging coats, bags and backpacks too large for the toilet hole. One or two solidly built men got stuck in the narrow hole. With emptied and repacked bags, and with shoving hands of helpers, they all eventually got through, but the delays put departures well behind schedule. When Eric Williams arrived to help close up the "trap," there was still a backup of escape traffic, and messengers had to be sent to those at the end of the list to wait to be summoned.

SBO Wings Day, last man on the list, was pretending animated support for the England rugger team, and trying not to worry about the delay, when a stooge eventually pushed in beside him in the crowd.

"It's time for you to be put down, sir," said the junior officer in a low voice.[1]

Day was a dour man. Paul Brickhill, the Australian author of *The Great Escape*, who became a friend of Day's, described him as looking like a hungry and unfriendly hawk in his POW days. But even Day couldn't hide a smile at the junior officer's turn of phrase. Casually, Day made his way to the Abort. Inside, his escape partner, Dudley Craig, was waiting for him with Williams and the other volunteers. The pair was put down, and Williams and others sealed up the hole in the sump wall and then climbed back up and fastened the toilet seat in place. Down below, thirty-three men were soon lying head to toe along the tunnel and filling the entrance cavern. Those in the cavern were taking turns working the air pump.

Up top, with the men all around him in good spirits, Williams sauntered back to his barrack block once the game ended. He was so excited by the fact the escape was under way that he never even took in who had won the rugby game. Most of his comrades also returned to their barracks. The camp's brick and concrete barrack blocks contained two long, open dormitories divided from each other by a central washroom and small kitchen. Using metal lockers and double bunks as dividers, the Allied airmen who occupied the two dormitories in each block had broken them up into twelve "messes," or dining groups, of eight men. Each mess cooked and ate together, sharing their rations, using their block kitchens for most cooking, only retrieving hot soup and other basics from the compound cookhouse.

"Dinner's an hour early tonight," one of Williams' messmates informed him when he arrived.

"Good show," Williams replied, knowing the reason for the change in schedule.[2]

The kriegies' decision to eat early was a pragmatic one. From experience, they knew what happened once an escape was discovered. They would be made to stand on the Appell ground for hours while the goons turned the entire camp upside down. If the Asselin tunnel was discovered before dinner, they would go without food. With food meager at the best of times, no one wanted to miss the meal.

In preparation for the inevitable camp shakedown, Williams and his friend Michael Codner had buried their cookhouse tunnel escape clothes and documents in the camp grounds, while Williams had sewed his precious escape map and compass into the waistband of his trousers. Williams and Codner had already planned their escape route if and when they got out—they would head south, for Yugoslavia, and hopefully link up with anti-Nazi partisans there.

Dinner passed with unusual merriment in the messes. Thirty-five places were empty: apart from the thirty-three men now down Asselin, two other prisoners had succeeded in making a break even before the Asselin boys entered the tunnel. At 3:00 p.m., Joe Bryks had been driven out of the camp with a British colleague named Morris, hiding inside the honey wagon's stinking storage tank, with the knowledge and assistance of the Polish driver Franciszek Lewandowski. Their escape had been approved by X Organization on the condition that it take place at the same time as the Asselin break, so that the Germans believed the pair had also gone out via the tunnel once it was discovered. Otherwise, if the Germans were to learn of their actual escape method, honey wagon driver Lewandowski would be a dead man.

In the town, at a little before 6:00 p.m., Stefania Maludzińska was preparing to leave Jeschke's store when Franciszek Lewandowski appeared and took her aside.

"Józef Bryks wants to see you," he said, urging her to accompany him.

Stefania's immediate reaction was fear and suspicion. As Lewandowski confided to her that he had helped Bryks and another POW escape and had hidden them in a house in segregated Schubin's Polish sector, Stefania's suspicions eased. She knew that Bryks had been planning an escape, just as she knew that Lewandowski was a good man. Deciding to trust Lewandowski, she went with him to the escapers' hideout. Stefania found Bryks and Morris wearing uniforms that had been dyed black. The barrel-chested, square-faced Bryks was pleased to see her.

"Do you have any more letters for me from my parents?" he asked.

"Yes, at home," Stefania replied.

"Let's take a walk, and you can give them to me."

"To my place?" Stefania responded, suddenly fearful of being caught in the open with an escapee, or of leading the Gestapo to her parents.

"Yes," said Bryks, smiling cheekily as he pulled on a hat and overcoat.

His charm and confidence soothed her fears. Plucking up her courage, she responded, "Okay, let's go."

Leaving Morris with Lewandowski, Bryks and Stefania set off arm in arm to walk to the house of Stefania's parents, where she lived. As they walked, Stefania told Bryks that there was an 8:00 p.m. curfew for Poles, and that, should they encounter German officials, soldiers, or police, Poles were required to bow to them. Moments later, several German policemen on night patrol came around the corner.

"Bow!" said Stefania in hushed tones to her companion before dutifully bowing to the policemen.

But, instead of following her example, a smiling Bryks tipped his hat to the police and said to them in perfect German, "Good evening."

Stefania glanced over her shoulder and saw the policemen looking back at the pair as they passed. But they kept walking. Upon reaching her parents' house, Stefania introduced her new friend to her mother and father without elaborating on how he came to be there. Mrs. Maludzińska brewed ersatz (literally, "substitute") coffee as Stefania went in search of the letters from Bryks' parents, and Joe made himself comfortable in an armchair.

When Stefania returned, Joe was telling her parents that he was an RAF pilot who had just escaped from the POW camp across town.

Mr. and Mrs. Maludzińska's hands were now trembling with fear—so much so that they couldn't hold their coffee cups without spilling the contents. Taking Bryks by the hand, Stefania led him from the house.

Outside, Bryks said, "Would you like to go to the cinema, or for a walk closer to the camp?"

Recognizing that her new friend was a dangerous daredevil who wanted to test the limits of his newfound freedom, young Stefania shook her head. "No, we must hurry."

Reminding Bryks of the 8:00 p.m. curfew, Stefania bustled him back to his hideout and left him in the care of friends of honey wagon driver Lewandowski.[3]

Back in the camp, the ghost escape volunteers slipped into the White House following dinner and made themselves comfortable in the attic. In the barrack blocks where the genuine and fake escapers had been housed—most came from Block 2—their bunks had been left padded with clothing under blankets to give the impression that the beds were occupied, should a ferret make a surprise inspection. The "bodies" were complete with fake heads covered with genuine hair the escapers had saved from haircuts over the preceding months, and pairs of boots jutting out from beneath the blankets.

Down in the tunnel, time seemed to slow. To save oxygen, the lamps had been doused, and escapers lay in complete darkness. The sound of the air pump couldn't be heard at the far end of the tunnel, where the oxygen was thinnest. Men breathed hard, and, rugged up in several layers of clothing, they perspired as if they were in a Turkish bath. Many had to fight down the fear of a cave-in. If that were to happen, with so many men crammed end to end in the tunnel, some of them wouldn't get out alive. The discomfort of the escapers increased when they realized that sewage had seeped in through the tunnel wall from the sewage pit. Soon it had impregnated the clothes of escapers, while those in the lowest section of the tunnel were lying inches deep in it.

Even though Bill Ash was at the end of the tunnel, and above the waste, he had crawled through it to get to the exit shaft and stank of it. He had never felt so uncomfortable in his life. "If ever I wanted to escape, this is that moment," Ash mumbled half to himself.[4]

As the time dragged by, worried questions were whispered from one man to the next, until, by the time they reached the tunnel's extremities, the messages were unintelligible.

"Shut up!" came Wings Day's hoarse exhortation from the cavern, and the nervous chatter ceased abruptly.[5]

Eddy Asselin, deciding that night must have fallen and that it was time to start digging the exit hole, pulled himself to his feet in the pitch black. Using the Klim can scoop, he hacked away at earth and roots above his head. Assisted by gravity, dirt came away easily, and the Canadian handed large clumps of it down to Ash, who knelt at his feet. Ash in turn broke up the clods and spread dirt around the tunnel floor. After a while, Asselin handed down a clod in which Ash felt grass. Raising it to his nose, Ash sniffed the aroma of living greenery. And then, with a hushed but exultant cry, Asselin broke through to the surface. Ash felt a rush of fresh cold air on his face. To the Texan, this was the smell of freedom.

Methodically, Asselin cut away the earth and roots that still blocked the exit. As the Canadian dug, Ash pummeled the last debris into the exit shaft floor. Behind them, grateful escapers felt the fresh night air on their faces as it flooded in. The man lying immediately in front of Robert Kee, number seventeen in the line of escapers, had been close to panic up to this moment as claustrophobia had begun to grip him.

"Thank God for that!" gasped number sixteen. It wasn't the air so much as the knowledge that Asselin had broken through to the surface. They were going to get out of this hole in the ground after all.[6]

Warily, Asselin poked his head up into the open. Sure enough, the exit shaft had come up dead on target, in an irrigation ditch running through the potato patch. Looking back the way they'd come, Asselin could see the wire and the camp beyond. Guards in the goon boxes had their backs to the tunnel as they slowly panned their searchlights around the camp grounds. To the west, the sheltering darkness of a wood beckoned the prisoner.

Hearing footsteps close by, Asselin froze in the exit shaft. A sentry with a rifle slung over his shoulder was patrolling on the other side of the perimeter wire. The German paced slowly by without noticing Asselin's head, the hole in the ground, or the steam rising from both. When the sentry was out of sight, Asselin heaved himself up. As he went, his feet scrabbled over Ash's head and the sides of the shaft, sending dirt down onto his friend. Asselin was out. In a running hunch, he scuttled to the trees, then dropped to one knee to look back to the tunnel exit. Ash now put his head out the hole. Spotting the sentry on his way back, he froze in place.

The sentry passed, never once turning his gaze outside the wire, and as he disappeared into the distance, Ash summoned up all his strength and hauled himself out the tunnel mouth. Flat on his stomach, he crawled in commando fashion, like a lizard, through the undulating potato patch. Stopping dead in another ditch, he waited for the returning sentry to pass, then rose and made a crouching dash to join Asselin, in dread that his every footstep must have been heard by the goons. Panting hard, he reached his friend. Ash would later say he never felt more alive, before or since, than he did at that moment.

After a last glance back at the eerily illuminated camp, the pair turned and set off through the trees at a brisk walk. Their objective was the Baltic Sea to the north and a port where they might emulate Philip Wareing and stow away on a ship to Sweden. Next out of the tunnel was Big X, Jimmy Buckley. He was followed by his escape partner, Jorgen Thalbitzer, a Dane who had enlisted in the RAF under the name of John Thompson so that relatives in German-occupied Denmark wouldn't be punished by the Nazis in the event that he was captured. Buckley and Thalbitzer were also heading for the Baltic.

Behind them came Otakar "Otto" Černý, a tall, gaunt, mustachioed Czech, and Stanisław "Danny" Król, a powerful little Pole who'd been a fencing champion before the war. Černý's Schubin messmates had given him their entire chocolate ration to eat on the run. Król, who had been part of the Warburg tunnel escape with Asselin and Bryks and would end up tunneling a third time at Stalag Luft 3, would become the model for Charles Bronson's Polish character, Danny, in the movie version of *The Great Escape*.

Each escaper had to wait for the patrolling sentry to pass, and this made the escape a stop-start affair for all who made the break that night. Consequently, it took a lot longer than planned to get escapers along the tunnel. Those with no experience underground struggled to get their baggage along the undulating tunnel in total darkness. Two candles had to be lit along the tunnel's length to help them see their way.

Wings Day, coming last of all, extinguished the candles as he made his long transit to the tunnel's mouth. On reaching the exit shaft, he encountered a problem. All the earth that had deliberately or accidentally been brought down from the tunnel entrance during the preceding departures had built up on the floor of the shaft to such an extent that tall, gangly Day couldn't get by. He spent a long time digging his way through, pushing the earth behind him. It was close to midnight by the time he struggled from the shaft and crawled to join Dudley Craig in the woods.

In contrast to the later Great Escape at Sagan, all the POWs participating in this break at Schubin made it out of their tunnel undetected. Back in the camp, many who knew about the break lay awake, expecting to hear shots that indicated the escape had been detected. Some eventually dropped off to sleep secure in the knowledge that the breakout had succeeded. Eric Williams, both excited and fearful for his escaper friends, didn't sleep a wink all night.

Just after dawn the next day, Saturday, yawning South African kriegie Don Gericke wandered into the main Abort. An X Organization member who was planning to escape via one of Schubin's other tunnels, Gericke knew about the Asselin scheme. He was amazed to find that the previous night's break had yet to be discovered by the Germans. Hurrying back to his barrack block, Gericke gathered up his escape gear, then, as casually as his excitement would allow, returned to the Abort.[7]

After prizing away the toilet seat and dislodging the fake wall between sump and cavern, Gericke entered the tunnel, crawled its length, and reached the end. Smaller than Wings Day, he squeezed his way into the exit shaft without too much difficulty. Putting his head up, he couldn't see any sentries looking his way, and even though it was now broad daylight, he decided to take his chances. Climbing out of the tunnel mouth, he crawled to the wood without being spotted. Thanking his lucky stars, Gericke pushed on through the trees and made good his escape.

Still the break went undiscovered. The 800 RAF and USAAF kriegies left behind ate big breakfasts that morning, and, expecting a long delay before the next meal, some even carried sandwiches in their pockets as they made their way to morning Appell and fell in. To confuse the goons, that morning they formed up in three ranks instead of the usual five. At a glance, all camp inmates seemed present. But Hauptmann Simms quickly noticed that it was the SBO's adjutant and not the SBO himself who stood at attention in front of the assembly and saluted him as he came up the slope from the gate.

Simms returned the salute. "Where is Mr. Day?" he inquired.

"He's not here this morning," the British adjutant casually replied.

"Ach, so?" The Wehrmacht captain looked along the ranks of prisoners standing looking back at him. All were grinning. With a mystified scowl, Simms realized that the kriegies were in only three ranks. "In fives, please," he said quietly. "Always in fives."[8]

The adjutant called on the prisoners to re-form, and with chuckles and mumbled witticisms, the POWs slowly jostled about and formed five ranks, after which Simms ordered the guards to proceed with the morning count.

As the count came back for each block and he completed the attendance roll, Simms looked more and more worried. In total, forty-six prisoners were unaccounted for. Simms called the compound's senior sergeant, who in turn called a soldier and gave a barked order. The soldier trotted away. Before long, the gates at the bottom of the hill opened, and a squad of troops in helmets and armed with MP40 submachine guns, so-called Schmeissers, marched stiffly into the compound from their barracks on the other side of Adolf-Hitler-Strasse, the secondary road that ran along the southern boundary of the camp. Forming up facing the prisoners, the guards leveled their weapons at them.

"Mass execution at Oflag XXI-B," whispered Michael Codner to his pal Eric Williams in the kriegie ranks.[9]

The German camp commandant, a Wehrmacht colonel who was rarely seen by the prisoners, then came storming through the gate and up the gentle incline toward the Appell ground with his open greatcoat flowing behind him like a cloak. Simms hurried to meet his colonel, and the pair stood talking animatedly for some minutes before the commandant departed and Simms rejoined the assembly.

"You will return to your quarters, gentlemen," Simms announced, a tight smile on his face.[10]

Once the kriegies had been herded back into their barrack blocks, the guards locked them in. They would be kept in there for the remainder of the day and all through the night. In the meantime, guards scouring the camp perimeter located Asselin's exit, and a prisoner from the adjacent Russian POW compound was sent down the tunnel to crawl its length and emerge in the Abort. But it was a matter of closing the barn door after the horse had already bolted. Thirty-six Allied POWs were loose in Poland with a nine- to twelve-hour start.

During the day, the Gestapo descended on Schubin town. They searched building after building, and scores of Poles were hauled in for questioning. Working in the Jeschke produce store, Stefania Maludzińska could barely hide her nervousness. Everyone around her was talking about the escape and the arrests. After being spotted by police in the street the previous evening in the company of a stranger, Stefania felt sure it was only a matter of time before the Gestapo came looking for her. But they never did.

No escapees, including Bryks and Morris, who hid in Schubin for several days before moving on, were located in the town. Escape accomplice Henryk Szalczynski would be arrested in April. Although his parents destroyed all evidence of his photographic work for the escapees, and the Gestapo could pin nothing on the teenager, the Germans suspected that he'd somehow been involved in the break via his regular visits to the camp. Sent southwest to the city of Posen

(Polish Poznań) by the authorities, Henryk would spend the rest of the war there as a forced laborer.

∎ ∎ ∎

AFTER WALKING ACROSS country for hours, Bill Ash and Eddy Asselin hid in a wood on their second night out. Searching troops with flashlights passed within inches of their hiding place, yelling and beating the undergrowth, without finding them. At dawn, the pair moved on. By nightfall it had become bitterly cold, so they risked hiding in a barn for the night.

The next evening, they came to a bridge over a river. As a bitter wind blew, German soldiers huddled in sentry boxes at either end of the bridge, emerging only occasionally to patrol the bridge's length before diving back into the shelter of their sentry boxes. The river was deep, its icy waters freezing, and Ash and Asselin decided to try crawling along the outer side of the bridge. At one point a sentry emerged from his box. He stood ten feet away from the cringing pair, looking over the other side of the bridge, before returning to his box like a dog skulking back into its kennel. The two escapees crawled on by, reached the cover of wood beyond the bridge, and continued north.

Over succeeding nights they hid in hedges. On their fifth night of freedom, they slept in the open near a railroad crossing. The next morning, they were awakened by a party of German farmers armed with pitchforks who'd stumbled on their hiding place. As the farmers surrounded the pair with pitchforks raised, bailing them up like foxes, a farmer's wife hurried away. Soon, she returned with armed German troops.

"Shoot them!" snarled the farmer's wife. "Shoot them now!"[11]

When the troops refused, the farmer's wife tried to grab a rifle from one of them, declaring she would shoot Ash and Asselin herself. As several soldiers restrained her, others searched the two escapees. One, an English speaker, found a letter on Ash, from his mother back in Texas. The soldier read it aloud, translating it into German for his comrades. After Ash had been captured, his mother had founded a charitable group in Dallas to support all POWs, and in this letter she wrote that she was baking apple pies for German POWs in North American camps because she was confident that German moms would be doing the same for American boys in German camps. This brought hoots of laughter from the German soldiers; if only Ash's mother could see the German mom who'd just wanted to shoot her son.

Ash and Asselin, their escape bid at an end, were carted off to a police prison in the town of Hohensalza (Polish Inowrocław) and thrown into a cell with German deserters and Polish pimps. After a few days, the pair was collected by Wehrmacht soldiers and returned to Schubin by truck. Both were disgusted that the journey didn't last long, indicating that, on foot and dodging detection, they hadn't traveled far from Schubin. After jumping down from the truck, the pair wasn't led back into the camp. Instead, they were tossed into the Oflag XXI-B Cooler, joining other Asselin escapees already crammed into the block's eight cells.

Ash and Asselin's six days on the run had been better than most of the others' outings. Wings Day and his partner, Dudley Craig, had been out barely thirty-six hours before they were betrayed by a child, a Hitler Youth boy who had gone off, they thought, to fetch them food, only to return with troops. Robert Kee stayed out a little longer, getting as far as Cologne on the Rhine by train before he and his escape partner were caught by an eagle-eyed German policeman at a railway station. The cop had become suspicious of the leather laces on their shoes: having run out of regular shoelaces in camp, POWs used thin leather strips for laces.

In little more than a week, thirty-three escapees were recaptured. Only Joe Bryks and two tunnelers remained unaccounted for. Like Ash and Asselin, all recaptured men were returned to Oflag XXI-B. With the Cooler's cells full, the last arrivals were locked up in White House punishment cells originally built to house boys when the camp was a reformatory. The ghost escapees had meanwhile soon been located in their attic hideout. Cheeky Joe Bryks remained on the loose for three months. He made it all the way to Warsaw, where he hid out before being betrayed and returned to kriegiedom elsewhere.

Two prisoners were never recaptured. Jimmy Buckley and his Danish escape partner, Jorgen Thalbitzer, reached Denmark, where the Danish resistance provided them with a canoe. One foggy night, Thalbitzer and Buckley set off to row across the Baltic to Sweden. Thalbitzer's body was washed up near Copenhagen the next day. He was still rugged up in his winter clothing, including a greatcoat, and it was speculated that the canoe had been unwittingly run down by a cargo ship and that the Dane had drowned before he had a chance to struggle out of his heavy gear.

No trace of Big X Jimmy Buckley was ever found. He never reached Sweden and never returned to Britain. He was presumed drowned. None of the Oflag XXI-B prisoners were aware of the fates of Buckley or Thalbitzer, and many spent the rest of the war believing that the pair had succeeded in getting home.

At the end of March, before any more escape bids could be made, the majority of RAF and USAAF prisoners at Oflag XXI-B were loaded onto trucks and sent by road convoy to Stalag Luft 3 at Sagan in Silesia, to the west of Schubin. At Sagan, the USAAF men went into South Compound, while the RAF prisoners were split between East Compound and the new North Compound, the latter to be the site of the Great Escape the following year. At the same time, most of the Russian compound at Schubin was also emptied. A few Russian prisoners were retained, occupying half of one of the three original Russian barrack blocks. The Russians slaved in work details around Schubin town, laboring fourteen to eighteen hours a day, every day, and were not permitted to mix with other camp inhabitants.

The recaptured Oflag XXI-B escapees undergoing solitary confinement punishment at Schubin remained behind. The maximum punishment allowed under the Geneva Convention was thirty days' confinement. Once their sentences were up, in early May, these men were also sent to Sagan. Their new Luftwaffe jailers deliberately split up the leading Asselin tunnelers, putting Bill Ash and Eddy Asselin in East Compound, while Wings Day and Danny Król were sent to North Compound.

Ash was still determined to escape, but Asselin had been appalled at how relatively quickly and easily the men from both the Warburg and Schubin breaks had been recaptured despite months of detailed preparation. After giving so much blood, sweat and tears to these tunnel escapes and achieving nothing, Asselin informed Ash he was giving up escaping for the duration in favor of a much safer and more profitable occupation. Much to Ash's disapproval, Asselin set up a card school in East Compound, with men betting the back pay they expected to receive once the war was over. Asselin would become a theoretically rich man over the next two years, fleecing gambling-addicted kriegies in his card school.

Eric Carpenter and Michael Codner, also sent to Stalag Luft 3's East Compound, were still determined to tunnel to freedom. Joined by Canadian Oliver Philpot, they would escape just six months later via a tunnel they dug from beneath a hollow wooden vaulting horse situated on the recreation ground. All three scored "home runs," making it back to England. With a 100 percent success rate, the Wooden Horse Escape was, percentage wise, the most successful tunnel escape of the war.

Meanwhile, Wings Day and other Schubin escape artists in Stalag Luft 3's North Compound, including Johnny Dodge and Danny Król, would join Roger Bushell, Paul Brickhill and others in preparing the Great Escape via tunnels Tom, Dick and Harry. On the night of the Great Escape, March 24–25, 1944, when seventy-six Allied POWs would bust out of North Compound via Harry, Bill Ash would be languishing in East Compound's Cooler after a failed solo escape attempt.

Back at Schubin, there were big changes. Prior to the RAF and USAAF prisoners being in residence, the camp had housed French POWs, and before them, Polish army prisoners. Now, with the transfer of the Allied airmen and removal of most of the Russian prisoners, and the court martial of the commandant and security officer Hauptmann Simms, Oflag XXI-B was renamed *Offizierslager* 64, or Oflag 64, and was made the destination for US Army officer prisoners and a small number of American enlisted men to serve as their orderlies. This would be the only German POW camp of the war dedicated to American officers. In June 1943, American ground force POWs began arriving at Schubin.

3

THE YANKS MOVE IN

It was the summer's morning of June 9, 1943, when the US Army's Second Lieutenants H. Randolph Holder and George Durgin marched the two miles west from a railroad station signposted ALT-BURGUND on the southeastern outskirts of Schubin. Through the sleepy rural town the POW group tramped, under guard, and along Adolf-Hitler-Strasse, the cobbled, tree-lined street running by newly re-branded Oflag 64. On their right, they passed a walled cemetery, then a gabled mansion with a sign on the gate: KOMMANDANT. Right next door, they came upon a sentry box and the pair of twenty-foot-high fences of barbed wire fringing the POW camp that was destined to be their home for quite a while.

At a command from the group's senior American officer, the column halted by the camp's tall latticed outer gateway, which was topped by a large carved German eagle and swastika. Holder and Durgin's group of 150 US Army officer prisoners had been transferred to Schubin from other camps. By October there would be 224 officer

POWs at Schubin, plus twenty-one American enlisted men serving as orderlies. In small groups, the new arrivals were herded into the space between the front gate and a new inner gate. In the open, German guards brusquely noted personal details, then sat each prisoner on a chair to be photographed holding a slate inscribed with their POW number for the Wehrmacht's *Personalkarte* record sheet and the ID card issued to each prisoner. Not surprisingly, no one smiled for the camera.

Holder and Durgin were best friends, tank platoon commanders with Company E, 1st Armored Regiment, 1st US Armored Division. Holder had commanded the second-to-last Sherman tank knocked out in a disastrous attack on Sidi Bou Said in Tunisia in February. Durgin had commanded the last Sherman to be destroyed in the battle, in which an American tank battalion took on two German Panzer divisions partly armed with Tiger tanks and was obliterated. Half of Holder and Durgin's fellow soldiers had been killed. Many of the rest, like Holder and Durgin, had been captured. That battle had been one of Nazi Field Marshal Erwin Rommel's last victories, but this was no recompense for the defeated Americans, who had been passed through other POW camps in Italy and Germany before ending up here at Schubin.

New arrivals who were already thinking about escape noted that coils of barbed wire filled the eight-foot gap between the two perimeter fences. Arc lamps high on poles every thirty feet or so lit the wire at night. Goon box towers mounting searchlights and Spandau machine guns sat high up on wooden legs at regular intervals around the wire. Twenty feet inside the perimeter fences, a low warning wire ran around the camp. Prisoners needed guard permission to step over that wire, or risk being machine-gunned from a tower.

Before the inner gates opened and the new party marched into the camp, handsome, mustachioed, twenty-seven-year-old Holder, from Moline, Illinois, saw the thirty-four Americans on the other side of the wire who'd made up the first American party to arrive in camp on June 6 along with Oflag 64's senior American officer, Colonel Thomas D. Drake. From Clarksburg, West Virginia, Drake had been commander of the 2nd Battalion, 168th Regimental Combat Team, when he was wounded and taken prisoner during the same February battle that had seen Holder and Durgin captured.

Holder spotted the avuncular colonel standing ramrod straight outside the White House as he watched the new arrivals brought in. A short man with a bushy mustache, Drake was neatly dressed and had an unmistakable military bearing. The goons at the front gate and in the guard towers watched the arrival, too, as the Americans' escort shepherded them into the compound.

At their last camp, Oflag IX-A/Z at Rotenburg, Holder and Durgin had shared a barrack with British officers. From the Brits, some of whom had been captives since 1939, they had picked up a little POW slang—kriegies, ferrets, stooges, goons. From them, too, they'd learned the source of the word "goon." Early in the war, British captives had kidded their German captors into believing that "goon" was an acronym for "German Officers Or Noncoms." In reality, goon was long-standing British slang for "fool" or "halfwit." It gave British and American POWs alike a kick to be able to call a Nazi a fool to his face and get away with it.

The Asselin tunnel had been destroyed by the Wehrmacht, and its starting point, the mass Abort on the western perimeter of the camp, was shut up. Another mass Abort was in use on the eastern side of the camp, behind the White House. The Germans had also combed the compound for more tunnels, in the process discovering and destroying the cookhouse tunnel and another begun from a barrack block. Several others remained undiscovered.

For the time being, the wire fence separating the three former Russian barrack blocks from the main compound was retained. Once the White House and two of those former Russian blocks were occupied with new American arrivals, and other blocks on the camp's north side were reopened, most of the separating fence would come down. The fence would remain around only one block, which would house the last forty Russian prisoners in camp and the Americans' Red Cross parcel store. The new inner gate had also been added for the Americans, creating a wired-off *Vorlager* area between the inner and outer gates for vetting new arrivals and to prevent the rushing of the outer gate.

As before, the administrative buildings immediately across Adolf-Hitler-Strasse from the camp gate contained the German *Kommandantur* (or command center), the Cooler, and the barrack of the guard company of a little over one hundred officers and men from the 813th Infantry (Grenadier) Regiment, plus a new security officer. In the wake of the recent tunnel break, camp security was being tightly enforced by that new security officer, Hauptmann G. Zimmermann, who would soon be hated by the American prisoners. From Bayreuth, onetime home of Hitler's favorite composer, Richard Wagner, Zimmermann was a Nazi Party member in good standing. Among other precautions, Zimmermann doubled the perimeter guard at night. In addition, these sentries patrolled outside rather than inside the wire, and some were accompanied by German shepherds straining on leashes.

One camp guard, Private Gottfried Dietz, would later remark that Zimmermann was very considerate with his own personnel. Zimmermann had told a friend of Dietz's in the guard company that he had to be strict with the prisoners to prevent escapes; otherwise, the SS would take over the camp and make life horrendous for everyone. Besides, any escape would result in Zimmermann's being sent to the Russian front, the apparent fate of his predecessor, Simms. It was in Zimmermann's own interests to keep the camp nailed down.[1]

SAO Colonel Drake had succeeded in obtaining some concessions from the camp's acting commandant, Oberstleutnant Le Viseur, after letting him know in no uncertain terms that he was an American officer, senior in rank to Le Viseur, and should be treated with respect. With Le Viseur's approval, the former RAF senior officers' residence would now be used as a schoolhouse by the American POWs. And Drake designated the hall in the White House that had been utilized by the British as a theater as one large dining hall for all his men, asking the commandant to allocate another camp building for use as a theater.

Holder, Durgin and their group from Oflag IX-A/Z were marched through a gate into the nearest redbrick barrack block, which was in the old Russian compound. As the camp filled with Americans and the northern barracks were progressively opened up, half of one of the former Russian barrack buildings, in the southwest corner of the camp, would be transformed into the cramped but intimate Little Theater, with the American kriegies building a small but professional stage at one end.

On the mild June morning when Holder and Durgin arrived, guards outside the barrack warned them away from the windows, so the curious new arrivals could only investigate the building's interior. It was as the previous occupants had left it in March, forbidding and bare but for bunks, lockers, tables and chairs. As the newcomers would later discover, RAF prisoners had left behind their medical supplies in the camp hospital, and these would be gratefully used by the US Army doctors in camp—the Germans would prove slow in providing the POWs with drugs, giving German patients first preference. The British had also been forced to leave behind a thousand books in the camp library, mostly English novels. Via the International Red Cross, the YMCA and family at home, American titles would be progressively added, with the Oflag 64 collection ultimately numbering 7,000 books.

Despite these previous occupiers' remnants, very few of the Americans who would now be housed in the camp had any idea that American and British flyboy POWs had previously called the place home. Nor would they become aware of the Asselin break, or of the existence of most of the other escape tunnels dug here. Clearly, that wasn't something their German captors were going to tell them about.

It wouldn't be until decades after the war that many Oflag 64 kriegies became aware of what had gone on in, and under, their camp when it was Oflag XXI-B. Eventually, as the camp filled with US Army POWs, the western mass Abort from which the Asselin tunnel had been dug would be reopened by the Germans, and Americans would use this latrine in complete ignorance of its part in POW escape history.

One of the men joining Holder and Durgin in the barrack on their first morning at Oflag 64 was Lieutenant Hill T. Murphy from Alabama. Murphy had picked up the nickname "Spud." He had also coined a nickname for Holder. At Oflag IX-A/Z, northerner Holder and southerner Murphy had frequently gotten into heated discussions about the Civil War, with Holder, in his deep, booming voice, accusing Murphy of being an "unreconstructed rebel." After Holder had been ordered to "shut up" by the SBO after he and a new British friend had talked long and loud into the night, keeping Murphy and others awake, Murphy had christened Holder "Boomer," and the appellation had stuck. Boomer Holder he would be to the rest of the kriegies of Oflag 64.[2]

Lunch was delivered to the latest arrivals in the barrack where they'd been locked—vegetable soup, but, unusually for a German POW camp, with a hint of meat. Compared to the rations the Germans would serve up over the next two years, it was almost gourmet fare. This was rare room service for kriegies, and, like meat in their soup, would not be experienced again. Around 2:00 p.m., Holder and Durgin were taken as part of a group of ten up to the second floor of the White House and into Room 28, a dormitory room with a window looking out onto Adolf-Hitler-Strasse.

Here, they were issued cutlery and a tin cup bearing the eagle and swastika, then told to select beds among the dorm's twenty double bunks. Each bed's mattress and pillow, filled with wood shavings, lay on hard wooden slats. Every man was issued two thin woolen blankets. The room was equipped with six wash basins and a single Abort, and was lit by five small electric globes. This was now their home sweet kriegie home.

Another new arrival that June was tall, thin First Lieutenant Craig D. Campbell, from Austin, Texas. Campbell was harboring a secret. As soon as he could, he shared that secret with SAO Colonel Drake. Campbell had been aide-de-camp, or ADC, to General Dwight D. Eisenhower, then commander in North Africa. Since 1941, Campbell had arranged Eisenhower's appointments, travel and accommodation, handled his correspondence, and had even looked after menial details such as organizing new footwear and accoutrements for the general.

For months, twenty-six-year-old Campbell had pestered General Eisenhower for an opportunity to briefly get away from his desk and see the war from the perspective of troops on the ground. In late March, when they'd visited the Tunisian front together, Eisenhower had given in to his young ADC and left him with the 9th Infantry Division, then in reserve, for a temporary posting behind the lines that was supposed to last three to four weeks. It was a case of being careful of what you wish for. Erwin Rommel launched a typically unexpected attack, and the unit to which Campbell was attached, 2nd Battalion, 47th Infantry, had been hurriedly thrown into action at Hill 369, near El Guettar.

The battalion had become lost during a night approach and stumbled into heavily dug-in enemy in a wadi. Raked by artillery fire, the unit was chewed up, suffering heavy casualties. Campbell had found himself with Lieutenant Sid Thal, who, sent forward to scout the situation for his CO, Lieutenant Colonel Louis Gershenow, had been cut off from the HQ company by the ferocity of the German fire. Throwing themselves into a deserted foxhole, Campbell and Thal had maintained covering fire as the battalion attempted to withdraw. Eventually out of ammunition and water, the pair agreed that surrender was their only option, and Thal had tied his white handkerchief to his Garand rifle and held it up. Campbell and Thal had joined Lieutenant Colonel Gershenow and six other officers and 205 enlisted men from the battalion who were taken prisoner that night.

For weeks after his capture, Campbell had kept his real job to himself as he maintained the sham that he was just another know-nothing junior infantry officer, all the while fearing that if the Nazis found out his regular role, they would torture him for information about Eisenhower, secret codes, planned troop movements, and everything else to do with the command of the Allied armies in North Africa. When Campbell shared his secret with Colonel Drake at Oflag 64, the SAO ordered him to continue to keep his mouth shut. From now on, Campbell would purposely keep a low profile and refrain from any activity that might draw German attention to him—including involvement in escape attempts.

General Eisenhower, meanwhile, had been devastated when he learned that Campbell was missing in action. He had ordered searches made of the area where Campbell and his 47th Infantry colleagues had last been seen, but when nothing turned up by April 12 he'd sadly written to the young man's parents, Mr. and Mrs. J. B. Campbell, in Austin, to tell them Craig was missing, and, hopefully, a POW.

"You cannot know how sadly I write these lines," Eisenhower told the Campbells. "Craig was not only my personal ADC, but my favorite young man in these forces."[3] On June 11, the relieved Campbell family received a telegram from the War Department stating that the International Red Cross had confirmed that their son was alive and a prisoner of the Germans.

Campbell would have been a celebrity among his fellow prisoners had his secret become known. There was already one celebrity in camp. Lieutenant Colonel John Knight Waters, whom Colonel Drake appointed his executive officer, or XO, at Oflag 64, was the son-in-law of the famous general George S. Patton. In 1934, Waters had married Patton's daughter Beatrice, or Little Bea. The handsome Johnny Waters was a professional soldier, a 1931 West Point graduate and cavalry officer. As commander of Lessouda Force, an armored battalion group, he had been forced to surrender to superior Axis forces at Sidi Bou Said during the same disastrous series of battles that had seen Drake, Campbell, Holder, Durgin and numerous other Schubin inmates snared by the Wehrmacht and more than one hundred American tanks destroyed. Waters, a tall, calm, composed man with a tight smile, could produce a steely gaze with his blue-gray eyes.

"Johnny Waters was an excellent choice for executive officer," another senior officer at the camp would say. "He immediately impressed everyone as an efficient, dedicated and level-headed officer."[4] Like SAO Drake, Waters believed that survival in captivity depended on the right mental attitude. Before arriving at Schubin, they had seen British officer prisoners wearing all manner of nonregulation clothing, growing untidy beards, even shaving their heads. Drake believed that he must never allow his men to forget they were US Army offi-cers, and as Drake's deputy, Waters enforced a strict adherence to mil-itary discipline. This included a dress and neatness code that required daily shaves and uniform inspections, which irked some kriegies but was essential to maintaining morale.

A keen sportsman, Waters encouraged POWs to get involved in sports in camp. He himself would play enthusiastically, especially vol-leyball, basketball and softball, becoming renowned for one day making a home run on a bunt. Later, when a more senior officer ar-rived in camp and became XO, Waters was appointed Oflag 64's wel-fare officer, but his duties and interest in the men under him remained basically unchanged. According to Waters' son George, "He believed, as Patton did, that if you took good care of your men, they will take care of you."[5]

The Germans left the POWs to run the internal affairs of the camp as they pleased. So, in addition to choosing Waters as his XO, Colonel Drake appointed Major Merle A. Meacham from Glenwood, Iowa, as camp adjutant, and established an orderly room at the front of the White House with two kriegie clerks. Drake also gave each bar-rack block a commander who was a lieutenant colonel. With each block divided into A and B sections by its central kitchen and wash-room, the men in each half were designated a platoon, with a major or captain commanding each.

The Americans' captors knew all about these appointments, but there was one they didn't know about. As far as the Germans were concerned, Lieutenant Colonel James Alger had no staff post and was unofficially in charge of entertainment in camp. Alger, from Brock-ton, Massachusetts, was a graduate of West Point, class of 1935, where he'd picked up the sobriquet Gentleman Jim. At the time of his cap-ture, Alger was in command of Boomer Holder and George Durgin's tank battalion when it was pounded into surrender in Tunisia. He'd been lucky to survive with only minor wounds after being blown off his Sherman by a German 88 mm shell.

At Oflag 64, in addition to his entertainment role, Gentleman Jim was also the SAO's S-2, his intelligence and security officer.

Alger's role included vetting all new arrivals in camp to ensure that they weren't Nazi plants. Camps had been infiltrated in this way on several occasions: after very convincing plants were removed from a camp for "punishment" or "hospitalization," never to return, the guards went straight to tunnels and hiding places of escape materiel, having been tipped off by their planted spies. S-2 Alger also kept an ear to the ground for useful information from and about the German military.

Most important of all, Alger was chief of the camp's secret escape committee, answering directly to the SAO with respect to all escape plans, which had to be submitted to Alger and approved by Drake. Adjutant Merle Meacham became Alger's escape committee deputy chief, and a number of escape plans would come via him. The SAO stipulated to the escape committee that the hospital in the middle of the camp, and the old chapel on its eastern extreme, which the American kriegies themselves renovated without stumbling on the entrance to the RAF tunnel there, were both off-limits for escape bids. The Geneva Convention protected hospitals, but, more importantly, once an escape was either detected in or took place from a hospital or chapel, the Germans could be expected to permanently deprive the kriegies of its use. Otherwise, everywhere else in the compound was fair game for escapers.

Instead of following the British example and giving Alger an exotic title such as Big X, the American kriegies called him S-2. His escape committee, rather than being the X Organization, was simply known as the security committee. Under Alger's aegis, too, came "the Bird," the radio receiver ingeniously built in camp by inmates and via which, each evening, a prisoner on secret listening duty noted down the war news emanating from the British Broadcasting Corporation (BBC) in London. The following day, throughout the camp, selected newscasters, including Boomer Holder, repeated the news to groups of kriegies after the summons, "The Bird is about to sing."[6]

The Germans regularly patched Nazi radio broadcasts into the camp via loudspeakers, and, while putting a German spin on events, these were remarkably honest throughout the war. But the Nazis were slow to confess to reverses. After D-Day, June 6, 1944, German radio would wait two days to mention Allied landings in Normandy. Via the Bird, Oflag 64's kriegies knew the day of the invasion that it had taken place. They had to contain their excitement in case they alerted their guards to the fact that they had a secret information source. When German media finally confirmed the Normandy landings, kriegies would quietly celebrate.

Gentleman Jim Alger's security committee brought the majority of camp inmates into the escape business one way or another. The American breakout organization at Oflag 64 was never quite so comprehensive as to include the sort of escape departments operated by the British at Schubin—no Gieves, Gammages, Thomas Cook, etc. Oflag 64 escape schemes were independent, small-scale affairs. Each American tunneling operation tended to involve a maximum of a dozen or so men, as opposed to the large-scale British tunnel schemes characterized by Asselin and the Great Escape. It was as if the British nationalized the escape business in their camps, while good old American private enterprise flourished at Oflag 64. This meant that those involved in each American escape project at Oflag 64 produced their own escape clothing, compasses, maps, and escape food, and there was no central forgery department.

Nonetheless, to protect all ongoing escape projects, Jim Alger's escape committee oversaw the distribution of earth from the tunnels that were soon being dug at Oflag 64. It also supervised the stooge program, posting lookouts throughout the camp to keep track of Germans when they were in the camp, especially the two ferrets in charge of searching for signs of escape activity—a sergeant nicknamed the Ferret, and his deputy, a mean-faced corporal dubbed the Weasel.[7]

"Ferret" and "stooge" were terms inherited from the British, who'd had three more years of imprisonment than most Americans in which to perfect their POW terminology. In British slang, the word "stooge" had a different meaning than the accepted American usage of a comic figure or secretly cooperative audience member used by comedians and hypnotists. To the Brits, to "stooge around" meant to hang around doing nothing in particular, and this was what stooges had to do a lot of when on boring lookout duty.

Several GIs had unsuccessfully attempted escape while on their way to Schubin, some more than once. But, by one estimation, only around 5 percent of American POWs in German hands thought of escape around the clock.[8] That 5 percent, inclusive of Boomer Holder and George Durgin, began planning a break from Schubin the moment they arrived. Back at their previous camp, Oflag IX-A/Z at Rotenburg, Holder and Durgin had contemplated escape, as they had on their way to Schubin. But they had never come up with the right plan or found the right circumstances.

This pair spent the first months of their captivity at Schubin making a detailed study of every aspect of Oflag 64, trying to find a flaw in German security. On July 28, there was a hullabaloo in camp when the ferrets discovered a tunnel, one of those left behind by the previous RAF occupants, dug from a barrack block. The following day, the Gestapo descended on the camp and turned it upside down. Unable to establish a link between the Americans and the tunnel, and finding no escape materiel, the Gestapo men left without charging any Americans. The tunnel was blown in.

Come September, discouraged by their inability to find a security flaw above ground, and encouraged by the progress the previous residents had apparently made tunneling during their occupancy, Holder and Durgin decided that the only way out was under the wire. Their interest in tunneling was conveyed to the escape committee, which had recently authorized a group of kriegies to dig a tunnel from the White House. Because Holder and Durgin were quartered in the White House and therefore had a good reason to hang around there, they were invited to join this tunnel scheme.

The White House tunnel team planned a tunnel that would go from the White House basement, under the southern wire and then under Adolf-Hitler-Strasse to cheekily emerge in the garden of the guard barrack on the other side of the street. Digging began that autumn, but the winter freeze meant it would have to be suspended by December—the first snows would fall on Schubin on November 5.

Digging could only resume the following spring, once the ground had thawed and conditions allowed a cross-country escape. The plan was to complete the tunnel by the end of April 1944. Because Holder and Durgin joined this tunnel team late, they weren't involved in digging. Like Eric Williams' part in the Asselin project, they were instead relegated to stooge duties, keeping a lookout for goons.

As the tunnelers began work in the White House basement in September, Holder, Durgin and the other lookouts frequently had to call a halt as the ferrets came nosing about. The suspicions of the Ferret and the Weasel were aroused by the number of men going down into the usually neglected basement, and by October, so little tunnel progress had been made because of interruptions that the escape committee deemed the project impractical and ordered it abandoned.

Undaunted, that October Holder and Durgin set their minds to perfecting another escape plot. If at first you don't succeed . . .

4

UNDER, OVER OR THROUGH THE WIRE

On October 18, 1943, a fleet of shiny new four-engine USAAF C-54 transport aircraft landed at Moscow's airport. In Indian file, they taxied to where an official Soviet reception party stood waiting in the subfreezing cold. Looking out his window, Major General John R. Deane, a passenger in one of the C-54s, could see the distant domes of the Kremlin, painted in wartime black.

Led by US Secretary of State Cordell Hull, Deane and the remainder of the sizable American party alighted and were met with handshakes and bear hugs from Soviet Foreign Minister Vyaacheslav Molotov and a gaggle of Red Army generals. Deane, a San Francisco native and a handsome, square-faced man with searching, intelligent eyes, had been a career soldier since 1917. Before the war, he'd served in China and Panama, and until this posting to the Soviet Union had been secretary of the Joint Chiefs of Staff in Washington, DC. He was arriving to take up the new post of chief of the American Military Mission to Moscow.

Previously, the US government had maintained army, navy and air force attachés at its Moscow embassy, but the Soviet government had refused to even talk to the attachés, let alone share military information with them. President Franklin D. Roosevelt's solution to a distinct lack of cooperation from America's Soviet ally was to send Moscow a new ambassador, Averell Harriman, and to establish this new high-level military mission under Deane to increase cooperation. The choice of Deane for this sensitive job had been very deliberate. He would have to apply his talents as both a diplomat and a military strategist to succeed in this new role.

The Russian officials conducted Hull, Harriman and Deane to a Red Army guard of honor lined up for the Americans' inspection. General Deane was impressed by the men of the guard detachment. Their uniforms and white gloves were impeccable, and their helmets shone. As the Americans passed in review, each soldier successively turned his head and eyes to the right with the precision of a robot. Deane thought the procedure very smart. Impressive, even.[1]

The American and Soviet officials then lined up in two ranks to watch the guard march past. The stiff, energetic goose-step style of Russian marching, which harked back to the days of the tsars, didn't impress Deane much. He thought the looser American style of marching, which concentrated on getting men from point A to point B, far preferable. "One for the Russians on the head and eye business," he thought to himself as he was escorted to his waiting car. "And one to the Americans on marching."[2]

His chauffeur-driven embassy car was a 1942 cream-and-brown Buick, which would always turn heads in austere Moscow. The British ambassador, Sir Archibald Clark-Kerr, was envious of the general's glamorous sedan. He nicknamed it Greta Garbo. As Greta carried Deane the five miles into downtown Moscow through gray streets filled with unsmiling Muscovites, Deane reflected on his mission. Back in Washington, his brief from General George C. Marshall, chairman of the Joint Chiefs of Staff, had been "to promote the closest possible coordination of the military efforts of the United States and the USSR." Deane was authorized to discuss American strategy, plans and operations with the Soviets at his discretion, and to use his charms to secure military cooperation from them in return.[3]

One area where Deane was determined to make inroads into Soviet cooperation was the rescue and repatriation of American prisoners of war in eastern Europe. "Of all the casualties of war," Deane was to say, "none elicit more sympathy from the American people than those known to be in the hands of the enemy. I felt a great personal responsibility in the matter."[4]

Ahead lay a difficult path for General Deane, whose efforts with the Soviets would impact the lives of thousands of American POWs in camps at Schubin and elsewhere that lay in the path of the Red Army's slow westward advance.

■ ■ ■

At Oflag 64, some kriegies weren't waiting around for the Russians to arrive and set them free. They had their own liberation plans. First, an American orderly, a sergeant, hid in the back of a departing truck that regularly made deliveries into the camp. The guards' search of the truck was perfunctory, and the sergeant was driven out of camp without being spotted. Unfortunately for him, the truck stopped right outside the Kommandantur just as a grenadier was passing by with his German shepherd guard dog. The dog, sniffing out the sergeant, began to bark. Result—time in the Cooler for the sergeant. He didn't have to walk far to reach his cell.

The 23rd Infantry Division's Lieutenant Colonel John H. "Jack" Van Vliet, Jr., from Red Bank, New Jersey, known as V.V. to fellow kriegies, had been perfecting his escape techniques ever since his capture in North Africa earlier that year. At Rotenburg, Van Vliet and Lieutenant Roy "Tex" Chappel from Refugio, Texas, had joined a British digging team that was making good progress until their tunnel was discovered by the Germans on a tip-off from a plant.

V.V. and Chappel had then tried various medicines to make them sick enough to be sent out of camp to a hospital, the plan to escape once outside the wire. But their captors had woken up to their scheme, and there was no transfer. Shortly after arriving at Oflag 64, Van Vliet had acquired a pair of wire cutters by bribing a Polish workman with cigarettes and chocolate. Van Vliet then put together an escape team comprising Chappel and himself plus Lieutenant Frank Aten, who had escaped briefly in Italy after being captured there, and Lieutenant William "Willy" Higgins from Boulder, Colorado.

V.V.'s latest scheme was as brazen as it was unlikely. He planned to get four men out by cutting through the wire under the guards' noses. With the approval of the escape committee and the SAO, the break went down one October evening at much the same time that General Deane was arriving in Moscow. Each evening, as the camp guard changed at dusk, kriegies were out and about in large numbers, getting their final breaths of fresh air for the day. Van Vliet and his escape team mixed with these men. In the half light of twilight, just before the fence lights came on and nighttime perimeter patrols began with the change of shift, the break went forward.

As accomplices staged a loud argument across the compound to distract guards, Lieutenant Richard W. "Dick" Secor from Des Moines, Iowa, acted as stooge for the break, keeping watch and waving quartet members forward when guards weren't looking. One by one, the four men stepped over the warning wire and bustled to a corner of the southeast fence by the commandant's residence. As V.V. had noticed, this location by the wire was shrouded from the eastern corner goon tower by a lilac bush in the commandant's garden. In a crouch, Chappel worked on the wire, swiftly cutting a hole big enough for a man to push through. Undetected, he progressed to the coiled wire and cut through that, too, before dealing with the outer wire.

In quick time, the first three men made it through the gap in the fences and walked as casually as they could east along the street and in through the gate to the old German Evangelical Cemetery adjacent to the camp.[5] The fourth man was just squeezing through the wire when the escapers' luck ran out. From across Adolf-Hitler-Strasse, an off-duty guard spotted the last man coming through the wire. He immediately raised the alarm.

Guards came on the run with weapons in hand and dogs on leashes.

As the last man through the wire was apprehended, guards dashed into the cemetery, firing pistols indiscriminately. After hiding behind a tombstone, V.V. and his companions slowly came to their feet with hands in the air. Meanwhile, the Appell bell rang, summoning the camp to an emergency assembly for a head count to determine the exact number of missing prisoners. Kriegies sauntered to the assembly, then milled about to confuse the count. They were kept standing for two hours while their numbers were counted and recounted.

Finally, security officer Zimmermann confirmed to new camp commandant Oberst Fritz Schneider, who had by this time replaced Oberstleutnant Le Viseur, that four prisoners were not present. As their kriegie colleagues went to supper late that evening, the recaptured escapees were locked up in the Cooler. The next day, Commandant Schneider sentenced the escapees to seven days' solitary.

The Germans also conducted an investigation into how the prisoners could have laid their hands on the wire cutters. With the escapers declaring they'd "found" them, the blame fell on Polish electrician Dariusz Musiał. Accused of carelessly leaving his tools lying around, Musiał was sentenced to six months in prison with hard labor and was never again seen at Oflag 64.

• • •

THAT SAME OCTOBER, Lieutenant J. Frank Diggs, an infantry platoon leader with the 3rd Division, came limping through the gate to Oflag 64 in a party of newly arrived Americans. Twenty-five-year-old Diggs, from Linthicum Heights, Maryland, had been wounded in the leg and captured in a battle near the town of Brollo on the north coast of Sicily. The invasion of Sicily, which followed the capitulation of Axis forces in North Africa, had seen 100,000 German and Italian troops escape to Italy with their equipment in an amphibious withdrawal across the Strait of Messina.

While American forces under General Patton had reached their Sicilian objectives, General Bernard Montgomery's British forces had failed to secure the port of Messina in time to prevent the enemy's evacuation. With limited success, Patton had used Frank Diggs' battalion in an amphibious landing behind the withdrawing German troops in an attempt to slow them down. It was, in Diggs' opinion, one of Patton's "less brilliant ideas."[6] When Patton tried the same amphibious maneuver a second time at Brollo, Diggs and his men had been cut off and overrun. The general would have an even less brilliant idea before the story of the Schubin inmates was over.

At Schubin, Diggs and another new arrival, Lieutenant Larry Phelan from Montclair, New Jersey, were assigned to Room 28 in the White House, joining Boomer Holder and George Durgin in that forty-bed dorm. The new pair soon teamed up with Holder and Durgin for bridge tournaments, and Diggs quickly became part of the Schubin establishment. For three years prior to being drafted in 1941, he'd been a journalist with *The Washington Post*, his tenure culminating with the job of city editor. Diggs put his newspaper experience to good use at Oflag 64. He and Captain George Juskalian conceived an outlandish idea—a printed monthly newsletter called *The Oflag 64 Item*, for distribution to every single Oflag 64 inmate. They put their concept to SAO Drake, who presented it to their captors. To Diggs' great surprise, Oberst Schneider also gave the idea his approval.

There was a print shop in Schubin that was run by a German soldier, Willi Kricks. A printer before the war, Kricks was now a member of the camp guard, working in the censors' office at the Kommandantur. While eight German soldiers with good English skills read and censored all letters to and from prisoners, Kricks, whose English was poor, checked all incoming parcels. Despite a crippled leg that gave him a limp, Kricks had been drafted into the Wehrmacht's local regiment once war broke out. At the same time, he'd acquired the Schubin print shop owned since 1920 by a Pole, Józef Kapsa.

The Kapsa family, like so many Poles, had been kicked out of their house and business by the Nazis in 1939 after being given just five minutes to collect their belongings. A thousand ethnic Germans had made up part of Schubin's population of 3,500 in 1939 when the Wehrmacht invaded this part of Poland. Some had roots going back generations to the 1700s and 1800s and the Prussian eras.[7] From 1939, other German settlers arrived from elsewhere, with Germans taking control of all of Schubin's government institutions and businesses. Willi Kricks had installed his German wife in the print shop to manage four Polish printers. Holding the contract for the printing needs of the 813th Regiment and the oflag, they also printed *The Item*.

Frank Diggs became convinced that his was the only POW camp newsletter in the Reich. It wasn't. Other camps were also allowed newsletters. The USAAF men in Stalag Luft 3's South Camp at Sagan, for example, put out their own camp newspaper. They called it *The Circuit* because it went around the camp. To produce *The Item*, Diggs assembled a team of a dozen kriegie writers, including his new friends and roomies Larry Phelan and Boomer Holder, and also used the illustrative talents of several inmates, including those of tall, dark, young Jim Bickers from Chicago. Between them, they put together a lively publication.

Most of Diggs' writers were amateurs, but for six months he was able to rely on the talents of another experienced journalist, Pulitzer Prize–winning Associated Press war correspondent Larry Allen, who had been captured while covering British navy operations in the Mediterranean. Allen penned an op-ed column for *The Item*, as well as regular war situation features, using the tongue-in-cheek byline "Schubin Bureau of the AP."

In May 1944, Diggs would receive permission to expand his press kingdom by also posting a handwritten daily newssheet, *The Bulletin*, on the camp bulletin board. Simultaneously, Allen's status as a noncombatant civilian would result in his being sent home to the United States via the Geneva Convention's repatriation provisions. It was great news for Allen, but Diggs missed his contributions.

As compensation, another war correspondent would land in Diggs' lap the following September. Wright Bryan—or "Write Bryan," as some kriegies described him—a former *Atlanta Journal* associate editor and subsequent war correspondent for that paper and the National Broadcasting Company (NBC), landed in France with US airborne forces on D-Day, only to be wounded and captured three months later while covering a firefight near Chaumont. Apparently because he was armed when captured, the Germans would not accord Bryan noncombatant status, so repatriation was out of the question for him. Bryan wrote for *The Item* and was editor of the Sunday edition of *The Bulletin*.

In addition, Diggs employed the skills of kriegie translators, a cartographer, and a prewar American printer. Diggs ran his crew with the care and efficiency of the editor of a big-city daily, and his team members were soon referring to him as "Chief." A lot of the paper's content covered activities in camp, including the kriegies' sports competitions and theater shows. In addition, *The Item* carried war news. The major source of information was the German radio and press, with Diggs' team taking the German news and putting an American slant on it.

All content had to pass the camp's German censors before publication, so Diggs was careful not to allow anything to appear that was too jingoistic. At times, too, Diggs knew, via the Bird, about Allied advances before the German media announced them. To keep the Bird safe, he wouldn't make anything known until after the German announcement. Diggs came up with a catchphrase for *The Item*: "Covers Oflag 64 like the dew."

Once a month from late October 1943, Diggs took copy and artwork for the latest issue of *The Item* under armed guard to the Kricks' print shop behind the former Kapsa house at 7 Paderewski Street, at the eastern end of Schubin. There, in contrast to the likable and easygoing Willi Kricks, his sour-faced wife, Anni, a dedicated Nazi, always greeted Diggs with a raised arm and "Heil Hitler!"

Apart from occasional typographical errors, the printers did a good job, and from the first edition of *The Item* on November 1, Oflag 64 readers looked forward to every monthly issue. Oberst Schneider no doubt thought these editorial activities, along with the POWs' active sports and theatrical programs, would distract his charges from thoughts of escape.

Unlike British officers in camps such as Stalag Luft 3, who displayed an unnecessarily "arrogant" attitude toward their German captors in the view of Swedish YMCA camp visitor Henry Söderberg, the Americans generally took a far more pragmatic and disciplined approach

to Schneider and his guards. This prevented unnecessary mass punishments for the stupid acts of individuals and also made the ferrets
less inclined to look too hard for signs of illicit activities.[8]

Several kriegies became friendly with German guards, who sometimes did them favors. For a time, Boomer Holder, a radio announcer
back home before the war, was permitted to broadcast "radio" programs of American music and chat over the camp's public address system, and was helped out by German *Sonderführer*. In the camp
library, librarian Lieutenant Leroy Ihrie from Lincoln, Nebraska,
found German guard Private Gottfried Dietz regularly climbing the
back stairs to his White House domain and running fascinated eyes
over the books on the shelves. Realizing that Dietz was interested in
improving his English, Ihrie loaned the young German several vol-
umes.

Dietz smuggled the American books out of the camp and read
them covertly before returning them to Ihrie just as discreetly. He
would have been in trouble if discovered in the act by his superiors.
These were the first books in English that Dietz ever read, and they
would encourage him to emigrate to the United States after the war.
He subsequently earned a Ph.D. at Princeton and became a professor
in Heidelberg, Germany. Dietz would always be grateful that his
American education had been launched in Schubin, courtesy of the
US Army kriegies there.

The prisoner-captor relationship at the higher level, between the
SAO and his staff and the German officers, was, Colonel Drake found,
businesslike and quite impersonal. Oberst Schneider always played
it by the book, often coming across as rigid and sometimes ridiculous. Drake found the German second in command, Oberstleutnant
Leuda, always fair, and the "lager officers," who were in charge of the
compound day to day, did their jobs without malice. The only German officer who was universally loathed was security officer Zimmermann, whom Drake considered petty in the extreme. There were
even times when Zimmermann, a Nazi Party favorite, appeared able
to reverse decisions of the commandant.

Overall, by not antagonizing the Germans, Schubin's SAOs were able to gain American prisoners concessions that were unheard of when the British were there—concessions such as the newsletter and the camp "radio" broadcasts. The Americans were also permitted occasional escorted walks through the countryside outside Schubin as well as winter ice skating, using YMCA-supplied skates, on a frozen pond where fish were raised across the street from the camp. These excursions beyond the wire, for groups of Oflag 64 inmates under guard, were a welcome break for kriegies sick of trudging around and around the short cinder Circuit, which followed the camp wire, for exercise.

The walks also allowed the escape committee to gain an accurate picture of the lay of the land immediately outside the camp for the information of Oflag 64 escapers. For, right under the Germans' noses, a range of escape plans were secretly being hatched by scores of camp inmates with the approval of Colonel Drake and the guidance of Jim Alger and the escape committee. Following the escape through the wire by the Van Vliet team, *Item* editor Frank Diggs ran a congratulatory note in the new camp paper, a note that escaped the attention of the German censors because it appeared in the sports section: "Good show, V.V. You and your team played heads-up ball against tough odds and bad breaks. You deserved to win. Better luck next time."[9]

Inspired by the efforts of Jack Van Vliet and his team, who had at least succeeded in breaking out of the camp, the frustrated Boomer Holder and George Durgin returned their attention to an above-ground escape. They came up with an idea that seemed so absurd it might just work. The pair would leave the camp the same way they came in, via the front gates. Holder and Durgin worked out that, on a rainy night, the sentries walking their perimeter beats and those up in the towers would hug their sentry boxes. At the same time, the rain could reduce visibility to almost nothing. On such a night, they hoped, they might be able to climb over the inner and outer gates without being spotted, and then, dressed like local Poles, walk away along Adolf-Hitler-Strasse as if they were locals.

To check their theory, they walked by the inner gate on several nights when light fog hung in the air. To their delight, the fog turned the light from the camp's arc lamps into a yellow haze that obscured their view of the guard towers at each corner of the southern perimeter. This also meant that the goons in those towers would have difficulty seeing them. The outer gate was made from latticed timber and would be a breeze to climb. The inner gate was topped with four strands of barbed wire angled back into the camp. But as the budding escapers discreetly studied the inner gate, they noticed that at one time it had been opened too violently and the metal strut on one side of those strands of wire had been bent back just enough to create a gap through which a man might squeeze. Excited now, they prepared a detailed escape proposal for S-2 Alger.

To give their plan every chance of acceptance, the pair drew a scale map of the camp's south side. Under the full gaze of the guards, they spent days casually pacing out distances and checking angles of sight from every direction. The gatehouse beside the front gate was just thirty yards from the inner gate, but it was unoccupied at night. As for the nearest goon towers, on the southern corners, they were far enough away for guards there not to see them if it was raining. Meanwhile, the sentries on foot patrol could be expected to be hunkering down.

Following their breakout, the pair intended to walk from Schubin to the port of Danzig (Gdańsk) on the Baltic, which they estimated was approximately one hundred miles to the north. They would then stow away aboard a ship bound for Sweden, where they would find a US consulate. Unwittingly, their plan followed an escape route similar to that used by Philip Wareing when the camp was Oflag XXI-B, a break that had resulted in a home run.

The pair planned to carry enough escape food for ten to twelve days of walking and two days of recon in Danzig to locate a suitable ship. To ensure that they weren't spotted or betrayed, they wouldn't approach locals for food or water, but instead would take along escape rations and a full water canteen to be refilled from streams en route. As for a compass, they had acquired a perfectly serviceable homemade one—a piece of magnetized metal on a mount—from Brits at Rotenburg and smuggled it into Oflag 64 when they arrived.

Submitting their proposal for escape committee and SAO approval, Holder and Durgin pointed out that the key to the success of their plan was its audacity. They knew that an escape via the gates was the last thing the Germans would expect. The escape committee agreed. SAO Drake gave his approval for Holder and Durgin's gate escape to proceed. To be able to walk all the way, the pair knew they would have to be as fit as possible, so they now began daily walking and running around the camp Circuit. To avoid drawing attention, they staggered their start times. After three months, they would be doing ten miles a day.

The Oflag 64 escape committee helped with a map and provided the pair with a briefing on the latest intelligence on port installation locations at Danzig, as well as troop concentrations to be avoided along their escape route. This information was gathered by Gentleman Jim Alger. Every time a new prisoner arrived in camp, or a kriegie went out of the camp for any reason, such as a hospital visit, he was quizzed by Alger on what he had seen.

Information also came from neutral camp visitors, who provided it sometimes unwittingly, sometimes wittingly, from Polish tradesmen occasionally working in the camp, and from a young Polish woman employed in the local station, Eugenia Grecka. Lieutenant Amon C. Carter, Jr., from Fort Worth, Texas, had to go the station under guard to collect private packages kriegies' families had sent via the Red Cross, and Eugenia left messages for him hidden in the station's wastepaper basket—until the day a German soldier found one.

"I could be promoted for reporting this," the German sternly told her, waving the piece of paper.

"Go ahead," Eugenia defiantly retorted.

He smiled. "Don't worry," he said, "I won't be such a swine."[10]

Eugenia would spend the rest of the war worrying that the soldier would report her to the Gestapo. He didn't.

By the time the Holder-Durgin escape scheme had been approved, winter had descended on Schubin, so, planning to make their break the following spring, the pair spent the winter making knapsacks just like the kind they saw on the backs of Poles walking by the camp. These knapsacks were carefully designed by perfectionist Durgin to carry precisely enough rations plus a canteen, made from a cookie tin, with a cork stopper. Durgin created his knapsack from gunny sacking, while Holder's started life as a fatigue jacket. Dyed brown with ersatz coffee, they ended up looking indistinguishable from Polish knapsacks.

• • •

IN LATE MARCH 1944, spring arrived, and with it, kriegie escape season opened in the Reich. Numerous escape plans were coming to fruition at Schubin, and elsewhere—the Great Escape took place on March 25–26 at Stalag Luft 3. At Oflag 64, Boomer Holder and George Durgin were almost ready to make their break.

The pair had waited until the last moment to prepare their escape rations to ensure that the food would not go off. The camp's medical officers had between them come up with a formula for a high-energy escape "cake" similar to the Fudge and Goo used by the Asselin escapers the previous year. Using this recipe, Holder and Durgin were happily making their escape mixture in their dorm, with ingredients piled beside them, when in walked the Ferret. Stooges had failed to call the usual warning, "Goon in the block!"

Thinking fast, Holder kept working, as if this was the most normal thing in the world to be doing. Kriegies sometimes made large community pies for whole mess tables, so Holder thought there was a chance he could bluff his way through.

"Making cake?" asked the smiling Ferret in German.

"Yes, yes," Holder replied, also in German. "Making cake is women's work. After the war, I won't be doing such a job."

Laughing, the Ferret went on his way.[11]

Breathing easy, the escapers kept working on their rations.

By the end of April, the pair was set to go. They had their knapsacks packed, and they were as fit as they'd ever been. Now the wait began for a rainy night. Day after day, they took turns staying awake until dawn so they didn't miss a downpour. Alas, the rain gods weren't smiling on them. Six weeks passed without a single wet night. Meanwhile, the pair's escape mixture became moldy, and they had to make a new batch.

Then another problem surfaced. Durgin had a skin condition, and in May it flared up on his hands. It proved so serious that the camp doctors could do little for him. Sent to the *Lazarett*, or military hospital, at Wollstein, for treatment, on medical advice he had to drop out of the gate escape on his return. A shattered Boomer Holder thought about going it alone, but eventually he and Durgin chose a running mate for him. Lieutenant Duane "Andy" Johnson from South Stanton, Iowa, was a White House roommate who got on well with both of them. Fit, and up for escape, Johnson eagerly took Durgin's place and his escape gear and joined Holder on the Circuit.

Several more weeks of nightly vigils passed, but while rain came during daylight, the nights were precipitation free. Then, in June came a promising overcast and windy night. Both men donned their escape clothes and waited. Nightly, three guards entered the compound after lights-out to conduct random dormitory checks. This night, Holder and Johnson didn't see where the German trio had headed. At the last moment they spotted the beam of a flashlight in the next room. As Holder dived for his bed, Johnson took a flying leap for his top bunk. Seconds later, the goons came into their room. In the dark, Holder and Durgin managed to pull blankets over themselves. Although undiscovered, the pair had to abort their escape that night.

In the following days and weeks, the weather continued to refuse to cooperate, and then Holder and Johnson were beaten to the punch by another escape. Serial escaper Jack Van Vliet had come up with a new plan, inspired by his time in the Cooler across the street. During his last incarceration there, he'd noticed through the barred window at the end of the Cooler's corridor that there was no barbed wire fence outside, just an open field, with woodland a quarter of a mile to the west. If a prisoner could get out that window, he would have a clear run for the wood.

There were three elements to the V.V. plan—a hacksaw blade, wire to pick cell locks, and time back in solitary. Acquiring the wire was the easy part. By the summer, Dick Secor, the stooge on the last Van Vliet break, came up with the required hacksaw blade, source unknown. As a result, he was recruited into the V.V. escape plot alongside Van Vliet, Tex Chappel, Frank Aten, and Willy Higgins. Also added was Lieutenant James J. MacArevey from Long Island. This created three teams for the break, each consisting of two running mates. The third part of the plan fell into place when a colleague suggested they create a drunken ruckus one night and get themselves thrown into the Cooler. Put to S-2 Alger, their plan received escape committee and SAO approval.

The Schubin escape committee maintained a protocol that required that no two escape bids could go ahead at the same time in order to prevent one escape from interfering with, or endangering, another. Van Vliet knew that Holder and Johnson were waiting for an elusive wet night to make their break. So he asked the pair's permission to go ahead of them because the Cooler gang was set to proceed immediately. V.V. assured the gate escape pair that, as his latest break would be from the solitary confinement block outside the camp, it would not impact their plan. Holder and Johnson agreed to hold off and give the Cooler break priority.

In the early hours of a June morning, Boomer Holder, asleep in his White House dorm, was awakened by the sounds of a raucous party in camp. He smiled to himself. The Van Vliet Escape, Mark II, was under way. For authenticity, the six escapers had soaked themselves in a raisin homebrew prepared by accomplices. For two hours, the partying band created a hullabaloo. But there was no move by the guards to stop them.

The group then commandeered a camp garbage cart and dragged it around, belting trash cans and shrieking with laughter. Because few in the camp knew about the escape plan, kriegies began calling out, telling the "drunks" to shut up and go back to bed. Even Holder tired of the group's antics, despite knowing what was really going on. Finally, several German interpreters came into the compound and asked the American gentlemen to please go to bed, as they risked being shot for being out after curfew. The band of merrymakers of course ignored them, so the Germans woke up the SAO and asked him to order his men back to barracks.

"Nothing doing!" declared Colonel Drake. "They're rowdy drunks, and deserve to be punished."[12]

So a dozen armed guards trooped into the compound, and the six "drunks" were dragged off to the Cooler. Secor even added to the effect by throwing up over the guards while being searched, which helped keep his hacksaw blade concealed. The next morning, after spending the night in the cells, the sextet was paraded before Oberst Schneider, who chewed out the Americans, especially Lieutenant Colonel Van Vliet, for conduct unbecoming officers. He sentenced them to fourteen days' solitary confinement. Perfect, thought the escapologists—plenty of time to prepare their break. All six had smuggled small pieces of wire past the guards, and Secor's hacksaw blade was still taped to the bottom of his boot.

No guard was stationed inside the Cooler, and over the next thirteen days Secor regularly picked his door lock, let himself out of his cell, and worked on the end window's six bars with his hacksaw blade. By the evening of the thirteenth day, the bars had been sawed almost all the way through and were ready to be removed with just a heave. In the meantime, American camp cookhouse orderlies had been smuggling in extra rations with the usual bread and water deliveries to the Cooler for the escapers to use on the run.

There was one hitch. Since the last visit of Van Vliet and his comrades to the Cooler, the ever cautious Hauptmann Zimmermann had put a sentry on patrol around the Cooler. This failed to put off the Cooler gang, but it meant that when they went out the window, they would have to be sure the sentry on this beat was on the far side of the building and unable to see them. To give themselves as much time on the run as possible before their absence was discovered the following morning, the escapers had decided to go before suppertime in the camp on the thirteenth night of their sentence, at a time when the sentries could be expected to be thinking about food and would be off their guard.

In the early evening, Aten and Higgins picked the locks to their cells' four-panel wooden doors, made their way to the window, and removed the almost sawed-through bars with brute force. Chappel, Secor and MacArevey also succeeded in opening their doors, but they were delayed because Van Vliet was having trouble with his lock. The guards were supposed to turn the cells' door key twice, double lock-ing them. They'd done this with Van Vliet's door, but had only given the other locks a single turn of the key. As a result, Van Vliet's lock was resisting all efforts to pick it. In the end, the colonel urged the others to go without him. Chappel, Secor and MacArevey left a per-spiring V.V. still working on his lock.

Aten and Higgins had meanwhile clambered out the window. Scooting along a drainage ditch, the pair reached the wood without being spotted. Back in the Cooler, their three colleagues peered out the open window. They knew better than to go the Hollywood route and jump the patrolling sentry—if they injured or killed him, they could expect death sentences if recaptured. In the end, the trio let their impatience get the better of them. Seeing no sign of the sentry, out the window they went.

From across the other side of Adolf-Hitler-Strasse, in the Little Theater in the southwest corner of the camp, Boomer Holder, Andy Johnson, George Durgin and others involved with rehearsals for the latest theatrical show had stationed themselves at windows to watch the break go down. They exchanged quiet cheers and handshakes when they saw Aten and Higgins reach the trees. Then they saw Chappel, Secor and MacArevey make their run from the Cooler win-dow. As the watchers were asking themselves where V.V. was, the pa-trolling sentry came around the corner.

Bent low as they ran, the trio was 500 yards along the drainage ditch. But the sentry spotted them and raised the alarm. Guards came running. Several went charging off on motorcycles, heading down Adolf-Hitler-Strasse to the west. *Hundeführer* with guard dogs con-verged on the window. Quickly picking up a scent, barking and strain-ing at their leashes, the dogs led their handlers at a trot across the field to the wood. A check inside the Cooler, where V.V. was still in his cell, made it immediately clear to the Germans that five prisoners were on the loose.

Boomer Holder and his colleagues went to supper shortly afterward, hoping that their friends had gotten away, or at least caused the Germans a pile of worry. Or both. At evening Appell, the kriegies were informed by the lager officer conducting the count that Chappel, Secor and MacArevey had already been returned to the Cooler. They would serve another stint in solitary, with the window repaired and a guard now stationed permanently inside the solitary confinement block. But Aten and Higgins were still on the run.

Holder and his roomies in the White House's Room 28 took turns keeping a vigil at their window through the night, in case there was any sign of Aten and Higgins being returned. Sure enough, around 2:00 a.m., a German staff car turned into the Kommandantur courtyard, and out of the rear struggled Aten and Higgins, under Gestapo escort. The clothes of the escapees were dirty. They were handcuffed and chained together. Caught by locals, they had been handed over to the police, who in turn had passed them on to the Gestapo. Fellow kriegie Lieutenant Clarence Meltesen, a former platoon leader with the 3rd Ranger Battalion, would learn that they had succeeded in getting two and a half miles from the camp before being nabbed.[13]

Oberst Schneider appeared, and there in the courtyard he bawled out Aten and Higgins for forty raging minutes. Boomer Holder, watching from his dormitory window a hundred yards away, couldn't hear what the commandant was saying, but he could imagine. Once this tirade ended, Schneider ordered the pair removed from his sight. Instead of being returned to the Cooler to join their four compatriots, Aten and Higgins were put back in the car, and driven away from the camp. The following morning, Jack Van Vliet was taken from his Cooler cell and paraded before the commandant.

"I must commend you on your good behavior, Lieutenant Colonel Van Vliet," said Schneider, unaware that V.V. would also have been on the run had it not been for a double lock. "I am very glad to see that you have learned your lesson."[14]

Van Vliet's original sentence having expired, Schneider returned him to the camp, where V.V. amused his fellow kriegies with his tale of the commandant's commendation.

When another day passed without any news of Aten and Higgins, SAO Drake asked for an urgent meeting with Oberst Schneider at which he demanded to know what had happened to his two men. Schneider, partly angry, partly embarrassed, admitted that the pair had been sentenced by the Gestapo to six weeks' hard labor at Hohensalza Prison—a place familiar to Bill Ash and Eddy Asselin. Drake, appalled, reminded Schneider that, under the Geneva Convention, the maximum punishment a POW could receive for attempting escape was thirty days' solitary confinement.

The pair's sentence was in contravention of the Convention. Declaring that he would take the matter up with representatives of the Swiss government, the "Protecting Power" under the Convention, and that he would hold the commandant personally responsible for the welfare of Aten and Higgins and this breach of the Geneva Convention, Colonel Drake left Schneider red-faced. The colonel got on the telephone, and Aten and Higgins were returned to Oflag 64 ten days after they'd entered the prison gates at Hohensalza.

"It was worse than awful there," the pair told Boomer Holder after their return. They had been forced to live on a daily ration of 300 grams of bread and a bowl of soup. "The SAO saved our lives."[15]

But Holder and Johnson weren't discouraged. With the Cooler break out of the way, they could now proceed with their gate escape.

5

DEATH SENTENCES

WHILE HOLDER AND JOHNSON WERE PRAYING FOR RAIN, A NEW TUN-
nel project was making good progress. A team led by artillery lieutenant William R. "Bill" Cory from Maryland was digging from
beneath Barrack Block 3A, one of the three blocks in the former Oflag
XXI-B Russian compound.

Unlike Stalag Luft 3, where the wooden barrack blocks sat above-
ground on brick foundations with open space between barrack floor
and ground, here at Oflag 64 the brick barracks sat on foundations
that ran all the way around them. This created an enclosed space
between floor and ground, but it could be accessed via a trapdoor,
and the ferrets regularly checked these spaces with flashlights. This
prevented both the digging of tunnels beneath the floorboards and the
disposing of tunnel soil down there. But there was a flaw in the block
design at Schubin that enabled the digging of a tunnel from a barrack
block. As was the case at Sagan, the blocks' stoves sat on broad concrete
bases that went all the way down to the ground.

Because all the Americans at Schubin ate in the one large mess, stoves in the small kitchens in the middle of each barrack block were rarely used. The Cory team realized, as did Big X Roger Bushell's tunnelers at Stalag Luft 3, that the barrack stoves' solid concrete bases could be burrowed through. This the Cory escapologists did, removing the grate beneath the stove and creating a thin new concrete base fitted with handles to cover the tunnel shaft's entrance. Laboriously chipping down through the solid concrete foundation, Cory and his fellow diggers succeeded in creating a narrow entrance shaft.

They then continued digging down through the earth for some twenty feet—deep enough, they hoped, to avoid German listening devices. Only then did the tunnel begin, heading west toward the wire. The Ferret and the Weasel regularly visited Block 3A, sniffing around with their probes and flashlights, but they never located the cleverly camouflaged entrance to the Cory tunnel in the now unused kitchen.

Dispersing the soil brought up from the tunnel did prove a problem. For one thing, it was a different color than the topsoil. Schubin's American kriegies quite independently came up with some of the techniques used in the Great Escape at Sagan, and one of these involved spreading tunneled soil on garden beds beside the recreation ground. Tunnel dirt was also spread on the Appell ground and the basketball/volleyball court.

But how could they get the earth from tunnel to gardens and sports fields? The Americans came up with the idea of earth-filled bags suspended inside trouser legs, just as the X Organization did at Sagan, where these soil dispersers were called "penguins." At Schubin, this method proved to take too long. Plus, there was much more soil than gardens or sports fields could accommodate—56 tons of it. Spreading it in the full view of the guards also proved difficult. Before long, this method was abandoned.

As Cory and his team cast about for other dispersal places, they discovered that Asselin soil had been packed into the space beneath the White House mess hall floor. Meanwhile, the ceiling above the top floor of the White House contained dirt from the old cookhouse tunnel. And then it dawned on the Cory crew that the solution lay right above their heads—between the ceiling and the roof of their own hut. Block 3A, being beside the west wire, was a long way from the front gate and even farther from the Kommandantur. If a ferret came in the gate, there was plenty of time for strategically placed stooges to signal a warning to escapers working in, and under, Block 3A.

But how would they get the dirt up into the roof space? Lieutenant Sid Waldman from Cleveland, Ohio, was a late sleeper and the best pantomime actor in the camp's Little Theater. He was also diminutive, hence his nickname, "Mouse." Mouse Waldman crawled up into the ceiling space regularly; a relay of helpers handed up Red Cross boxes filled with earth from the tunnel below. Waldman happily spread earth over the ceiling, but on one occasion he slipped and put a foot through the ceiling. Trapped there, he had to be hauled out. Waldman left a gaping hole, which would have tipped off the Germans, so kriegies quickly repaired the hole and covered the cracks with toothpaste mixed with dust. They got away with the cover-up, too. Digging continued belowground while earth spreading resumed above.

To shore up the tunnel, the escape committee required all kriegies in camp to make a donation of bed boards. Second Lieutenant Billy Bingham, a 168th Infantry officer captured in Tunisia in February 1943, would complain that he was left with just three boards to sleep on. The boards were smuggled to the tunnel entrance and taken underground to line walls and ceiling, as had been the case with the RAF's Asselin tunnel. Consequently, the claustrophobic tunnel was less than three feet high and three feet across.

Conscientious Hauptmann Zimmermann began to suspect that bed boards were being removed. So he had his assistant quartermaster do a count of every bed board in camp to see if any were missing, and if so, how many. The kriegies easily got around this. While the methodical German was counting boards in one block, the Americans snuck boards into the next one, so that all bunks appeared to have their full quota of boards when he passed through.

The Cory tunnel had the luxury of air-conditioning, courtesy of

Second Lieutenant Louis W. Otterbein, the handiest handyman in the camp. He was in charge of creating staging and props for the Little Theater, located right next door to the block containing the tunnel entrance. In James Bond terminology, Lou Otterbein was the Oflag 64 escape committee's "Q," the gadget man. Following in the footsteps of the Asselin tunnelers, but independent of his predecessors, Otterbein built bellows to pump air into the tunnel and air lines made from linked Klim milk cans. When the Cory shaft began to fill with water, Lou the "Q" Otterbein built a suction device that efficiently sucked the water out.

Hauptmann Zimmermann was meanwhile convinced that a tunnel was being dug somewhere in the compound, but while his ferrets regularly searched all camp buildings, they never came up with anything. So Zimmermann resorted to drilling ten-foot holes outside the camp perimeter and setting off explosive charges in order to cave in tunnels. This blasting exercise moved progressively around the camp, and when it was opposite Block 3A, the kriegie moles abandoned their hole and crossed their fingers.

The Cory tunnel stood up pretty well to the nearby blast, but men lying on their bunks quickly evacuated 3A when it swayed to and fro, fearing that tons of earth would cascade down onto them from above. The ceiling also held up. As Zimmermann moved on with his explosives, the tunnelers went back to work. Digging was slow, and a projected spring 1944 escape date had to be revised. At their current rate of progress, the Cory team anticipated reaching open ground beyond the western perimeter fence by late summer, before the autumn chill set in at Schubin.

■ ■ ■

IN EARLY JULY 1944, Colonel Drake was summoned to Oberst Schneider's office and informed that fifty Allied airmen had been shot by the Gestapo after they had escaped from Stalag Luft 3. This was the Great Escape.

While they had come from thirteen countries, most of the executed Stalag Luft 3 men were Brits. The others included Canadians,

Australians, New Zealanders and Poles. Contrary to the story conveyed by the movie version of *The Great Escape*, no Americans took part in that breakout. Several Americans, including Colonel Albert "Bub" Clark and Major Jerry Sage, had been integrally involved in the break's preparations, but that was before Americans were removed from Stalag Luft 3's North Compound. Clark had been Big S, in charge of X Organization security for the compound, while Sage had run diversions.

Once in that camp's South Compound, Clark became Big X there, and Sage a member of the three-man escape committee, and they set about planning their own mass escape until they learned that their friends from North Compound had been shot by the Gestapo. Men who had busted out of Schubin via Asselin, including Peter Fanshawe and Danny Król, were among those executed. Other Asselin escapers, including Wings Day and American Johnny Dodge, had been among the minority of recaptured Great Escapers to avoid the execution list. That pair was sent to Sachsenhausen concentration camp. They would survive the war.

Oberst Schneider warned Colonel Drake that the Gestapo was now threatening to shoot all recaptured escapees and urged him to pass this information on to his men. Escaping, the commandant said, was now deadly. Drake was shaken by this news and issued an order halting all existing escape schemes and banning any future escapes.

He was not alone. Across the Reich, SAOs and SBOs gave the same order at numerous POW camps. Kriegies were told by their senior officers that they would have to just sit tight and wait for Allied armies to fight their way to their camps and liberate them. Some more pessimistic prisoners didn't think that would happen anytime soon. Up until that June, Oflag 64's Billy Bingham had been predicting that the war would not end until 1983. After D-Day, he would revise his forecast to 1950.[1]

Boomer Holder and Andy Johnson were infuriated by the escape ban. One night, just days after the colonel issued the standing order, Oflag 64 was blanketed by rain, creating the perfect conditions for their gate escape. The members of the Cory tunnel team were similarly crushed by the "no escape" order. Two disappointed young tunnelers, Second Lieutenants Reid F. Ellsworth and John O. Kadar, had their break all planned, right down to their escape route and destination: Hungary.

Ellsworth differed from most Schubinites. He was a B-17 navigator from Idaho serving with the 346th Bomb Squadron, 99th Bombardment Group, and had been captured in Italy that January. As USAAF, not US Army, he shouldn't have even been at Schubin, but he'd been captured with US ground troops. From the outset he'd teamed up with Kadar, who had also been bagged in Italy in January. They had gone through other camps together on their way to Schubin. Being good soldiers, they, like all budding escapers, obeyed orders and put their ambitions for freedom on hold. For now.

To ram home the message that escape was a dangerous idea, the German authorities subsequently had posters printed in English with the message "THE ESCAPE FROM PRISON CAMPS IS NO LONGER A GAME!" and advising "ALL POLICE AND MILITARY HAVE BEEN GIVEN THE MOST STRICT ORDERS TO SHOOT ON SIGHT ALL SUSPECTED PERSONS." These posters were distributed to all American and British POW camps. At Oflag 64, the unpopular Weasel and another corporal arrived in the American admin office at the White House to pin up several of the posters. When the German corporals strode into the office, posters in hand, assistant adjutant Second Lieutenant James "Jimmie" Schmitz from Ottawa, Illinois, was sitting at his desk. Before he would permit the posters to be displayed, he demanded to read them.

Once he had taken in the posters' content, Schmitz objected to them, considering them offensive to American officers because they accused the American government of "gangster warfare." Telling the two Germans to wait, he hurried away to find the SAO to back him up. The SAO was unavailable, so Schmitz returned with Lieutenant Colonel William H. Schaeffer. A battalion commander captured in Sicily, Schaeffer had suffered a serious leg wound and still needed crutches to get around. Tall and heavy-set, he had a reputation for being ornery at the best of times, and he never lost an opportunity to bait the Germans. At a previous camp, he had more than once waved a crutch at guards. As a consequence, he'd racked up seven weeks in the Cooler there.

Schaeffer was in sympathy with Schmitz and told the Germans so in no uncertain terms. But the posters went up, with an additional line scrawled across the top by the Weasel: "Removing will be punished." As the Germans turned to leave, a fuming Schmitz stood in the doorway, folding his arms and blocking their way. One of the Germans pushed Schmitz. Reluctantly, he stood aside. And the two guards departed.

The matter seemed to have passed until, several days later, both Schaeffer and Schmitz were summoned by the commandant and charged with "obstructing the functions of the German Reich." Some months later the pair would be tried in a German civilian court. Defended by a German lawyer, they would be acquitted. Until that trial, Jimmie Schmitz remained at Oflag 64. The troublesome Schaeffer was transferred to Oflag IV-C, the infamous Colditz Castle maximum-security POW camp.

Four more Schubin kriegies were also hauled into a German court during this period, George Durgin among them. They were in a group of kriegies taken to Posen for dental treatment. As they were walking through the city, their guards ordered them off the pavement and into the street. Only German citizens were permitted to walk on the sidewalk. Allied POWs encountered this discrimination until the end of the war. George Durgin and three others refused to leave the sidewalk and, like Schaeffer and Schmitz, were charged with obstructing the functions of the German Reich. Once brought to trial, they, too, would be found not guilty and returned to camp.

All of these cases would be suddenly revived a short time later with terrifying potential consequences.

■ ■ ■

THIS SAME MONTH of July, Stefania Maludzińska was walking along Adolf-Hitler-Strasse past Oflag 64. The previous December 31, using the excuse of visiting friends to celebrate New Year's Eve, Stefania had traveled with Mrs. Łucja Karczewska to the small fishing port and prewar resort of Heisternest (Polish Jastarnia) on the Baltic. Oflag 64's escape committee had asked the women to help American krie-gies then tunneling to freedom—the Cory tunnelers. The women hoped to convince the captain of a particular boat to take the escap-ees to Sweden once they broke out of the camp. To their regret, they hadn't been able to gain the cooperation they'd sought.

As Stefania passed the camp now, her thoughts were on the young Americans behind the wire and her failed mission to help them. The usual practice for Poles passing the camp was to keep looking directly ahead. Drivers of horse-drawn vehicles would slap the reins along the backs of their steeds to speed by. Defiantly, Stefania looked in the di-rection of several young American officers standing outside the White House, not far from the wire. According to Boomer Holder, Stefania was "quite comely," and the Americans inside the wire gave her a dis-creet wave. Not so discreetly, Stefania waved back.[2]

A guard in the Kommandantur was also watching the girl pass, and he saw her wave to the POWs. Guards came on the run, and Ste-fania was arrested in sight of the Americans. Tried in August for consorting with the enemy—simply because she'd returned that American wave—Stefania would be sentenced to twelve months' im-prisonment. The young woman was sent to Hohensalza, the very same prison where Schubin escapees Bill Ash, Eddy Asselin, Frank Aten and Willy Higgins had been locked up after their recapture.

After two months behind bars at Hohensalza, Stefania would escape while working outside the walls. Walking part of the way home, she then hitched a ride on a wagon and then on the back of a bicycle ped-aled by a Schubin man. For the final leg, she boldly rode in a railroad car reserved for Germans. Back in Schubin, Stefania went into hiding with distant relatives. During this period, her mother was arrested for giving bread rolls to passing POWs, and sentenced to four months' solitary confinement. Stefania's mother never returned from prison.[3]

■ ■ ■

MAJOR JERRY SAGE was a new arrival at the camp in July 1944. Twenty-seven years of age, tall, lean and mean, a graduate of Washington State University, Sage knew all about escapes. He had helped prepare the mass escape at Stalag Luft 3. Five months before the Great Escape occurred, paratrooper Sage had been among 300 Americans transferred out of Stalag Luft 3's North Compound to the new South Compound.

That transfer had probably saved Sage's life. Otherwise, he would have been one of the Great Escapers; being a serial escaper, he would almost certainly have been one of the fifty shot by the Gestapo. He shouldn't have been at Stalag Luft 3 in the first place, for the camp was for air force officers. Because paratroop forces were part of the Luftwaffe in the German military, and the Luftwaffe ran the Stalag Luft camps, Sage had been initially lumped in with the flyboys. Considered a troublemaker, he had subsequently been sent to Oflag VII-B at Eichstätt in Bavaria.

Oflag VII-B was an all-British camp, and when the commandant there offered Sage a transfer to a camp for American ground force officers at Schubin, Sage jumped at the idea. He knew that Schubin was hundreds of miles closer to the Russians than to American forces advancing from the west. Changing circumstances dictated changed plans. Instead of escaping west into Germany, Sage now plotted to go east, link up with the advancing Russkies, and do as much damage to the Nazis as he could in partnership with the Reds.

Sage had been looking for a fresh escape opportunity ever since he was separated from the escape committees at Stalag Luft 3. Jerry Sage was no ordinary prisoner. While ostensibly an airborne division soldier, Sage was in reality "Dagger," a secret operative of the Office of Strategic Services, the OSS, forerunner of the Central Intelligence Agency. Captured during a behind-the-lines mission in Tunisia in 1943, Sage was a highly trained silent killer and saboteur, and he had been raring to get out and get to work behind enemy lines ever since. On being welcomed to Oflag 64 by Colonel Drake, Lieutenant Colonel Waters and Major Meacham, Sage was informed of Drake's new standing order banning escapes. Sage didn't agree with the order, but he respected it and settled in to await the approach of the Russians.

That July, too, as Colonel Drake called a halt to escapes from Oflag

64, he managed an escape of his own. He was advised that he had sat-isfied German and Protecting Power doctors that he was sufficiently crippled by his wounds to be repatriated to the United States under the provisions of the Geneva Convention. Drake was shipped out of Schubin on July 27 in the company of a Protecting Power represen-tative. Within a head-spinning ten days, he was back home in the States, soon to be discharged from the US Army. Over the coming months, Drake would write to the families of men he'd left behind at Oflag 64. Craig Campbell's parents in Texas would hear from him in November. Assuring them that Craig was holding up well and would eventually come home to them, Drake also told the Campbells a little about conditions in the Schubin camp.

On September 8, Leo Fisher, a burn victim, was also repatriated from Oflag 64. He was home by September 18 and soon began to write press articles about the plight of his buddies back at Schubin. Al-though repatriation was rare, it did offer a way to get home fast, and frustrated tunneler Reid Ellsworth now had an idea. Ellsworth had no serious wound, but one of the grounds for repatriation was severe mental illness.

Many kriegies became clinically depressed behind the wire, often after receiving bad news from home. Then there were the young of-ficers who, questioning their own decisions and courage, fretted about men who had died fighting under them. A few kriegies began to with-draw into their shells. At Schubin, this depression became known as "kriegieitis." At its worst, it could lead to suicide attempts; a British officer at Schubin when it was Oflag XXI-B had reputedly taken his own life by jumping from the White House roof.

One American kriegie who was determined not to succumb to kri-egieitis was Second Lieutenant Edwin O. "Ed" Ward, from Clewis-ton, Florida. A 1st Division infantryman captured near the Kasserine Pass in Tunisia in early 1943, he'd been in the first group of Ameri-cans to arrive at Oflag 64. To keep his mind active, he got involved in sports, the theater and camp bridge tournaments. He was also one of five business-minded kriegies who set up and ran the Schubin Mer-chandise Mart, a popular points-system bartering scheme that operated in the camp schoolhouse one day a week, trading Red Cross food and cigarette allowances.

In a letter home to his young wife, Mildred—they'd married in September 1942—Ed asked for a warm knitted cap for the winter. Months later, a parcel containing a knitted cap arrived from Mildred. As twenty-seven-year-old Ward studied his fine new headwear, he came across a name tag inside: "Jones."

"Who the hell is Jones?" Ward exclaimed aloud.[4]

Despite the ribbing of his fellow kriegies, who suggested that his wife might have found herself a boyfriend named Jones, Ed Ward never doubted his wife's fidelity. But others fell into deep depression or began acting strangely after receiving unsettling news from home or, worse, opening "Dear John" break-up letters from wives or girl-friends.

What if, pondered Reid Ellsworth, he could convince the doctors that he was crazy and win an early ticket home via repatriation? Approaching escape committee deputy chief Major Merle Meacham, Ellsworth put up his scheme, assuring Meacham that he would be able to pull it off. Officially, escape was now off the agenda at Oflag 64. But Ellsworth's plan, if successful, would see him sent home with the acquiescence of the Germans and without the dangers now associated with being on the run in the Reich.

Meacham gave Ellsworth approval to implement the "insanity project," as they called it. But for the project to work, said Meacham, none of the American medical officers at the camp could be told that Ellsworth was playacting. To get past the German doctors, Ellsworth would first have to convince American MOs that he had lost his mind. Having seen other men become mentally unstable by degrees, Ellsworth began gradually developing his "symptoms."

■ ■ ■

IT WAS NOW dangerous for American and British POWs, both inside and outside their camps. Earlier in the war, American and British prisoners had been excluded from harsh measures ordered for other troublesome POWs. But by the fall of 1944 the attitudes of Adolf Hitler and his SS chief, Heinrich Himmler, had been hardened by the Great Escape and by the unrelenting bombing of German civilian targets by the USAAF and RAF, whose aircrews were now labeled "terror fly-ers" and "gangsters" by the German radio and press. Downed Allied aircrews were being lynched and beaten to death by German mobs—frequently led by women in the absence of their menfolk who were at war. Seven American airmen suffered this fate after their B-17 crashed in German territory. Not only did Himmler approve of these mur-ders; German police and soldiers who protected Allied aircrews from such mobs were reprimanded.

That September, there was another mass execution of Allied pris-oners. On September 5, forty-six British and Dutch prisoners and one American were taken from various Nazi prisons to the Mauthausen concentration camp fifteen miles outside the city of Linz in Austria. In official SS records, all were listed as "pilots." They were in fact agents of the Special Operations Executive (SOE), Britain's espionage agency, who had been parachuted into Holland and Belgium and caught by German Abwehr counterespionage agents.

All these men had been captured wearing civilian clothes, and all had been imprisoned for up to a year until their transfer to Mauthau-sen. Upon arrival, they were informed they had been sentenced to death as spies. At 7:00 a.m. on September 6, nineteen of the condemned men were stripped to their shirts and underwear, and, barefoot, es-corted to the camp's stone quarry, dubbed the Vienna Trench. There were 186 steps leading down into the Vienna Trench. Mauthausen inmates called them the Steps of Death.

Down the steps the nineteen men were bustled. Each was given a twelve-pound rock. Ordered to carry their load up the steps, one after the other, they were beaten all the way. It was hard enough for the weak prisoners to walk up 186 steps without pause, let alone do it carrying a heavy load. Some fell under the weight, often toppling onto men behind, sending them falling like dominoes, which the guards thought hilarious. Prisoners were then taken back down into the quarry, made to pick up even heavier stones, and forced to climb the steps again.

This continued until the prisoners could no longer stand. All were then dragged to flat ground above the quarry. Told that freedom awaited them beyond the camp wire, they were told to run, walk, or crawl toward the fence. As they did, they were cut down by rifle and machine-gun fire. All nineteen were dead by 9:00 a.m. The following day, the remaining twenty-eight prisoners suffered the same horrific fate. SS camp records noted that all had been killed while "attempting to escape from their place of work."[5]

Mauthausen would be the scene of the execution of more Americans the following January. On December 26, eleven American OSS agents, six British SOE agents, and ace American Associated Press war correspondent Joe Morton would be taken prisoner in Slovakia during the culmination of the largest and most disastrous OSS Central European operation of the war. Although all but two were captured in military uniform, every one of the OSS and SOE agents was sent to Mauthausen. They were brutally interrogated at length by the SS before an execution order came through from Berlin. These men weren't consigned to the Steps of Death. Senior camp personnel came up with what they considered an even more amusing fate for these prisoners, who were not informed they'd been sentenced to death.

In late January 1945, the eighteen prisoners would be taken, naked and one by one, into a basement room and stood before a camera. They were told by the camp commandant that their details were being taken for the records, after which they would be sent to a POW camp. As each man stood there, expecting to be photographed, an apparent height-measuring device, operated by an SS captain, was slid up behind them. It fired a bullet from a concealed gun into the back of the prisoner's head. The SS thought their execution device a hoot. German radio would announce that these prisoners had been shot as spies. Three more American OSS agents captured in Austria in February would be executed at Mauthausen. A fourth OSS agent also captured in Austria, a US Navy lieutenant, would somehow survive Mauthausen and be liberated by the US Army in April 1945.

As these cases proved, military uniform was no longer protection for Americans on the run in the Reich, and any escaped POW was

on notice that he would be shot. The safest place for American kriegies in 1944 was behind the wire.

■ ■ ■

WITH THE DEPARTURE of the repatriated Colonel Drake, Colonel
George V. Millett, Jr., took over as Oflag 64's SAO and was almost
immediately thrust into an escape crisis. Lieutenant Harry T. Schultz
managed this same month to get out of the camp by exchanging identities with an enlisted man being transferred to Stalag XXI-D at Posen. When Schultz reached Posen, Brits of the camp's X Organization
equipped him with escape clothes and forged ID papers, and on July 14
he had succeeded in breaking out of Stalag XXI-D.

Riding trains in plainclothes as a passenger, Schultz had reached
the Czechoslovakian capital, Prague. At Prague station, an alert Gestapo officer found flaws in his forged papers. Accused of being a
spy, Schultz was arrested. Instead of being returned to his camp of
origin, Oflag 64, Schultz was shunted by the Gestapo from one dun-
geon cell to another in Breslau, Dresden, Posen and Bromberg, each
time getting a little closer to Schubin but always under threat of death.

Hearing of Schultz's plight from a Protecting Power representative, Colonel Millett lodged a formal protest with Oberst Schneider.
As a result, the Gestapo handed Schultz over to the Wehrmacht in
Bromberg. He was returned to Oflag 64 in a railroad car fitted out
with punishment cells in which it was just possible to crouch. After
serving twenty-one days in the Schubin Cooler, Schultz rejoined
the kriegie population. He was lucky to be alive, and the harrowing
experience in Gestapo hands had cured him of further thoughts of
escape.

Three months into Colonel Millett's tenure as SAO, in October
1944, a more senior colonel arrived with a new batch of prisoners, and
the new man immediately took over as SAO. This was the very tall
and gangly Colonel Paul R. Goode. Formerly the commander of the
175th Infantry Regiment, 29th Division, fifty-three-year-old Goode,
the oldest American in camp and a thirty-one-year army veteran, was

from Corvallis, Oregon. Goode's hair had turned white after an escape attempt had gone wrong the previous August.

Captured in France two months after the D-Day landings in Normandy, Goode had been heading for Germany on a train packed with Allied prisoners when he'd ordered a junior officer to make a hole in their boxcar floor. At the next stop, fifteen officers had escaped via the hole, but 200-pound Goode couldn't fit through. The 359th Infantry's First Lieutenant Brooks E. Kleber from Trenton, New Jersey, was due to be next man out after Goode. Hearing submachine guns firing outside, Kleber was glad he hadn't gotten out.

Two companies of Waffen-SS troops were traveling on the same train, and, as the senior American officer, Goode was hauled out of the boxcar and handed over to the SS unit's commander. Brooks Kleber saw the colonel lined up beside the train with four other American officers. A shallow grave was dug, and an SS firing squad formed up. Goode, convinced he was about to die, slipped off his cherished West Point ring and passed it to one of his men. The firing squad went through the motions without firing and then stood down. Goode and the others were herded back onto the train.

The SS did shoot a French parachute sergeant who disobeyed the order for all prisoners to lie flat and keep their heads down while Goode's mock execution took place. Goode lived in fear of being executed over the coming weeks until he arrived at Schubin. In the meantime, his hair had whitened and he'd shed thirty pounds. The experience had aged him so much that the men at Schubin came to refer to him as "Pop" Goode.

Once at Oflag 64, SAO Goode reorganized the senior levels of prisoner staff, appointing George Millet as his executive officer, replacing Johnny Waters in that role. Major Kermit V. Hanson became assistant XO, while Major Merle Meacham retained the role of adjutant and Jim Alger remained S-2. Goode found a new post for Waters—welfare officer, a role he had previously been filling in part as XO. This allowed the popular Waters to continue doing what he did best, keeping up the military spirit and morale of the prisoners.

Apart from senior officers serving as block commanders, the appointments under Colonel Goode included the camp's medical officers and dentists, as well as officers in charge of all the smaller departments, from the tailor and barber shops to the library. To ensure that all department heads were on their toes, Goode appointed Colonel Fred W. Drury as his inspector general.

The single most important department as far as kriegies were concerned covered food distribution. Under a lieutenant colonel, this encompassed the cookhouse with its boring kriegie diet of soup, potatoes, cabbage, turnips, and ersatz coffee, a little horse meat, and the packaged food from the Red Cross parcels that had been coming into the camp each month until then. When Colonel Goode took charge in October, there was a plentiful store of Red Cross tinned food at Oflag 64, with 350 cans a day being opened. There were also a million cigarettes in store, even cigars and pipe tobacco.

But the tenth of October marked the end of Red Cross food parcel deliveries until December 3. Allied bombing was causing such problems for the German railroad system that millions of dollars' worth of Red Cross food for POWs was backed up in Switzerland. Without Red Cross food, Oflag 64 MOs found that their kriegies lost an average of nine pounds during this period.[6]

Goode, like Drake before him, was opposed to escape attempts now that the Germans were known to be shooting escapees. Not only did he reiterate Colonel Drake's order banning escapes, he shut down the escape committee and ordered those men who had been digging tunnels to immediately fill them in. This order did not go down well with some Schubin kriegies.

Yet Goode's reasoning was simple and sensible. He knew, as a result of the bloody end to the Stalag Luft 3 escape, that the Gestapo was shooting escapees. Nor were the Germans hiding the fact they would shoot any escapees they caught—the posters now hanging in the camp's administrative offices made that very clear. More and more, the Germans were imposing group punishments on bunches of kriegies for the infractions of one or two. If a tunnel was discovered at Oflag 64 by the Germans, they would naturally track it to its source. In the current climate, it wasn't implausible that the Gestapo would shoot all the men in a block where a tunnel entrance was discovered. Pop Goode wasn't having that on his watch.

As unhappy kriegies transferred earth back from hiding places to fill in tunnels, Bill Cory's team tunneling from Block 3A rebelled. Deciding to keep their hole in the ground as an insurance policy, they only filled it in partway. The day would come when they would cash in that policy in an unusual but ultimately successful escape.

···

IN THE SECOND half of 1944, as the war increasingly turned against the Germans, conditions in POW camps worsened steadily. Apart from the disruption of Red Cross food parcel delivery, both the Americans and their Wehrmacht jailers had to contend with the interference of the Gestapo in their lives. Ever since the Great Escape in April, and the July attempt to blow up Hitler by his own officers, the Gestapo had tightened its grip across the Reich.

Over November 14 and 15, plainclothed Gestapo agents descended on Oflag 64 in force. Looking for tunnels, escape materiel, and contraband, they turned the camp upside down. Wherever kriegies were at the time, they had to stand to attention while the Gestapo rifled through their few possessions and storage places. The previous month, the Americans at Oflag 64 had seen their best combat uniforms confiscated—for German special forces to wear during the Battle of the Bulge, they later learned.

When the Gestapo arrived on this latest occasion, Frank Diggs and several members of his editorial team were sitting in *The Item*'s office, the small unheated washroom off the Little Theater. Lieutenant Leo W. Fisher was one of those team members. Badly burned and having suffered two compound leg fractures when his Sherman tank was knocked out in Tunisia's Faïd Pass in May the previous year, Fisher had his name down for repatriation. In the meantime, Diggs was keeping him mentally active by employing his talents as a writer. In the middle of their editorial meeting, one of their colleagues hurried in from the theater.

"The Gestapo are on the prowl!" he warned.

Hearing Germans shouting in the theater, Diggs urged his colleagues to quickly hide their stash of chocolate and cigarettes, which far exceeded the German daily allowance. German voices grew louder.

"Here they come," said Diggs contemptuously, a cigarette wagging in his mouth as he spoke. "Smell 'em!"

The door burst open, and Weasel the ferret corporal strode in. *"Achtung!"* he bellowed.

As required by German camp protocol, the Americans came to their feet—casually, as required by kriegie camp protocol. Several Gestapo men in their signature long black leather coats entered the room behind the Weasel, accompanied by a pained-looking Oberst Schneider.

One of the Gestapo men walked up to Frank Diggs and, standing inches from his face, shouted, "You will not smoke when the Oberst is in the room! Understand, you?"

Without a word, Diggs took a drag from his cigarette, then dropped it to the floor and ground it out with his heel.

The Gestapo man took in the layout for December's upcoming issue of *The Item* spread on the editorial table. "You are a journalist?" he queried.

"Yes," Diggs replied.

"Ah, yes, one day a great story you will write! You are indeed fortunate to be in Germany at such a time when history all about you is being made. Isn't it not so?"

Diggs could only snort in response.

While this was going on, the Weasel had been searching the room. To the delight of Oberst Schneider, his subordinate unearthed the kriegies' cigarette and chocolate hoard. The prisoners were only allowed two packs of cigarettes and one chocolate bar a day to prevent them from building up stocks to bribe guards or to use during escape bids, which was exactly why the kriegies were saving them. The editorial room stash was confiscated, and the Germans withdrew, on their way to annoy other kriegies.[7]

. . .

IN NOVEMBER, THE July charges against Lieutenant Colonel Schaeffer and Lieutenant Schmitz were revived by the Germans, this time in a Wehrmacht court-martial, with the accused allowed legal representation by Schubin kriegies and lawyers Clarence Ferguson and Lemund Wilcox. In their December retrial, Schaeffer and Schmitz were found guilty and sentenced to death. Under the Geneva Convention, the Protecting Power had three months in which to appeal on behalf of the condemned men. During the appeal, Schaeffer was returned to Colditz and Schmitz to Schubin.

George Durgin and the other Americans who had refused to walk in the street in Posen were also subjected to Wehrmacht court-martial on the old charges. They, too, were found guilty and sentenced to death. With the same three months' grace for a Protecting Power appeal, Durgin and his comrades came back to their usual barracks at Oflag 64 to wait out the time. Durgin assured his best friend, Boomer Holder, that he wasn't worried: he intended to bust out of the train on the way to the eventual appeal hearing. A worried Holder began collecting rations for his buddy's break.

Meanwhile, all new arrivals were being warned of the fatal consequences of escape attempts. Tank platoon commander Lieutenant Mays W. Anderson from Springville, Utah, had been captured in November during the Battle of the Bulge. After he'd gone through arrival processing at Oflag 64, he received a terse warning from a guard NCO: "Do not attempt to escape. Guards will shoot without warning."[8]

Even for the Germans guarding the kriegies at Schubin, by December 1944 life was becoming tough. Rations for the guards were little better than those being given to the prisoners, and the likes of chocolate were a rare luxury for Germans now. There were still hopes in German ranks that the drawn-out German offensive in the Ardennes would turn the war around for them. But with the Russians pushing relentlessly closer every day from the east, not every German at Schubin really believed that Germany could still win the war.

One day that December, Private Gottfried Dietz was on telephone duty in the German Kommandantur across the road from the camp when he put a call through to the commandant. Young Dietz respected old Oberst Schneider and felt a little sorry for him. Schneider came from an old Junker family in Prussia with large landholdings in Pomerania. He had been severely wounded in the leg during World War I. His limp, and his age, had meant that he'd been sidelined to running a POW camp in this war. It wasn't a job Private Dietz envied. Schneider never expressed sympathies for Nazism within Dietz's hearing. As far as Dietz was concerned, the colonel did his job to the best of his ability and barely tolerated the security officer, Hauptmann Zimmermann, who had the ear of the Nazi Party.

Dietz knew what this incoming phone call was all about. Two of the camp's guards had deserted and tried to get home to their families. The private listened in as the colonel was informed that both deserters had been caught and shot.

"They were out of luck," said Schneider with a sigh before hanging up.[9]

6

THE RUSSIANS ARE COMING

IN EARLY JANUARY 1945, TENS OF THOUSANDS OF AMERICAN SER-
vicemen taken captive during the Battle of the Bulge continued to
flood into POW camps across the Reich, almost overwhelming the
capacity of the Germans to house them. By the second week of January, there were close to 1,600 American prisoners, mostly officers, at
Schubin. A section of the White House mess hall was partitioned off
to create a new prisoner dorm. Once that filled up, the latest arrivals
had to bed down in the barn on the northeast side of the camp.

When these measures proved insufficient, the Wehrmacht decided to create a sub-camp, Oflag 64-Z, at Schokken (Polish Skoki),
due south of Schubin. Lieutenant Colonel Doyle R. Yardley was transferred from Schubin with several junior officers and enlisted men to
establish the Schokken camp. Yardley, a Texan, had been commanding the 509th Parachute Infantry Battalion in Italy when he was
captured in September 1943. Shortly after Yardley's group established the command staff at Schokken, Colonel Hurley Fuller arrived with a batch of new prisoners and took over as Oflag 64-Z's

SAO. By January 21, there would be 190 officers and twenty-two enlisted men at Schokken.

Lieutenant Craig Campbell was sent with Yardley to serve as his XO. By this time, Campbell's captors knew that he had been General Eisenhower's ADC. His secret had been exposed the previous November, apparently when a letter arrived for him from Mamie Eisenhower, the general's wife. The letter's sender and contents had alerted the camp censors to the fact that Campbell was known to the Eisenhowers, and Campbell had been hauled in for questioning by the Germans. To his relief, the young lieutenant had subsequently been returned to the camp population. So much time had passed since Campbell had worked for the general, and Eisenhower's position and location had changed so much during that period, that the Germans decided that they could extract no information of value from him. Besides, the Abwehr already had a very thick file on Eisenhower.

Another way to relieve crowding in the camps, at least a little, was to repatriate wounded men. In all, 478 wounded Americans were sent home in early January, taken from seven German POW camps, including Oflag 64. Fifteen seriously wounded men were flown from Marseilles to the United States. The remaining repatriates were sent home aboard the M.S. *Gripsholm*, which would sail into New York on February 21.[1]

To the frustration of Reid Ellsworth, he wasn't included in this latest repatriation round despite having perfected the insanity project to the extent that Schubin MO Captain Ernest M. Gruenberg had genuine doubts about his sanity. New Yorker Gruenberg, who had trained at Yale University and was an intern at St. Elizabeth's Hospital in Washington, DC, before the war, had a strong interest in mental illnesses. Following the war, he would become director of the New York State Mental Health Commission and a noted professor of psychiatry at Baltimore's Johns Hopkins University. In contrast to Gruenberg, whose opinion they would not consider, the Germans were unconvinced by Ellsworth's act and would not sign off on his repatriation.

Red Cross parcels arrived at Oflag 64 by rail from Switzerland on January 18, the first delivery in six weeks. Not knowing when, or if, the camp would see another delivery, Colonel Goode ordered the conservation of most of the parcels. Their guards, meanwhile, punctured the cans of Red Cross supplies as they were distributed, so that the contents had to be consumed immediately and thus could not be stored for use in escapes. With the Red Army moving closer with each passing day, the Wehrmacht suspected that many American POWs would attempt to escape to link up with them. They weren't wrong.

■ ■ ■

AT 7:00 P.M. on Saturday evening, January 20, Pop Goode called all his senior officers and block commanders to an urgent meeting in the White House administration office. George Durgin was duty officer that day and was kept busy scurrying around the camp conveying the colonel's messages.

"I've heard we are to be evacuated, deeper into Germany, tomorrow," Goode advised the meeting. He ordered his subordinates to have their men make all preparations to depart. According to Goode's information, the camp inmates would march to a nearby railhead, from which they would be taken by train to another camp in Brandenburg in northern Germany. The men at Oflag 64-Z at Schokken would evacuate at the same time. Goode now authorized another distribution of Red Cross parcels for the men to take on the march.

"Are you rescinding the standing order not to escape, sir?" called Jerry Sage to Goode.

"Not at this time," the colonel replied, noting that SS troops might follow the column and pick off escapees.[2]

Someone else, voicing concern about the treatment escapees could receive from Red Army soldiers, suggested that escape to the Russians might not be such a good idea anyway. America and the Soviet Union might be allies in this war, but Russian troops on the ground were an unknown quantity at this point.

The camp's senior medical officer, Captain Floyd M. Burgeson from Des Moines, Iowa, asked Goode about the fate of men who were unable to march because of wounds or illness.

"The Germans have given permission for those who are wounded or too ill to march to remain behind at the hospital," Goode advised.[3] The two dozen sick men at the Wollstein Lazarett would also be permitted to remain where they were. The final decision as to who stayed at Oflag 64's hospital would be in the hands of the Germans.

Goode's officers hurried away to make preparations for the evacuation. Kriegies realized this was all for real when, for the first time ever, the Germans permitted the lights to be left on in the barracks all night. As prisoners packed for the march to Germany, not knowing when they might eat again, they feasted on contents from the latest issue of Red Cross parcels.

■ ■ ■

MO CAPTAIN BURGESON moved along the rows of beds in the overcrowded camp hospital, accompanied by his taciturn Wehrmacht counterpart, Hauptmann Pongratz, a staunch Nazi. As they progressed from bed to bed, they discussed each patient. Originally, there had been twenty-two beds in the camp hospital, and daily sick call usually saw an average of thirty men on Burgeson's sick list. But an influx of new wounded "Bulgie" prisoners, plus a wave of sickness brought on by the winter cold and the poor camp diet, meant that one hundred men were now packed into the hospital's rooms and corridors. Upper respiratory tract infections, which were widespread in German-run POW camps, proved the most common ailment. Battle wounds, stomach problems, skin conditions, and cuts and bruises filled out the remainder of the sick list.

Dr. Pongratz, the German physician, was not popular with kriegies. On his word alone, the more seriously sick POWs had been transferred to the hospital at Wollstein for treatment by Polish surgeons, and it had always been difficult to convince Pongratz of the severity of American cases. This same Dr. Pongratz, when Colonel Goode had proposed that MO Lieutenant Harry Abrahams join the camp hospital staff, had rejected Abrahams because he was Jewish, cynically suggesting he be appointed camp latrine inspector.

Now, as Burgeson came to Private Jonel C. Hill's bed, Pongratz was wearing a sour expression and was at his uncooperative best. Or worst. Dr. Pongratz had the final say on who would be spared the evacuation march. Already, he'd ordered several American patients to dress and join the main camp population for the march.

Nineteen-year-old Private Hill, from southern Minnesota, had been an infantryman with the 1st Division's 26th Infantry when captured by German paratroopers near Aachen seven weeks earlier. Sent to Oflag 64 as an orderly, he'd swept the officers' barracks and served them two meals a day in the mess. For the past two days he'd been laid low by a fierce fever that had him hallucinating—he was certain he was being nursed by his girlfriend from back in the States.

Standing with Pongratz at the end of Hill's bed, Burgeson declared that the private had appendicitis and begged the German to let him keep the German-provided surgical instruments in order to remove Hill's appendix.

"Nein!" grunted Pongratz before moving to the next bed.

Hearing this, Hill was scared stiff. Without a word to the teenager, Burgeson joined Pongratz to assess the next patient. Young Hill would hardly sleep a wink that night, so terrified was he that his appendix was about to burst and kill him. The following day, an American orderly assured Hill that he had only a bad case of gastritis. Hill had been a pawn in Burgeson's attempt to retain the hospital's surgical instruments. With such instruments in short supply, Pongratz would take them with him whenever he departed the oflag. But Burgeson had succeeded in bluffing the German doctor into believing that Hill's case was more serious than it was. Hill was permitted to remain behind.[4]

War correspondent Wright Bryan was another of the kriegies excused from the march by Pongratz. One of Frank Diggs' team producing *The Item* and the *Daily Bulletin*, the tall, lean Bryan had taken a bullet in the left leg when captured in France the previous September. By the time Burgeson and Pongratz did their final ward round together, Bryan's wound had flared up. Gruffly, Pongratz agreed that the war correspondent was not fit to walk any distance and could remain behind.

The future of the men slated to stay at the camp hospital would be just as uncertain as that of those marching west.

7

THE BIG BREAK, DAY ONE

SUNDAY, JANUARY 21, 1945, DAWNED GRAY AND THICKLY OVERCAST at Schubin. Standing in rank after rank on the Oflag 64 Appell ground, stamping their feet and blowing on their hands to try to keep warm as the icy winter chill seeped into their bones, more than 1,400 American prisoners wanted to know what the holdup was. They had formed up by barrack block platoon, in ranks five men across, creating a column that trailed from the gate back to the Appell area. Half of these GIs were married. More than half had attended college. One had a Ph.D. They were from every state in the Union, and the Territory of Hawaii. The youngest among them were just nineteen. Their average age was twenty-seven. And all these young men just wanted to survive the Nazis, and the winter, and get home.[1]

According to camp thermometers, the temperature was several degrees below freezing. The cobbled road running past the camp was four inches deep with ice and snow. Icicles hung from tree branches and telephone wires. Poles would say this was the coldest winter their country had experienced in thirty years. Starting here in Poland, over the next few days the German military would commence moving more than 300,000 Allied POWs from the eastern part of the Reich to the west, away from the Russians, deep into Germany. In these conditions, the German guards from the 813th Grenadiers would have thought that any man contemplating making a break was insane. Yet the scene was set for the largest American prisoner-of-war breakout in history, and the largest Allied escape of the Second World War.

At the head of Block 9A's platoon stood Captain Thornton V. Sigler, previously a company commander from Pop Goode's 175th Infantry Regiment. Like Goode, Sigler had been captured in France just weeks after D-Day. With a grunt, he adjusted the improvised pack on his back and looked around at his comrades, laden with clothes and food and shivering in the snow. "Never have I seen such a conglomeration of makeshift packs as we carried," he would note. Sigler recalled that someone, sometime, had said that Americans would win all their wars because of their talent for improvisation. That was certainly in evidence here.[2]

Thornton Sigler had made his backpack from a pillowcase, cutting up a towel to make the straps. The backpack was crammed with two spare uniforms, two jackets, two hats, two sets of underwear, two unopened Red Cross ration parcels, an overcoat, toiletry articles and a scarf. A pair of rolled blankets sat on top of the pack. Sigler estimated his load weighed close to forty pounds. "How I moved is still a mystery," he would say.[3]

Nearby, Lieutenant Ted Ellsworth was toting a knapsack made from the cover of the mattress on his prison barracks bunk. Ellsworth was using socks for gloves and had stuffed his pockets with food and the contents of seven hoarded cartons of cigarettes—which he intended to use as currency when he made his intended escape bid.

Many kriegies with their makeshift packs envied those men in the column who had piled their loads on sleds, and who stood with towing ropes over their shoulders as they awaited the order to move out. Most of these conveyances had been fashioned from bed boards and bookshelves. Boomer Holder and his best friend, George Durgin, had built themselves a sturdy sled from timber they'd stripped from the stage in the Little Theater, lining the runners with metal bands from Red Cross boxes.

Holder's 1st Platoon of some fifty White House men was nearest the gate. Durgin had been in the 2nd Platoon, but he'd swapped places with a kriegie in the 1st so he could help Holder haul their sled. In addition to filling their backpacks, the pair had piled that sled high with all their rations and possessions. Holder had even brought along a book on Spanish grammar so that he could keep up his Spanish studies on this trip. Holder was an optimist.

The Cadillac of sleds was the one in the possession of *Item* editor Frank Diggs and his friend Lieutenant Nelson Tacy from Otis, Massachusetts. Six feet long, this was a regular Polish sled, elegant in design and, most important, lightweight. Diggs and Tacy had stumbled on it in the White House basement long before and had hidden it for a day like today. Ready to haul their sled like a pair of Santa's reindeer, Diggs and Tacy stamped their feet and blew on their blue hands for warmth.

All the kriegies in camp had been called to this Appell at 8:45 a.m. They'd been told that the guards would make a distribution of bread from Schubin's German bakery for the march, and sure enough a van drove up, and black bread was handed out at the head of the column. But 150 loaves did not go far among thirty platoons.

"We've been had!" grumbled Ranger Clarence Meltesen after bread failed to reach his 22nd Platoon way back in the column.[4]

Now, it was approaching 11:00 a.m., and the prisoners had been standing here for over two hours as the guards made head count after head count in the freezing weather.

"Cold enough to bring a brass monkey inside," grumbled twenty-four-year-old Lieutenant Harry B. Long from Punta Gorda, Florida, his breath steaming his round eyeglasses. Long, a 318th Regiment surgeon's assistant, wasn't weighing himself down. Traveling "light," he was wearing British boots, a French overcoat and two pairs of long johns. Extra socks and shirts were stuffed down the long johns. It wasn't pretty, but it was practical.

Long had been told they were marching to a new POW camp farther west. No one apart from the commandant seemed to know where they were bound, but one of the guards had told Long they would only have to march fifteen kilometers to a rail siding, where they would board boxcars for the remainder of the journey. Long didn't believe the German. He guessed, correctly as it would turn out, that they would be in for a longer walk than that. Much longer.[5]

Most of Long's colleagues did seem to believe that they were only in for a short stroll before trains took them on the next leg of their relocation. As a result, the mood among the prisoners had been generally upbeat by the time they fell in on Sunday, as it had been ever since news of the evacuation was passed along to them the previous evening. The move was positive news to men experiencing boring, depressing POW camp life. Besides, relocation west would put them closer to the advancing US Army and, theoretically, freedom.

It would be impossible to take along all the thousands of Red Cross parcels delivered to the camp just three days earlier, and so, on Saturday, and again on Sunday morning, the prisoners had eaten better than they had at any time since their incarceration. After that, they filled their packs, pockets and sleds with more Red Cross food. It was with full stomachs and high expectations, then, that they had answered the last Appell bell.

On Adolf-Hitler-Strasse, a continuous procession of carts, wooden farm wagons drawn by bony horses, and civilians on foot or pushing bicycles had been rolling silently by since dawn, heading west toward Germany, continuing the refugee stream that had begun a week earlier. Most of the greatly outnumbered men among them were elderly. Wagons were laden with women and children, some blank-faced, most clearly scared.

The thousand or so German residents of Schubin town were included in this unholy exodus. Some of the refugees were Germans who'd been settled on Polish soil early in the war. Along with locals whose German heritage went back generations, and who had lived all their lives in Poland, the new settlers dreaded what the Russians would do to any German once they arrived. Reports of what the Red Army had done to German civilians when they overran East Prussia were bloodcurdling.

Standing in a platoon near the gate, thirty-three-year-old Second Lieutenant John N. Dimling, Jr., from Winston-Salem, North Carolina, watched the refugees filing past. In February the previous year, Dimling, a history major at Durham's Duke University just prior to the war, had found himself in no-man's-land outside the Allied perimeter at the Anzio beachhead in southwest Italy. A massive German counterattack had swept by, and he'd been captured. There seemed no possibility of a massive German counterattack here at Schubin. The German army was clearly stretched too thin.

Most of the refugees took no notice of the ranks of prisoners lined up inside the camp, but Dimling saw one German woman on an overloaded wagon glaring at the POWs through the wire as her wagon rolled by.

"It's all your fault!" she called bitterly to the Americans.[6]

Dimling couldn't figure out whether she was blaming America for being in the war, or for being too slow to get to Berlin to end the conflict before the Russians got this far. The bitter German woman may well have been Anni Kricks, wife of print shop operator Private Willy Kricks, who, along with the Kricks' eight-year-old son, had joined the refugee tide. Kricks himself was somewhere in the guard detail as it prepared to escort the Americans west. As for Dimling, he wasn't thinking about escape. He was focused only on surviving the march that lay ahead.

Ed Ward stood with ninety other men from the two Barrack Block 3 platoons, a homemade knapsack on his back and all the clothes he could wear on his body. The knitted cap his wife had sent him from Florida, the one with the "Jones" name tag, was pulled down over his stinging ears. Ed wasn't thinking about escape. Not yet. He'd had a taste of escaping after being on the run in Tunisia two years earlier. With John Creech, Jim Bancker and a bunch of other American prisoners, Ward had been placed in a cattle car for the ride to Tunis after they'd been captured. They'd made a hole in the bottom of the car, and dropped through. The choice of locale for their break had not been ideal, and they'd ended up wandering in the desert for days. They found an oasis and received food and water from local Arabs, who then sold them to the German army. If Ward was going to escape again, it would be with more thought than the last time.

Heading up another block platoon, escape king Jack Van Vliet had no immediate plans for a break. In 1943, he and Captain Donald B. Stewart had been sent by their captors to Katyn in the Ukraine. There, with several British officers, they had been shown the mass graves of executed Polish army officers and told by the Germans that the massacres had been carried out by the Russians. At first disbelieving the Germans, over time Van Vliet had come to accept their version of events. He had been given photographs from the scene, which he now had in his pocket with the intention of passing them on to US Military Intelligence along with his report on the incident. But he knew that if the Russians found these damning pictures on him, he was a dead man. Van Vliet had every intention of escaping, but not until this evacuation took him deep into Germany, away from the Red Army and closer to the advancing US Army.

Others in the column could think of nothing but imminent escape. At the head of the men from his barrack block, his face almost completely masked by a balaclava, Jerry Sage was planning to soon make a break, but not until the right opportunity presented itself. That morning, Pop Goode had delegated permission for escape on the march to his platoon commanders, and Sage had already given himself permission to make a break. Sage intended to travel as light as the bitter cold would allow. Tied in a horseshoe around his neck were two blankets, one made for him by a British friend at Oflag VII-B. Inside the blankets, Sage carried meat, cheese and bread. Two pairs of heavily darned socks covered his feet, while his other clothing consisted of long johns, two pairs of trousers, a shirt, paratroop battle dress and greatcoat.

The balaclava on Sage's head gave him a sinister appearance that only enhanced the aura of threat that surrounded him. The efficient chief ferret at Stalag Luft 3's North and South Compounds, the Luftwaffe's Oberfeldwebel Hermann Glemnitz, had once told Sage, as he released him from solitary confinement, that he was one man he would not like to run into after the war. Sage, known as the Cooler King in South Compound, would be a model for Steve McQueen's character, Virgil Hilts, in the screen version of Paul Brickhill's *The Great Escape*.

Sage would need no weapons for his intended break. At the OSS's secret Camp B2 in Maryland, he had instructed others on a score of ways to kill with their hands. Sage's favorite was the sentry kill— attacking an enemy from behind, left arm snaked around his neck while the right fist punched into his kidneys, after which the right hand jerked the man's head back, breaking his neck. None of Sage's fellow Oflag 64 officers knew of his secret OSS role, or of his plan to escape and join the Russians.

Frank Diggs and Nelson Tacy had a well-rehearsed escape plan ready to go when the time was right. Their escape gear was hidden on their Polish sled. For Tacy, this consisted of clothing that would make him look like a Polish worker. For Diggs, it was gray trousers, a German-style greatcoat, a cloth cap fashioned into the shape of a German coal scuttle helmet, and a length of wood that Diggs had carefully carved into the shape of a rifle. They were hoping that, in poor light, the pair would pass for a Pole and an escorting German soldier and be able to walk right by their guards to freedom.

At the head of the column now, talking with short, portly Wehrmacht camp commandant Oberst Schneider, stood the unmistakable tall, white-haired figure of SAO Colonel Paul Goode. Incongruously, the colonel was carrying a set of bagpipes that he had been trying to learn to play for months, and he seemed determined to take them with him. On night stops on the march, the colonel would annoy kriegies with occasional attempts to blow a few whining notes. Boomer Holder was to observe, "Most of us thought he could not have chosen a less useful piece of baggage to carry."[7] Neither Holder nor the Germans knew that, right under their noses, Pop Goode was carrying the Bird, the kriegies' secret radio receiver, in his instrument's tartan wind bag.

Goode was very much aware that many of his officers were keen to make escape bids. The previous night, he had received requests from scores of men, including Ted Ellsworth, who'd wanted to attempt a break from the camp that very evening while the guards were distracted as they prepared for Sunday's departure. Goode had ruled that out as too risky and likely to bring reprisals down on the escapers and others if they were caught. The colonel had told those who wished to make a break to do so once the march west had begun, when the chances of success would be greater.

Goode would have liked to join the escapers. But as SAO, he felt obliged to stay with the bulk of his men for the duration of the march, wherever it took them. Other senior officers had agreed to stay with Goode to maintain order and ensure that their German guards did the right thing by the men on the march. Duty-bound Lieutenant Colonel Johnny Waters was one of them.

As it was, Goode was leaving more than a hundred of his men to an uncertain future—two dozen sick men in the hospital at Wollstein and ninety-one men in the Oflag 64 camp hospital. The men in the Schubin hospital included seventy-eight sick and injured American officers, tended by US MO Captain Robert Blatherwick, who'd won the assignment after splitting a deck of cards with another camp MO. Blatherwick was joined by Catholic chaplain Father Stanley Brach from Newark, New Jersey, who had volunteered to stay, and ten of the fourteen enlisted men who had been serving as hospital orderlies.[8]

Goode had put Colonel Fred W. Drury in charge of the hospital group. While commanding the 3rd Cavalry Group the previous September, Drury had been captured in a German ambush at Gravelotte in northern France. All ninety-one hospital stay-behinds had been told they would have to wait at the camp until the Wehrmacht provided transport for them. And all were hoping that German transport failed to eventuate, which would mean they'd fall into Russian hands once the advancing Russian army reached Schubin.

Among the Americans planning to attempt escape was twenty-nine-year-old medical officer Captain Ernest Gruenberg, who, apart from his medical duties, had also headed up the high school department at Schubin's Kriegie Kollege. The short, sharp-faced MO had been serving with the 317th Parachute Battalion when he was captured on June 8 the previous year, just two days after landing in France with the 101st Airborne. He and his twenty-nine-year-old colleague, Lieutenant Frank H. Colley from Washington, Georgia, were intent on making a break as soon as an opportunity presented itself on the march.

Like their fellow kriegies, Gruenberg and Colley knew that General Patton's forces were still many hundreds of miles to the west and that it was pointless trying to escape west or south. Via the Bird, the pair also knew that the Russian army was only a few days east of Schubin and continually pushing back the retreating German army. Once they made their break, Gruenberg and Colley planned to head toward the Russians, with the ultimate aim of making it all the way to Moscow and the US embassy there.

Reid Ellsworth was another man planning to escape. After failing to convince the repatriation board that he was nuts, a few weeks earlier Ellsworth had abandoned the insanity project. He now intended to make a run for it when the time was right. So, too, did twenty-two-year-old Lieutenant William R. Shular, Jr., from Oconee, Georgia. A G-2 (military intelligence) officer who had married his high school sweetheart before being shipped to Europe, Bill Shular had history as an escapee. Wounded and captured in Italy when leading a 30th Infantry patrol, Shular had escaped from a boxcar with an Indian Army officer and headed for Switzerland. Seven German paratroopers had been airdropped to catch them, which they did. Shular had surrendered, and was worked over by the paratroopers, who shot the Indian.

Shular had been so badly beaten up that he was sent, unconscious, to a hospital in a Polish women's forced-labor camp. Later moved to a Polish POW camp, he taught eager Polish kriegies demolition techniques. He and a group of these Polish POWs were smuggled out of the camp in its honey wagon, after which Shular led his resistance team to Berlin to blow up trains. All had been caught and sent to Belsen concentration camp.

Shular had been saved by former world heavyweight boxing champion Max Schmeling, who had become a German paratroop NCO in 1941. Schmeling had won his boxing crown from, and lost it back to,

American Jack Sharkey, and had knocked out Joe Louis in New York City. The German pugilist had retained a liking for Americans, and for fair play. Learning through paratroop circles of Shular's fate, Schmeling had tracked down the young American. Despite his low Luftwaffe rank, Schmeling retained influence with fellow Germans as a result of his sporting achievements and gentlemanly reputation. Using that influence, Schmeling was able to have Shular removed from the concentration camp and trucked to Oflag 64.

Now Shular was scheming to escape and link up with the Polish underground as soon as an opportunity presented itself outside the camp. Looking around the camp perimeter, he could see that the goon towers were empty. The machine guns had come down from their perches. The camp's one hundred guards would be sharing the rigors of the march with the prisoners, plodding through the snow on either side of the column, several with guard dogs on leashes. Like the kriegies, the goons were being made homeless by this evacuation. The commandant's battered staff car and two horse-drawn wagons, one piled with Oberst Schneider's personal possessions, the second carrying his officers' belongings, now stood on Adolf-Hitler-Strasse outside the Kommandantur and guard barrack blocks.

Bulging packs on the guards' backs contained their worldly possessions. Some of these grenadiers were only teenagers. Many were senior citizens drafted into military service late in the war, men as old as seventy. Others were soldiers wounded earlier in the war who'd been given "soft" duty as POW camp NCOs. They all wore jackboots, greatcoats and forage caps. Some had the luxury of gloves. Enlisted men had Mauser rifles over their shoulders and bayonets on their belts, while NCOs were armed with Schmeissers.

Still the prisoners were made to wait. The delay in departing the camp had been caused by the repeated prisoner head count. At Oberst Schneider's insistence, it was being done for the fifth time that morning. Half a dozen prisoners were missing, and repeated German searches of the camp had not located them. Colonel Goode knew where four of those prisoners were. A quartet of lieutenants—Bill Cory, Bill Fabian, Hervey Robinson, and Boomer Holder's verbal sparring partner, Spud Murphy—was hiding in the abandoned escape tunnel beneath the kitchen in Barrack Block 3A.

This was the tunnel they'd helped dig, the tunnel they'd previously told Goode they had completely filled in. Their insurance policy. The previous evening, Cory and his fellow diggers had gone to Colonel Goode and sought his permission to hide in their tunnel until the rest of the prisoners had marched away on the Sunday. Goode had agreed to their plan, as they were unlikely to be found in the underground hiding place that had already remained a secret for so long. Where the other missing men were, Goode had no idea.

One of those missing men was the combative Lieutenant Colonel Tom Riggs from Huntingdon, West Virginia. Previously commander of the 81st Combat Engineer Battalion, he was a Bulgie captured while defending Saint Vith in Belgium in December. A prisoner for just several weeks, the indomitable Riggs had never settled into the POW malaise of acceptance that seemingly gripped some men at Schubin who'd been prisoners for close to two years.

A little while back, in Oflag 64's mess hall, the ever vigilant Riggs had noticed a gap between the top of the large walk-in ice chest and the ceiling, just large enough for a man to hide in. This morning, once the mess hall had emptied following breakfast, Riggs had climbed up in there and waited. Five times, following each head count on the parade ground, the guards had searched the mess hall looking for Riggs and the other missing prisoners, the last time using a guard dog. But even with the dog, they had failed to find Riggs.

Oberst Schneider's patience finally gave out. When the fifth head count produced the same number as the previous four—1,471 American officers and enlisted men on the parade ground and 91 in the hospital—and the searches of the camp failed to produce any more to give a figure that accorded with the precise German records, Schneider decided that he had done all that was humanly possible to locate every one of his prisoners. The march must begin. The commandant entered the compound to give his final speech to his charges.

The kriegies had become accustomed to Schneider's occasional addresses to them. He would spout a short sentence in German, then, as a noncommissioned officer translated it into English for the assembled Americans, Schneider would move a single pace sideways to the left, crablike, and wait for the translation. Followed by another sentence, and another sideways move. Schneider was a figure of authority that the Americans neither feared nor respected. Some thought he belonged in a comic opera.

"We are going to Germany," the comical colonel began. "We will walk, but later we may get a train. My orders are to get you there. You treat me well, and I will treat you well." And then he added, coldly, "I advise you not to attempt to escape." The outcome, Schneider said, would be fatal for those involved. It was not advice that hundreds of American officers were going to take, this day, and over the succeeding few days.[9]

Orders rang out. Guards took stations on either side of the formation. German shepherd dogs strained on leashes. Just after 11:00 a.m., the gates were opened, and guards halted refugee traffic passing along Adolf-Hitler-Strasse to permit the kriegie column to exit onto it. The pair of Wehrmacht wagons heading the column began to roll slowly forward along the street. The commandant's sedan sat at the roadside; Oberst Schneider would bring up the rear of the column. Crunching through the snow with some tugging sleds along behind them, 1,471 prisoners turned left, then marched off the Appell ground in their platoons. They passed through the inner gate, then out the ornate latticed second gateway, and turned right, toward Germany.

The course of the column from the Appell ground to the gates took the prisoners curving past the front of the camp hospital. Clarence Meltesen, marching in the 22nd Platoon, glanced up at the hospital windows and saw kriegies on the sick list sadly waving good-bye to their buddies. Men who were remaining behind to look after the sick-list kriegies were at the hospital building's front door, similarly waving. And then Meltesen noticed a man from the column step to one side, do a quick about-face, take several backward steps toward the hospital door, then begin waving to the passing column.

Not a single guard noticed. The Germans assumed this prisoner to be one of the men permitted to remain behind at the hospital. A

smile washed over Meltesen's face as he realized that the clever kriegie had just initiated the simplest of escapes from Nazi custody. And
he kicked himself for not having thought of it himself. Too late, his
platoon had passed the hospital. The window for using the same escape ruse had closed.

It was game on! The greatest POW escape of the war had begun.

8

GAME ON

Peering out a hospital window in a crush of American patients keen to bid farewell to their departing comrades, war correspondent Wright Bryan watched until the long column trudging through the snow was out of sight. Oberst Schneider's little German staff car, carrying the commandant and several of his officers, brought up the rear, crawling along with smoke curling from its exhaust. And then the road was reclaimed by the flood of refugees. An eerie silence fell over Oflag 64.

Right up until the time the camp was evacuated, Bryan had not known whether German guards would be left with the men at the hospital, or whether Wehrmacht vehicles would arrive for the hospital patients. With a general lack of German motorized transport, and an even greater lack of gasoline available to the Wehrmacht in 1945, the latter seemed an unlikely prospect. But nothing was certain. Not even their captors seemed to know exactly what was going on. In the end, no convoy of vehicles had arrived for the men in the hospital. At the last moment, Hauptmann Menner, Oberst Schneider's soft-spoken

Austrian adjutant, had handed the gate keys to Chaplain Brach, urging him to keep the gates locked to prevent local Poles from looting the camp.

Father Brach had been captured in North Africa in 1942 and had thought that he'd been liberated from an Italian POW camp the following year when its Italian guards deserted their posts with Italy's capitulation to the Allies. The Wehrmacht had promptly taken over Italy, along with the POW camps in that country, shattering hopes of freedom. With that experience in mind, Brach didn't want to build up hopes of liberation among the Schubin hospital patients. Just the same, he urged those men who could do so to paint large red crosses on bedsheets. These were draped out hospital windows, and several enterprising orderlies clambered onto the roof and tied a couple there.

The best estimate was that the Russians were fifty miles away. How long they would take to reach Schubin was anyone's guess, but Colonel Drury assured his charges that there was enough food and coal in the camp for the men in the hospital to survive comfortably for several weeks.

"The Russians will be here either tomorrow, or the next day," Drury told them. "Or next week. Or next month. We don't know when. But they will be here."[1]

During the day, four perfectly fit kriegies walked into the hospital and reported to Colonel Drury. Ever since the order to form up for the evacuation march on Sunday, Cory, Murphy, Fabian and Robinson had been hiding in the unfinished tunnel they'd dug from their barrack's kitchen. When Drury told them that the Red Army would organize transport for the Americans at the camp, the quartet decided to hang around.

■ ■ ■

Across town that same day, Polish friends went to the Schubin hiding place of Stefania Maludzińska.

"The Germans have gone!" they excitedly assured her.[2]

Stefania emerged from hiding for the first time in months. Like her friends, she held no fears that the Nazis would return to Schubin.

The rapid departure of all German troops, police and officials from the town, combined with the shambolic procession of German refugee wagons that would continue to trundle through Schubin for the remainder of this day and all the next, told them that they had seen the backs of the Nazis for good.

Stefania was free. Now, all she had to worry about was how the Red Army would treat her and her fellow Poles once it rolled into Schubin.

. . .

ON THE ROAD west, the refugee exodus extended from horizon to horizon across the flat, snow-covered Polish landscape. Wagons crawled along nose to tail on one side of the road, with the American POW column walking beside them. In its now ragged ranks, the column was strung out for a mile. Even at their slipping, sliding walking pace, the POWs moved faster than the creeping train of wagons. No one spoke. The silence was broken occasionally by the neighing of horses, the impatient encouragement of their drivers, and the colorful curses of Americans who lost their footing.

As the column left the camp behind, Jerry Sage noticed a road sign pointing to Exin, twenty-four kilometers, or fifteen miles, away. To Sage, that march to Exin would eventually seem more like 124 kilometers. All around him, Americans fell on the snow and ice and had to be helped to their feet. Before long, one man could go no farther, and a sled was emptied for him. Friends subsequently hauled the invalid along on the sled. Sage was among the many who fell. Feeling foolish, the OSS man hauled himself back to his feet and trudged on.

Ernest Gruenberg, slogging along in the ranks with his belongings weighing heavily on his back, noticed that not all the refugees in the endless stream being passed by the POW column were German. He overheard some speaking quietly in Polish. Over the coming days, kriegies would learn that not a few Poles feared the coming of the Russians more than they cheered the departure of the Germans and were heading away from the Red Army. Gruenberg also saw a bunch of Polish forced laborers being herded along like cattle by German guards.

Still, the majority of these tens of thousands of miserable, now homeless people on the roads of Poland were German, and a large proportion were women and children. Gruenberg passed many frightened German housewives. As his eyes met theirs, several cursed him. He recalled a story in camp of a Jewish American kriegie who'd been spat on by a German grandmother in the street on his way to Oflag 64. At one stop on the way to Schubin, Gruenberg himself had witnessed a German officer ask German Red Cross girls to give hot soup to his group of American prisoners. The young women had refused because several of the Americans were clearly Jewish, they said.

As the column pushed on, Gruenberg saw a few perspiring middle-aged German men struggling through the snow, some clutching briefcases. These were low-ranking regional Nazi Party officials on the run. What good was their party creed to them now? Despite Gruenberg's own parlous state, there was something comforting in the Nazis' misery. Gruenberg even saw some Polish refugees try to help a few kriegies by hitching sleds to the back of their wagons. But with the POW column moving faster than the wagons, this only ended up with kriegies becoming separated from their sleds.

Before long, prisoners found that their homemade sleds were either too heavy or too fragile and broke apart. Sleds were increasingly abandoned. Boomer Holder and George Durgin realized they'd made a big mistake after just a mile and stopped to lighten the load on their sled, with Holder gently cursing perfectionist Durgin for having insisted on building their sled with cross braces, which had only made the thing heavier. Some passing kriegies made fun of them and their cumbersome conveyance, while others eagerly accepted anything they offloaded. The pair resumed the haul, but after laboring for another mile and a half, Holder and Durgin again pulled to the side of the road.

"It's either the sled or us, George," said Holder.[3]

Durgin agreed. They retained food, one blanket and a greatcoat each from the sled. Holder also kept a copious kriegie diary he'd been secretly maintaining in a YMCA notebook for a book he intended to write one day. They handed out the rest of their sled possessions to passersby. Everything was snapped up, even the Spanish primer.

Other kriegies were also keen to take over their sled, so the pair happily handed over the deadweight to new owners. Their load considerably lightened, Holder and Durgin slogged on toward Exin. When they reached for their cookie-tin canteens for a drink, they found that the contents had frozen, splitting open the canteens. Tossing them aside with disgust, they kept walking.

John Dimling was marching light, with just a backpack made from a woolen undershirt, which he'd loaded with nothing but Red Cross rations. Ever since the previous October, as Red Cross rations diminished, Dimling had also diminished, losing close to twenty pounds. He wasn't planning on losing any more weight from his already slender frame. As Dimling walked, one of the men from the German guard company tramping beside the column kept pace with him. The guard was overloaded with his own personal possessions, and within fifteen minutes of leaving the camp Dimling noticed the German sweating profusely.

All the guards had their steel coal scuttle helmets dangling from their belts. When the guard beside Dimling thought no one was looking, he unfastened his helmet and cast it away into the snow. Dimling smiled to himself, wondering if the German's Mauser rifle would be next to be offloaded. Up to this point, Dimling had been weighing the possibility of escape. The sight of the guard getting rid of his helmet was a turning point for him. "That moment clinched my idea that I wasn't going into Germany," he would say.[4]

■ ■ ■

KNOWN AS KCYNIA to the Poles, Exin was a railroad junction. When the column reached the town late in the day, it was crowded with desperate local Germans making a hurried departure. There was a train at the station, its locomotive hissing steam and tooting its whistle urgently. But the train wasn't there to give the POWs a ride. This train was for German civilians, who clamored for a place on board. Even the town's German police were taking this last train out of Exin. The exhausted kriegies were ordered to continue marching.

Beyond Exin, Colonel Goode and the Oflag 64 column were di-

The Oflag XXI-B and Oflag 64 White House (right) and hospital (center) at Szubin (Schubin), present day. A Polish war memorial stands in the foreground. *Courtesy of Mariusz Winiecki, Szubin, Poland.*

At Oflag XXI-B, in 1943, honey wagon escapee Joe Bryks (left) and Asselin tunnel escapee Otto Černý (second from right), with (from left to right) Australian Ambrose Haley, Briton John Ireton, and Czech Pablo Cryanski (far right). *Photograph: Australian War Memorial, Canberra. P11249.004.*

Schubin woman Stefania Maludzińska, photographed after the war. She helped POWs escape from the Schubin camp at risk to her own life. *From the Collection of the Muzeum Zienni Szubinskiej, Szubin, Poland.*

Generals Dwight D. Eisenhower, George S. Patton, Omar Bradley, and Courtney Hodges, Germany, 1945. Both Eisenhower and Patton had men close to them behind the wire at Schubin, while Bradley was critical of Patton's mission to free Schubin prisoners. *Photograph: Library of Congress, Washington DC. LC-USZ62-135308.*

The Wehrmacht Oflag 64 POW identity card of escapee Lt. Bill Shular. *Courtesy of Mary Shular Hopper.*

American kriegies playing baseball at Oflag 64, July 1944. *Courtesy of the International Council of the Red Cross, Geneva.*

At Oflag 64 in July 1944, senior American officer Colonel Thomas Drake; International Red Cross delegate Dr. Mayer; Lt. Colonel William Schaeffer, who would be sentenced to death by a German court; American camp XO, Lt. Colonel John Waters, son-in-law of General George S. Patton; and American camp adjutant and escape committee deputy chief Major Merle Meacham. *Courtesy of the International Council of the Red Cross, Geneva.*

American escapee Lt. Reid Ellsworth, who had earlier devised the unsuccessful "insanity project" to escape from Oflag 64. *Courtesy of the Reid Ellsworth family.*

On far right, escapee Lt. Craig Campbell, General Eisenhower's personal aide, photographed at Oflag 64. He found himself a prisoner there after asking to see some action. Also in this picture (from left to right) are Lt. Frank Smith, tunnel king Lt. Bill Cory, and Lt. Tony Cipriani. *Courtesy of Oflag 64 Association.*

Photographed on the steps of Oflag 64's hospital, escapee Lt. Billy Bingham (second from left, back row), the pessimist who predicted that World War II would not end until 1983. *Courtesy of Oflag 64 Association.*

Part of the first group of American prisoners to arrive at Oflag 64 in June 1943. Escapee Lt. Ed Ward is on the far right in the bottom row. Beside him is Lt. Sid "Mouse" Waldman, who was in charge of soil dispersal from the Cory tunnel. *Courtesy of Ed Ward Jr.*

Escapee Lt. Alfred Nelson, who came within seconds of being shot by a Russian firing squad following his escape. *Courtesy of Linda Kreuger.*

Baron von Rosen's Wegheim manor house in Poland, present day. A number of American Schubin escapees gathered here following their break. *Courtesy of Mariusz Winiecki, Szubin, Poland.*

Nine Wehrmacht Hetzer tank destroyers, like this one photographed at Hammelburg, stood in the way of the successful rescue of Schubin kriegies held there. *Courtesy of Peter Domes, www.taskforcebaum.de, Germany.*

Unsuccessful escapee Lt. Jack Hemingway, in Cuba with his father, author Ernest Hemingway, and half-brothers Patrick (left) and Gregory (right) in 1945, just after the end of the war in Europe. *Photograph: The Hemingway Collection, President John F. Kennedy Library, Boston.*

American escapee Lt. H. Randolph "Boomer" Holder, back in the United States shortly after the war, as he begins his career in commercial radio. *Courtesy of the Holder Family personal archives.*

Dr. Ernest M. Gruenberg, when he was professor of psychiatry at Baltimore's Johns Hopkins University in the 1980s. In January and February 1945, as Captain Gruenberg, he led the Moscow Trio, the first Schubin escapees to make it back to the United States. *Photograph: 'Ernest M. Gruenberg,' #241148, ca. 1982, Courtesy of the Alan Mason Chesney Medical Archives of the Johns Hopkins Medical Institutions.*

verted down a road at right angles to the one they'd traveled. Grim-looking, hollow-eyed German infantry stood at the intersection, weapons cradled in their arms as they silently watched the POWs pass. Reid Ellsworth, tramping along in the ranks, was sure they were SS. Supposed to stop the armored Russian advance, these German infantry had the appearance of dead men. Soon, many of them would be just that.

It was after dark when the vehicles leading the column turned off the road in the vicinity of Wegheim (Polish Sierniki). The column trudged up a drive for 150 yards through a little wood, to a manor house. This, the kriegies were to learn, was the estate of Baron Hans von Rosen, a Wehrmacht lieutenant colonel who had been regional military commander here until very recently. Rosen had inherited his large Wegheim property, known as the Grocholin Estate, in 1933, the year the Nazis came to power in Germany.

The baron had recently hightailed it to Berlin, leaving the estate in the hands of his Polish farmworkers. Behind the handsome but dilapidated two-story manor house, a courtyard extended, lined in a *U* shape by impressively large farm buildings—a three-story brick residential block for estate workers, a gristmill, barns for cattle, sheep and pigs, and well-stocked hay and equipment sheds.

Billy Bingham, the pessimist, had struggled on the march and was at the very end of the column as it came up the baron's drive. He noticed that as the column filed into the courtyard, the guard bringing up the rear walked on by him to say something to another guard ahead, leaving the tail of the column unguarded. All of a sudden, Bingham felt a hand on his arm. The short, bespectacled Bingham looked around just as his kriegie friend Captain Bob Kroll dragged him out of the ranks. Before Bingham could protest, Kroll drew him into a narrow alleyway between farm buildings and put a finger to his lips.

No guard raised the alarm. In the darkness, the pair's departure had gone unnoticed. With pounding hearts, they waited there in their hiding place as the column's last men shuffled into the courtyard. At the other end of the alley, a Pole appeared. Grinning, he gave a thumbs-up and beckoned the pair to follow. Bingham and Kroll looked at each other, then decided to take their chances with the man. Like a bloodhound with a scent, the Pole led the way across the fields. When the Americans asked where he was taking them, he answered in German.

Bingham, being a pessimist, became convinced that the Pole was only going to turn them over to the Germans for a loaf of bread. And the Germans, he was sure, would shoot them for attempting to escape. But Kroll was more trusting. After walking for two miles, their guide took the pair to a barn, told them to bed down among the cows, then disappeared. Too exhausted to do anything else, the suspicious Bingham and his escape partner introduced themselves to the Polish cows and snuggled in among them.

They were the first Americans to escape the Oflag 64 column on the march. But they were not the last. The Schubin break had begun with the men who'd avoided the column back in camp. Now, with Bingham and Kroll, the break was becoming a trickle, like a small hole in a levee. Before long, it would be as if the levee had broken, and the break would become a rushing torrent.

■ ■ ■

BACK IN THE darkened courtyard at the Rosen estate, 1,468 kriegies were made to wait in their platoons on the cobblestones, until, finally, they were dismissed and told to bed down in the barns. Inside, they found the buildings filled with livestock and smelling very rural. The haylofts above provided the most comfortable sleeping places, and these were grabbed by the first men inside. Those who came behind had to try to sleep among the animals on the cold stone floors, but at least they had the body heat of the animals to warm them.

More escape plans were already in motion. One group of four kriegies led by Major Robert "Bob" Crandall from Northwood Narrows, New Hampshire, simply walked out the rear door of their barn without waiting to bed down and burrowed into a haystack nearby. They figured they could hide out in the haystack until the column marched on the next day.

Meanwhile, in another barn, Boomer Holder and George Durgin

discussed making a break that night. They were always going to attempt to escape. With the December death sentence still hanging over his head, Durgin couldn't afford to end up in another German POW camp. The problem was finding both the opportunity and the physical strength for a break. Requiring each other's help just to get the packs off their backs that evening, they agreed that they should aim for a good night's sleep to regain their strength before they tried anything.

Apart from the bread a few had received, the kriegies' only food that day came from the Red Cross rations packs they carried. They ate what they could, cold, and lit up cigarettes. Many exhausted marchers were soon asleep, but, with a number of men around him smoking in the hay, Boomer Holder worried that one would set the place alight, and they would all be fried in their sleep. Despite his concern, his exhaustion sent him into dreamland after a while.

■ ■ ■

JERRY SAGE, SLEEPING on the ground in one of the cow barns, was gently shaken awake in the early hours of the morning. Opening his eyes, he saw, leaning over him, thirty-one-year-old Major John "Jack" Dobson, commander of the First Ranger Battalion in the same disastrous Italian operation that had netted Clarence Meltesen. In January 1944, near Cisterna just outside the Anzio beachhead, 767 Rangers had one morning advanced against German positions. Only six had returned to American lines that afternoon. Dobson and Meltesen had been among one hundred American officers captured during the Anzio battles to arrive at Oflag 64 in April 1944.

Dobson was, like Sage, a hard man and keen to escape. He had tried straggling behind the column on the march that day, hoping to slip away unnoticed, but the German rearguard had gathered him up and pushed him back to the marchers. Now, Dobson was ready to use the darkness for a break.

"I'm bugging out, Jerry," Dobson whispered to Sage. "Want to go with me?"

Sage and Dobson had previously discussed a joint break, and Sage was immediately up for it. But when he tried to move, his legs would not respond. It was as if he were paralyzed from the waist down. To his frustration and embarrassment, his ambulatory state, or lack of it, had been caused by the freezing cold.

"Go ahead," Sage told Dobson. "I'll have to make my move when my legs start working."[5]

As Dobson slipped away, Sage began vigorously massaging his legs. After a while he wrapped them in spare clothes and inserted them between the warm bodies of two obliging cows, which helped return feeling to his limbs. Before the sun came up, Sage struggled to his feet and limped from the barn. With no sign of guards, he crossed the courtyard to the baron's farmhouse. Finding a basement window at the rear that would open, he slithered down through the opening, landing on a large mound of vegetables. The entire cellar was filled with piles of rutabagas. Sage buried himself in a pile. As the sun peeked over the flat horizon in the direction of the advancing Red Army, Sage heard the German guards yelling impatiently for the kriegies to form up for the new day's march.

"Fall in!" American platoon commanders called to their men.

Boomer Holder and George Durgin, like most of their colleagues, came trotting out into the courtyard under the eyes of the waiting guards and joined their platoons in march formation. A number of men decided to try hiding in the haylofts until the column departed, but a corporal of the guard was alert to this. Walking into a barn and taking a Schmeisser from his shoulder, he yelled that if hiding prisoners didn't come out, he would shoot. When there was no movement, the corporal loosed off a full magazine into the hay. Miraculously, he hit no one. A dozen Americans now emerged from the hay, hands raised.

Angrily, the corporal shoved them up against a brick wall as he reloaded, making them think he was going to gun them down. They were saved by a German captain attracted by the gunfire. Apparently, this was Hauptmann Menner. The captain convinced the corporal to take the dozen culprits to the head of the column, where they would march under close escort.

The guards didn't wait around any longer. Anxious that every passing minute put the Russians nearer, they didn't bother to search every potential hiding place. The column was herded from the courtyard and back toward the road. As Boomer Holder passed out through the courtyard gate, he saw several guards trying ineffectually to count them all, and he cursed to himself. He and Durgin knew that some kriegies who'd hidden in the hay hadn't emerged when the corporal let loose. Realizing that, in this rush to resume the march, the Germans would never be able to make an accurate head count, Holder figured that he and Durgin could have succeeded in escaping by joining the kriegies in the hay. But it was no good being wise after the event. With more than 1,400 others, the pair resumed the march.

At that same time, in a barn two miles away, Billy Bingham and Bob Kroll had awoken after a warm night among the cows and found themselves looking at another smiling Pole. He gave them cups of warm, sweet milk, and black bread spread with pig fat, which they swiftly devoured. Contrary to Bingham's fears, they were not turned over to the Germans. Instead, they were now in the hands of the Polish underground, which, over the coming days, would move them four to five miles a day, from one Polish house to another.

* * *

GRADUALLY, AN HOUR or so after the column had departed the Rosen estate, kriegies began emerging from their hiding places around the courtyard. Among the thirty kriegies who had escaped the column was Reid Ellsworth. Now acting very sanely, and cautiously, he remained in his barn hiding place.

In the cellar of the manor house, Jerry Sage had been walking back and forth to get the circulation going in his legs. When he gauged that his limbs might support him, he crawled out through the window that had admitted him. All was dead quiet. Pulling himself to his full height, Sage looked at the sky and tasted his first day as a free man in close to two years.

"Thank you, Lord!" he exclaimed to the heavens.[6]

Limping across the courtyard, Sage realized he would not yet be able to walk far, and he made the decision to remain at the baron's farm for a day or two to build up his strength. Now he saw grinning fellow kriegies leaning out of basement windows, barns and haylofts. Mays Anderson was one of them. John Dimling was another; he'd hidden in the hay overnight and had held his nerve when the corporal let rip with his Schmeisser. Like Jerry Sage, Dimling, Ellsworth and most of the others decided to stay at the farm for the time being, expecting the Russians to reach them before long. As comrades snuggled back into their hiding places, Sage returned to his basement hideout, resettling among the vegetables to await nightfall.

Jack Dobson was one of the minority of escapees at the Rosen farm who decided to keep moving. After parting from Sage, he'd hidden in the hay until the column marched away. He subsequently linked up with Captain William R. Bond, Second Lieutenant Peter N. Gaish, and another officer, who had all hidden in the hay. They shared a concern that SS troops sweeping behind their retreating comrades could turn up at the estate at any time and find them. So, deciding to avoid the roads in case they ran into the SS, Dobson and his three new companions left the barns and set off overland, heading east.

Bill Shular was another who was not waiting around. In the cow barn he'd been assigned to, he woke before dawn. Nearby, Second Lieutenant Dale S. Barton, Jr., was also awake, and the pair agreed to team up and hide in the hay. Several hours after the column's departure, Shular and Barton warily left the farm buildings and walked to the main road. Refugees were still passing in an endless stream, heading for Germany. Against the slow-moving tide, Shular and Barton turned east, toward the Russians.[7]

■ ■ ■

THAT SAME DAY, back at Schubin, the men in Oflag 64's hospital began what they expected would be another nerve-wracking day waiting for the arrival of either Wehrmacht trucks or the Red Army. The road outside was now deserted. Refugees no longer passed. Like the lull before a storm, it was creepy. At breakfast time, an American came in swearing he had seen a Russian light tank and two American-built

Studebaker 6x6 trucks drive past. Polish residents would record that two Russian tanks passed rapidly through Schubin early that day. Meeting no resistance in Schubin, those tanks had surged on, heading west, pursuing the retreating Germans.

Just after 10:00 a.m., Wright Bryan and others watching from the hospital windows saw a light armored vehicle pull up in Adolf-Hitler-Strasse between the Kommandantur and the guard barrack. A handful of troops in white winter parkas piled out and went through the two blocks. Bryan could not make out whether they were Russian or German. The vehicle then turned and drove through the camp's open outer gate and up to the locked inner gate. That was when Bryan recognized it as an American-made three-quarter-ton reconnaissance car of the kind the United States had given the Soviet Union under the Lend-Lease program. Bryan's heart began to beat faster. His prayer that these were Russians was answered when a bulky Red Army captain stepped from the car.

Colonel Drury and Chaplain Brach opened the gate for the Russian, Captain Kakkonen. Led to the hospital, Kakkonen demanded to see written proof of the identities of all the men present. After studying the kriegie ID cards produced by Drury, Kakkonen was satisfied that these were American POWs. Jonel C. Hill, still weak from gastritis, was lying in his hospital bed when the Russian captain strode into his ward. Hill was to describe him as a bear of a man.

"Anybody here from Minnesota?" called the captain in broken English, looking up and down the row of beds.

Hill overcame his surprise. "Yes, here!" he called.

Captain Kakkonen strode to Hill's bedside, and the pair struck up a lengthy conversation about Minnesota. It turned out that the Kakkonen family had emigrated to the United States early in the twentieth century, and the captain had grown up in Minnesota and Wisconsin. In the 1930s, in response to calls from the Communist government for Russian expatriates to return to Mother Russia to help build the Soviet Union, the Kakkonen family had gone back to their homeland. The captain plied Jones with questions about Minnesota and Wisconsin and spoke wistfully about his American job, his salary, his prospects, and about his family, all of whom had been killed by the Germans in Russia.[8]

During the day, more Russian vehicles from reconnaissance and armored units passed speedily along Adolf-Hitler-Strasse. Some troops halted at the camp, among them men from Captain Kakkonen's company, who were billeted in camp barracks. Two groups of Russian officers arrived during the afternoon and spoke with Colonel Drury. These officers were alert and businesslike as they asked to see the Americans' papers. Once satisfied that the camp's occupants weren't Germans, the Russians saluted Drury and relaxed.

None of the Americans spoke Russian, and none of these latest Russian arrivals knew more than a few words of English. It eventuated that the word "Studebaker" immediately brought smiles and nods from the Russians—the reliable 6x6 trucks being used in great number by the Red Army were American-built. And a three-word phrase invariably won the approval of the Russkies: "Stalin, Roosevelt, Churchill."

"*Da! Da!*" came the grinning response.

"We want to go to Moscow," Drury told one of the afternoon's Red Army visitors.

"Not Moscow, no," the Russian officer came back. "I go to Berlin."[9]

Drury was ordered to keep his men where they were until the Soviets organized transport for them, although the Russian officers could not say how long that would take. Meanwhile, the hospital inmates quickly created makeshift American, Russian and British flags and ran them up the camp flagpole by the gate, where the Nazi swastika had been flying for more than five years until the previous day.

■ ■ ■

AS THE KRIEGIES in the column trudged another fifteen miles on the second day of the march, which was now angling north, there was no more talk from guards of hopping a train. The Americans began to think they might have to walk all the way to Berlin.

The nonstop line of refugee wagons still crawled along on one side of the road, with each vehicle maintaining its place in line in regimented German fashion. On one wagon they passed, driven by an elderly woman, Boomer Holder saw three small children sitting on the back among a pile of furniture. One sad-eyed little German girl of three or four caught his eye and tugged at his heartstrings when she smiled sweetly at him. Breaking off a piece of Red Cross chocolate, he handed it up to her.

"*Danke schön*," she said softly in thanks.[10]

Holder and Durgin were making much better progress without their sled. Wiping icicles from his eyebrows and mustache, Holder observed the guards beside them. Like their prisoners, the goons making hard going of the march. The Germans looked tired and regularly glanced over their shoulders toward the eastern horizon for signs of the approaching Red Army. Holder guessed that the Russians were still fifty or sixty miles away, but dull explosions off to their right during the day suggested that they were closer. Hoping to find out where they were headed, and where the Russians were in relation to the column, Holder attempted to strike up a conversation with a Sonderführer he knew from the camp who was walking with a guard dog on a leash. But the Sonderführer was too depressed to volunteer any useful information.

Frank Diggs and Nelson Tacy, still tugging their efficient Polish sled, were keen to escape the column and kept testing their guards to see if they could successfully slip away. But, as weary as the goons were, they were quick to notice stragglers and lingerers. Diggs saw one group of marchers attempt to escape by hiding in a culvert. Guards spotted them, and a German NCO—possibly the same trigger-happy corporal who'd opened up in the barn—sprayed the snow by the culvert with a Schmeisser burst. The would-be escapees quickly emerged from their hiding place, and, with hands aloft, scurried to rejoin the column. With one eye warily on the shepherding goon with the gun, they were pushed to the head of the column with other recaptured kriegies.

"The snow has stopped falling, thank God," said Diggs with a sigh as they kept putting one foot in front of the other in the middle of the column.

"Still can't be more than 12 degrees," Durgin estimated.[11]

The column plodded on, with the Americans kept in the dark about where they were going. At a rest halt in the small town of Netz-thal (Polish Osiek nad Notecią), just beyond the River Netze (Polish Noteć), Boomer Holder and George Durgin's platoon stopped right outside a Polish bakery. The bakery owners came out and pressed bread, buns, and water on the lucky few, and whispered that the Russians had now taken both Schubin and Exin behind them. The Americans stifled cheers. The Red Army and liberation were now surprisingly, tantalizingly close. The local Poles felt sure the Russians were only a day away. But still the column plodded away from liberation.

Come nightfall, the column spent the night in barns at Eichfelde (Polish Polanowo), a small town with a single street lined with farmhouses. By this time, an increasing number of men were falling by the wayside sick or exhausted, and, with Oberst Schneider's permission, twenty-five prisoners who were unable to walk another step were carried to Eichfelde's village church so the MOs could keep an eye on them.

Philadelphia native Lieutenant Alan Dunbar, from the 106th Infantry Division, was one of these men. His foot and leg had become progressively swollen over the past two days, and he could no longer walk. Johnny Waters had convinced the guards to allow Dunbar to ride on one of their wagons, and, at the end of the day's march, Waters personally carried Dunbar from wagon to barn. Dunbar would credit Waters with saving his life.

During the night, Colonel Goode obtained Oberst Schneider's approval to send the men in the church, who could obviously no longer keep up with the column, back to Oflag 64. Schneider even arranged for several wagons, which the kriegies would have to drive themselves, to carry the men. Goode put Colonel Edgar A. Gans in charge of this group, which set off in the darkness before the Germans could change their minds. Gans planned to retrace the column's steps back to Schubin and the Oflag 64 hospital via the Rosen estate.

MEETING THE RUSSKIES

AT THE ROSEN ESTATE, JERRY SAGE AND THE OTHER ESCAPEES HIDING out at the farm had kept under cover through Monday in case German frontline troops put in an appearance. The Americans only emerged that night, going into the rundown manor house in search of food. The estate's Polish farmworkers welcomed the escapees, soon cooking up a huge pot of vegetable soup for them. The kriegies reciprocated by sharing their Red Cross chocolate and coffee rations—luxuries the delighted Poles had not seen in more than five years. The next morning, the Americans in the house heard the unmistakable clatter and rumble of approaching tanks.

"Lord, they can't be Jerry tanks," said John Dimling, who could distinguish one tank from another by the noise of their engines and clanking treads. "They sound like M4s—Shermans."[1] The Red Army used Lend-Lease Shermans.

Jerry Sage, the most senior officer then at the estate, volunteered to take a look and hopefully make contact with the Russians to arrange truck transport for the escapees. The previous day, Sage had removed a pair of small silk US flags that had been hidden in the lining of his battle dress since before he'd been captured and sewed them prominently on the upper arms of his uniform. Walking down the estate's driveway, Sage saw a massive tank churning toward him. Smiling, he waved his arms back and forth above his head.

The tank came to an abrupt halt in front of him. Its turret turned, pointing the tank's big gun at the manor house. The monster's two 50-caliber machine guns both pointed at the American major. With a clang, the turret hatch was thrown open, and out popped the largest Russian that Jerry Sage would ever see in his life.

Sage now used the little Russian he knew to tell the giant Russian tanker that he was an American major named Sage. When the tanker frowned and pointed to Sage's shoulders, the American explained that these were US flags. Apparently, the Russian was unfamiliar with Old Glory.

"Amerikanski officer, escaped prisoner," Sage tried to explain. "Where is Marshall Zhukov?"[2]

The giant pointed back over his shoulder, indicating that the Russian commander was somewhere to the east. Sage was now joined by a Pole from the estate—possibly the same man who'd helped Bingham and Kroll. The Pole satisfied the tank commander that Sage was who he said he was, and the giant broached a broad grin. Declaring that he was on his way to Berlin and couldn't stay to chat, he retreated inside his metal monster. Spewing smoke from its exhaust, the tank withdrew back down the driveway.

Back at the manor house, where the other American escapees waited nervously, a Pole suddenly burst in. "Russkie! Russkie!" he exclaimed with joy, having seen Sage talking with the Red Army tanker.

The Poles in the house sang a hymn in thanks, after which John Dimling, joined by his American kriegie comrades, sang "God Bless America." "And how we meant it!" Dimling would say.[3]

Jerry Sage remained at the estate gate as more Russian tanks rolled by on the road that was still carrying thousands of refugees, who were now going east. After a while, a Red Army lieutenant stopped to question Sage, and the American asked for trucks to start his comrades and himself on their way to Moscow.

As the lieutenant drove off toward Exin, Sage returned to the manor house. There he got into conversation with the newly arrived Lieutenant Colonel Charles Kouns, who had escaped from the column and made his way back to the estate. Kouns, an 82nd Airborne officer from Ardsley-on-Hudson in New York, had been captured in Sicily in 1943. The pair agreed that if no Russian transport turned up that day, they would walk into Exin the following day to see what they could organize.

During the afternoon, a Red Army tank lieutenant walked into the house. Speaking with Kouns, with a Pole interpreting, the Russian said he was very pleased to see the Americans. He proceeded to shake hands all around, then produced a bottle of vodka, which he shared with the kriegies. In return, they gave him cigarettes. Then with a salute, he went out the door.

"Got to keep going to Berlin," he called back over his shoulder in Russian as he departed.[4]

• • •

IN THE BARNS at Eichfelde on Monday night following the departure of the Gans group, almost unbelievable news had spread through the column. Oberst Schneider and his guard company had departed, apparently to take part in the fight against the Russians. Only Hauptmann Menner was left with the column as a token Wehrmacht representative. Colonel Goode and his staff promptly moved into the best house in town to access hot water for their men and to plan what they should do next with the column.

Most kriegies happily went back to sleep, convinced that by the time they awoke the next morning, the Russians would have arrived. But Colonel George Millett received permission from Pop Goode to head back to Schubin with another group of around one hundred men who were eager to seek out the Red Army rather than wait at Eichfelde for the Reds to come to them. Major Merle Meacham, MO Ernest Gruenberg and his escape partner, Frank Colley, were in this group of one hundred. Hauptmann Menner had no objections, and few other kriegies noticed when the party slipped away.

At sunup on Tuesday, January 23, Colonel Goode ordered his remaining men not to wander off; he wanted to ensure that they presented to the Russians as one manageable group. But hopes of imminent freedom were dashed when, around 1:00 p.m., instead of Russians appearing, the hated camp security officer Hauptmann Zimmermann marched back into Eichfelde at the head of a detachment of a dozen tough infantrymen from a Latvian unit of the Waffen-SS. Resuming control of the POW column, Zimmermann ordered the Americans to prepare to march to Germany at 3:00 p.m.

Leery of the murderous reputation of the SS, Boomer Holder and George Durgin took this turn of events as their cue to go into escape mode. Burying themselves in hay in the middle of an Eichfelde cattle barn, they had their friend Captain Bucky Walters cover them.[5]

First Lieutenant Alfred C. Nelson from Kentucky, who'd been captured in Italy the previous July while leading a deep penetration behind German lines, also decided it was time to "go native." As the column reformed in preparation for the 3:00 p.m. restart to the march, Nelson and a new acquaintance, Lieutenant Nicholas Munson from Williamsport, Pennsylvania, prized a board from the back of their barn and slipped through the gap.

Hiding behind a haystack in the compound, Nelson and Munson avoided detection by Zimmermann's dozen guards, who had their hands full managing 1,300 prisoners. Once the column marched from sight, Nelson and Munson scurried from the compound and made it to a nearby pine forest unseen. There they built themselves a lean-to bivouac from pine branches. They would spend the next three days there in the forest before setting off to find the Red Army.

Holder and Durgin, hiding in the hay, had also avoided detection as the SS men made a cursory check of the barn. Long after the column had marched off, they remained where they were, continuing to hide even when farmworkers later came into the barn. After several hours of silence, the pair emerged and identified themselves to a little old Pole feeding the cattle.

"Amerikanski?" said the old man, beaming.

Aided by local Poles, Holder and Durgin, joined by a young escaped Russian POW, would remain there in Eichfelde for several days. Their escape odyssey was just beginning.

■ ■ ■

As THE MEN in the column tramped on through the afternoon of that third, reduced day of marching, four kriegies slipped away as the marchers passed through a thick wood, with comrades screening their departure from the diminished guard. The column paused in the middle of Charlottenburg (Polish Falmierowo) on the last of its ten-minute rest breaks before bedding down for the night in the massive barn of a large dairy farm on the outskirts of town. Following a distribution of black bread, the kriegies were ordered to sleep in the barn's haylofts.

This farm compound was surrounded by a ten-foot barbed wire fence, and SS sentries were posted at its entrance. As usual, inside the compound, the Americans were left to their own devices. This suited Frank Diggs and Nelson Tacy, who changed into their escape outfits of German soldier and Polish worker. In the twilight, the pair hauled their packed sled from the barn. Tacy then took over the hauling, with Diggs following along behind, posing as Tacy's escort as he brandished his "rifle" and cursed him in German. Snow was falling lightly as they headed for the farthest, darkest corner of the compound fence.

Out of the blue, a patrolling SS guard yelled something to them. Diggs waved dismissively, and the pair kept going. The guard ignored them, turning away. On reaching the fence, Tacy climbed to the top. With a monumental effort, Diggs hoisted the sled up to him, and Tacy managed to get it over. With a thud, the sled fell to the snow on the far side. Diggs climbed to the top, and then both men dropped to the earth outside the compound. Standing with ears pricked, the pair heard not a sound. No shouts, no shots. Getting onto a road, they headed away from the farm, with Tacy continuing to haul the sled alone and Diggs bringing up the rear, still in the guise of an escorting soldier.

Hands thrust deep in his pockets, a Polish civilian heading home after work hurried toward them through the falling snow. Diggs and Tacy stopped him.

"Do you speak English?" Diggs asked.

The surprised Pole shook his head.

"Amerikanischer offizier," Diggs then said, to explain who they were. In his rough German, he went on to say they needed a place to hide.

The Pole nodded. In German, he replied that, at a farmhouse a few kilometers down the road, there lived a Mr. Dudziak, a member of the Polish underground. Mr. Dudziak would be able to help them, the workman assured the escapees, describing the house they should look for. Thanking the Pole, the pair moved on, both of them hauling the sled now, as the snow began to thicken on the ground. For close to two hours they labored, until, outside the village of Wirsitz (Polish Wyrzysk), they found a farmhouse fitting the description given to them by the man on the road. Hoping it was the Dudziak house, they went up to the door and knocked. The door opened a few inches.

"Mr. Dudziak?" said Diggs. "Amerikanischer offizier. Can we come in?"

The door was flung open by a weathered farmer in his fifties, and the pair was hauled indoors. So too was their sled. They found themselves inside a basic, three-room farmhouse.

"Momma, food!" cried the farmer.

Mrs. Dudziak, a tiny, industrious woman, quickly rustled up something for the Americans to eat as the couple's children clustered around—two boys in their twenties, plus a boy and a girl in or close to their teens. In the light of a kerosene lamp, Diggs and Tacy ate and answered a barrage of excited questions from the Dudziak family. The Dudziaks, devout Catholics, were more worried about the coming Communists than they were about the departing Nazis. When Diggs and Tacy asked to stay in the barn, the Dudziaks would not hear of it. The Americans were led to the residence's double bed and told they must sleep there. As Diggs and Tacy eased wearily down onto the bed, they found themselves lying on a feather mattress for the first time in years.[6]

···

BACK AT THE column's overnight stop in the giant dairy barn, more kriegies were progressing with escape plans. Ed Ward and five friends from Schubin's Block 3A found hiding places in the barn and waited for dawn.[7]

A dozen guards were always going to struggle to contain so many prisoners, and the Latvians had their hands full the next morning just forming up the column. With neither the time nor the manpower to conduct detailed searches, and with head counts a thing of the past, Hauptmann Zimmermann got the column under way after just a cursory search of the barn, which failed to find Ward or his colleagues.

Ward's party remained in hiding in the barn through the day, joined by another eight kriegies who escaped from the column while it was on the march that day. The fourteen escapees would remain in the barn for the next seventy-two hours as German patrols passed by and Russian aircraft bombed unseen German targets in the vicinity.

···

REID ELLSWORTH WAS still at the Rosen estate. He was not impressed by Colonel Gans when he arrived with the party of sick kriegies from Eichfelde. Deciding to remain at the estate, Gans took over as SAO there. Ellsworth considered Gans indecisive and lacking in the qualities he expected of an SAO in their situation. Several more Russian tanks had rolled past the manor house during the day. Sending a junior officer to locate the Russians and have them send an officer to him, Gans produced a homemade American flag he'd been carrying with him, spread it on a table, sat down and waited for Russians to arrive.[8]

Later that day, the Red Army sent word that trucks would be provided for Americans at the estate in three days and that the kriegies should sit tight until they arrived. Roy Chappel, former Van Vliet escape team member, was another who hid out at the estate, and he now became involved in cooking for the growing group of Americans there, slaughtering one of the baron's sheep and commandeering some of the Rosen vegetable supply for a veritable feast that night.

Reid Ellsworth had already decided to remain in the army after the war, and he began to worry that his insanity project had been too successful and that, back in the States, fellow Oflag 64 inmates would tell the US Army he was mentally unstable. He was delighted that Major Merle Meacham had returned to the manor house during the day; taking him aside, Ellsworth begged the major to tell the others present that his craziness in camp had all been part of an approved escape plan. Meacham happily complied, and after their fine dinner that night he addressed their fellow escapees and passed on the insanity project secret that he and Ellsworth had shared.

"I'll be damned!" exclaimed MO Ernest Gruenberg, who had spoken with Ellsworth in the course of his charade. "The only thing that would have gotten you out of the camp faster would have been a sloppy suicide attempt."

"Such plans had been in process, doc," Ellsworth replied, bringing hoots of laughter from his comrades.[9]

■ ■ ■

JERRY SAGE AND Charlie Kouns walked back to Exin from the Rosen estate the following day, on a road now clogged with Russian military vehicles. Ernest Gruenberg and Frank Colley accompanied them, and while Sage and Kouns spoke with Russian officers at Exin about securing trucks for the kriegies at the estate, Gruenberg and Colley kept on walking to nearby Wegheim. There Gruenberg and Colley found a Red Army field hospital busy with Russian battle casualties. The Russian MO in charge was a female major, and when Gruenberg offered to help out, she welcomed his aid. For the time being, Gruenberg and Colley remained at Wegheim.

Meanwhile, Alfred Nelson and Nicholas Munson had left their forest bivouac. They pushed east in the night only to come upon a series of German machine-gun nests that were almost invisible in the snow. Fortunately for the Americans, the German troops were looking east, and the pair was able to crawl by the positions. Once clear, Nelson and Munson disagreed on which direction to take. So, with mutual good wishes, they split up. Nelson continued on alone for several days, at one point slipping on the ice and cutting a knee to the bone. Limping on, he spied a light on the other side of the frozen Bromberg Canal (Kanał Bydgoski).

"That's for me," said Nelson to himself and, slipping and sliding, he crossed the ice to the far side of the waterway.[10]

The light was at a Red Army encampment, but Nelson didn't receive a warm welcome from the scruffy Russian troops he encountered. Suspecting him of being a German deserter, the Russians stripped him of his clothes, tied his hands behind his back, and put him against a wall. A firing squad lined up.

"Stalin! Roosevelt! Churchill!" the terrified young American kept repeating to the Russians as he attempted to convince them he was an ally.[11]

Ignoring his protestations, the Russians had their rifles aimed at Nelson when a Red Army officer arrived on the scene. He put a stop to the proceedings, saving Nelson's life. Not sure whether to believe that Nelson was American, the officer took him to the nearest town— Nelson had no idea what town it was—and lodged him in the basement of the mayor's house with a sentry at the top of the stairs. After a time, Nelson noticed that his guard had disappeared, and, taking his chances, he crept from the house in darkness. Locating railroad tracks, he jumped a passing train and hoped and prayed it would take him to someplace where he could link up with fellow Americans, and keep him *out* of the hands of the Red Army.

10

MOSCOW OR BUST

JERRY SAGE AND CHARLIE KOUNS HAD RUN OUT OF PATIENCE. IN EXIN on Thursday, January 25, they met a Russian lieutenant who thought they stood a better chance of securing transport east if they were in Schubin and took them back to their old camp in his truck.

At the Oflag 64 hospital, Sage and Kouns found Colonel Drury and his hospital group still waiting for transport. The pair decided they would walk to Moscow if they had to. After helping themselves to Red Cross rations from the old parcel store, they set off. Making Warsaw their first objective, they hitched a ride with an empty Russian supply truck that took them as far as Mogilno, a town thirty-five miles east of Schubin.

Dropped in Mogilno's main square, they were quickly surrounded by curious Poles. To this point, the Red Army had not bothered with Mogilno, and the locals were hoping that these Americans had come to liberate them. Once they overcame their disappointment on learning that Sage and Kouns were merely escaped POWs, the villagers conducted them to a small hotel on the square that had been taken over by the Polish Red Cross. The pair was welcomed by the all-female Red Cross staff and provided with a spotless second-floor bedroom with a bathroom and two beds complete with crisp white sheets, something Sage hadn't seen in years. Fed sausage, bread and soup in the dining room, the Americans in return doled out Nescafé and chocolate from their Red Cross packages.

The following day, Sage and Kouns spoke with a number of townspeople, one of whom proudly declared he'd been granted US citizenship in Milwaukee thirty-two years earlier. A Mogilno woman said she had a son in Buffalo, New York. Late that afternoon, when the two Americans were back in their hotel room, a boy ran into the hotel lobby.

"The Russkies are coming!" yelled the youth excitedly before dashing away again.[1]

Villagers quickly disappeared from the street, and as Sage and Kouns watched from their second-floor hotel window, a column of Red Army infantrymen trudged by. All wore quilted jackets, fur caps and high boots. Some had ornate looted lace Polish bedcovers draped around their necks. One wore a toilet seat as a necklace. The troops seemed to have passed through the village, but, after dark, Sage and Kouns heard the sounds of nearby revelry, including guns being fired in the air. The Russkies had stayed.

Five Red Cross women operating the hotel became increasingly frightened, and they welcomed an invitation to join the Americans in their room. There, one young woman hid under a bed while two others skulked in the bathroom. The remaining pair joined Sage and Kouns at the table, trying to teach the Americans a Polish card game. As they played, Sage had the two Polish women also teach him a particular phrase in Russian in case he needed it.

The sounds of Russian revelry drew closer. And then the rampaging Reds were downstairs in the hotel. The bedroom door opened, and a teenager who had been working in the kitchen dashed in. Blonde, blue-eyed, and a beauty, she was eight months pregnant. Terrified, she hid in the closet. Doors banged downstairs, then on the second floor. The Russkies were going from room to room.

Inevitably, the bedroom door burst open. Two Russian soldiers stood in the doorway, semiautomatic rifles in hand. Seeing the two women at the table, their eyes lit up.

Sage, glaring at them, jabbed a finger in the direction of the first man and unleashed his newly learned Russian sentence. "Get out! These are ours!"

The first soldier blinked. He'd clearly been drinking heavily. Swaying, he frowned disconcertedly as he took in the powerfully built foreigner.

"Get out!" Sage repeated, pointing down the hallway. To emphasize his point that possession was nine points of the law, he put an arm around the shoulders of the Polish woman sitting next to him.

Mumbling incoherently, the leading Red turned. Pulling his companion with him, he lurched off down the hallway.

"Thank you, Lord," said Sage half to himself as he closed the door. "Amen!" echoed Charlie Kouns.[2]

The six women remained in the room that night under the Americans' protection. Sage and Kouns slept on the floor.

■ ■ ■

BOOMER HOLDER AND George Durgin had been joined in their barn hideout by another American escapee, Lewis Bixby, and, together with their young Russian POW comrade, the trio ventured to the village of Polanowo. Locals told them one house had previously been occupied by a Nazi official, a Herr Kuss, so the Americans figured it was fair game. But a Polish family living in the house—Herr Kuss' servants—were reluctant to admit the escaped prisoners, fearing that their former master might return and punish them. Nothing was going to dissuade Holder and his companions, and they convinced the Poles that it would be all right for them to come in for a while.

There, stoking up the coal fire and boiling water, the kriegies were able to shave for the first time in weeks and dined on Herr Kuss' hoard of vegetables, berries and applesauce. Their band was soon enlarged by the arrival of two more Oflag 64 escapees, Polish captains who had been captured in Italy fighting with the US Army and sent to Schubin.

On January 27, after several days enjoying life in Herr Kuss' house, the group heard Russian tanks in nearby woods. Going out into the street, they came face to face with a dozen fellow Schubinites who, to their surprise, had also been hiding in the town. The kriegies then encountered their first vodka-soaked Russian soldier, who babbled something before lurching away. Local Poles told Holder and company that the Russian had said his comrades had just liberated the nearby town of Wirsitz. Able to see a church steeple in the distance, Holder and his companions immediately set off to walk toward Wirsitz. On reaching the town, they met an armed Polish underground fighter wearing an identifying armband.

"Safe at last," thought Holder.[3]

Moments later, three Luftwaffe Messerschmitt Bf 109s hurtled past overhead, flying low. There was still a sting in the retreating scorpion's tail. With guns chattering, the Messerschmitt fighter-bombers dropped bombs on a concentration of Russian vehicles at a crossroads on the outskirts of Wirsitz, then banked away. Boomer Holder ducked into a doorway to shelter. Never again would he speak too soon. Emerging from cover and proceeding cautiously, the Americans met grim-faced Russian infantry in the middle of town. While keeping an eye on the Me-109s, which continued to swoop on Russian vehicles outside the town, the Russians nonetheless shared the contents of their canteens with the kriegies—vodka, of course.

Polish residents led the Americans to an abandoned building, a local brewery, where Holder and his companions bedded down. They didn't get much sleep. Throughout the night, both Russian soldiers and local Poles visited the brewery, liberating the contents of its beer kegs. The following day, Holder's group was joined by more Schubin escapees, including Captain Bruce Martin from Pittsburgh, Pennsylvania, bringing their number to thirty-six.

As the senior officer present, Martin took charge and sent several men to locate better quarters as an alternative to the stinking brewery. On a hilltop on the edge of town, the scouts found an abandoned local Nazi Party headquarters, an impressive solid steel and concrete bunker covered with camouflage paint. The previous occupants had left their last meal partly uneaten on the table. Martin transferred the kriegie party there. Taking over the building, the Americans helped themselves to Nazi souvenirs and laid out beds of straw in the building's gymnasium.

To round up any more kriegies who might be wandering around, and to ask locals to direct escaped Americans to the bunker, Captain Martin meanwhile went back into Wirsitz. Walking along the main street, he saw a horse-drawn wagon approaching, carrying Russian troops and three Americans. One of the Americans was Major Bob Crandall, who, along with two Schubin escape partners, had been captured by the Russians twelve miles east of Wirsitz and forced to accompany them back to the town.

Seeing Martin, Crandall jumped from the wagon and made a beeline for him. The scruffy Russian officer in charge promptly pulled his pistol and dived after the American. The next thing Bruce Martin knew, he had the Russian officer's weapon at *his* temple. Martin soon realized that the Russian officer was drunk and that he would have to play his hand very carefully. When he tried to explain to the inebriated Russian that Crandall and he were American officers, and that another three dozen Americans were in a building on the outskirts of town, the Russkie decided that all the Amerikanski should join his troops fighting the Germans.

With the gun at his head, Martin was marched all the way back to the Nazi Party HQ with Crandall and his companions also in tow. There, in the gymnasium, one of the two Polish kriegies, Captain Ted Radvanski, a fluent Russian speaker, engaged the Red Army officer in conversation. Soon talking at length about himself, the Red completely forgot why he was there. Eventually, he kissed Martin and Radvanski on both cheeks and cheerily departed. With the Americans left unmolested in their bunker, Crandall became the group's SAO.

Through the day, generous townspeople came to provide them with food, and a tide of Schubin escapees found their way to the bunker's door. *Item* editor Frank Diggs and his escape partner, Nelson Tacy, still dragging their efficient Polish sled, were among them.

When they arrived, the pair discovered George Durgin parading around in a Hitler Youth uniform he'd found in the bunker. Diggs thought his fellow kriegie looked pretty snappy in the outfit, shorts and all, but suggested to Durgin that being seen in the Nazi rig-out was a sure way to get himself shot by a Russian or a Polish partisan. Durgin quickly disrobed.

The following day, Diggs and Tacy went exploring in Wirsitz, only to discover that German troops were still in the town, hiding in basements. The Krauts were routed out by Russian troops who were systematically looting the town. Diggs and Tacy witnessed a party of quaking German enlisted men with raised hands being shoved behind a building by three Russians carrying burp guns. There was a burst of automatic fire. Only the Russians reemerged, grinning at the Americans before strolling away. Searching for steeds at a nearby horse farm, Diggs and Tacy found that the horses had gone. An elderly German woman lay in a pool of blood, riddled with Russian bullets, on her farmhouse doorstep.

By the time a sober Russian major came to the Wirsitz bunker on January 29, there were 110 escaped American Schubinites sheltering there. The major urged them to leave and, with German counterattacks expected in the area, the kriegies didn't have to be told twice. Leaving four sick companions in the town's Catholic church, the remaining 106 Americans packed up, some making homemade sleds in an attempt to emulate Diggs and Tacy's sleek conveyance, and hit the road.

As a group, they headed for Nakel (Polish Nakło nad Notecią) via Sadke (Polish Sadki). On their way out, they walked through the crossroads that had been bombed by the Me-109s and was littered with blackened vehicles and bloated corpses of horses. Along their route, the Americans passed numerous feet, denuded of footwear, poking out of the roadside snow. These corpses of both German and Russian soldiers had been stripped of their boots by passersby.

While trailing at the back of the American party, medical officer Harry Abrahams had his greatcoat stolen at gunpoint by a passing

Russian infantryman. Russian hardware regularly rolled past the tramping line of kriegies, much of it American Lend-Lease equipment. In the back of Studebaker 6x6s, Russian troops were frequently drunk. At one bend, a Russian soldier was bounced from his precarious position on a truck and fell into the road beside the Americans. He was run over by the next truck in the convoy, whose driver made no attempt to avoid him. Russians in both trucks laughed and applauded, and the convoy roared on without stopping.[4]

From the back of the American line, Harry Abrahams ran to the man to see if he could help him. A passing Russian foot soldier beat Abrahams to the victim. Grabbing the man's feet, the soldier dragged him to the roadside. But instead of trying to help him, the Russian rifled the man's pockets, taking his wallet. As Abrahams was examining the victim, who was well and truly dead, the Russian infantryman spotted the American's wristwatch and demanded it. Relieved of his timepiece, Abrahams the Good Samaritan unhappily trotted to rejoin his fellow kriegies, who had kept moving. Boomer Holder would see as many as six purloined watches on the wrists of some Russian soldiers.

When the group reached Nakel, on the River Netze in northern Poland, they found the town a smoking ruin after recent savage fighting during a German counterattack. Knocked-out Russian tanks filled the streets, as did drunken Russian troops who had retaken the town after German troops had initially fought their way back in.

Finding the Russians here not particularly welcoming, some of the kriegies decided to return to the comparative safety of Schubin. Diggs and Tacy were among them. On January 30, finally ditching their sled, the pair began walking. When a massive Russian tank came along heading in the direction of Schubin, they flagged it down. With the mention of Amerikanski, the commander offered the pair a ride. In thanks, Diggs raised his last pack of Camels, offering the commander a cigarette. The Russian took the entire pack. But at least the pair rode the last dozen miles to Schubin, hanging onto the back of the careering tank.

Walking back through Oflag 64's gates, passing a Russian sentry who took no notice of them, Diggs and Tacy found Colonel Millett, who was in command of a handful of escaped American kriegies, plus a motley band of other Allied POWs and a small detachment of Russian troops under two sergeants. Among the kriegies back in camp was Ed Ward. His group had been taken into Wirsitz by Russians, and from there Ward and three others had tramped to Nakel and back to Schubin. When Ward walked in through the oflag's open gates, he'd found three other Americans there and, in a massive pile of undelivered letters at the Kommandantur, seven letters from home addressed to him.

Diggs and Tacy reported to Colonel Millett and claimed beds in the White House. Millett himself had earlier returned to Schubin via the Rosen estate. On January 25, SAO Colonel Drury had been driven by the Russians to Hohensalza, where he'd won a promise from the Red Army's General Alexander Kotikow that a road convoy would be sent to collect the men at Oflag 64. By January 28, with no sign of the convoy, Colonel Millett left the camp to find out where it was.

That same day, while he was away, a Red Army convoy of twelve Studebaker trucks had rolled up to the camp. At 2:00 that afternoon, the convoy had departed Schubin, carrying Colonel Drury and 107 other Americans as well British, French and Italian POWs who had congregated in Schubin by that time. Returning to find an empty camp, Millett decided to wait there for the time being. The convoy, meanwhile, took the Drury party to Rembertów, a little east of Warsaw, in three daily stages.

Not long after Diggs and Tacy arrived back at the oflag, Boomer Holder and George Durgin also trudged in. After going full circle, the exhausted kriegies were back where they'd started. But at least they were no longer prisoners.

■ ■ ■

THE OFLAG 64 column, meanwhile, continued on the march northwest into Germany. Five days after its regular guards had left, Colonel Goode led the column into a German town where they came upon Oberst Schneider and his grenadiers, who resumed duty guarding the column. The Americans hooted them derisively, and the colonel and his men looked genuinely embarrassed.

• • •

FINDING NO TRANSPORT heading east via Mogilno, Jerry Sage and Charlie Kouns hitched a ride back to Schubin on a Red Army truck. Like the kriegies who'd returned ahead of them, Sage and Kouns were ordered by Colonel Millett to remain in camp until further Russian transport could be organized.

Millett had no idea when he and the other escaped kriegies who continued to arrive back at the camp could expect Russian transport to enable them to follow the Drury group. As Oflag 64's SAO, Millett made Jerry Sage the camp's mess officer, and Sage and Kouns claimed bunks in the White House with other returned kriegies. In his new role, Sage was in charge of the old Red Cross parcel store, which still contained several thousand parcels from the January 18 delivery. Sage guarded these parcels zealously, rightfully considering them American property vital for the feeding of the Americans then in the camp and others who might reach it after escaping German custody.

The day after returning to the camp, Sage was summoned urgently by the young officer he'd put in charge of the parcel store, because Russian troops were looting the Red Cross rations. Running to the store, Sage discovered a quartet of Red Army soldiers removing Red Cross boxes under the direction of an officer and loading them onto a handcart.

"Stop!" bellowed Sage in Russian. In English, he explained that these were American parcels. The soldiers ceased what they were doing and looked sheepishly to their officer. When the Russian officer ordered his men to continue what they were doing, Sage's anger flared. "Stop!" he yelled again, this time stepping in among the Russians.

Again, the soldiers froze. After glaring up at the much taller Sage, the Russian officer yelled at him, then picked up a parcel and held it out to one of his men. Without a moment's thought, Sage knocked the parcel from the officer's grasp. It clunked to the floor. Enraged now, the Russian reached to the pistol holstered on his hip. His OSS training and experience kicking in, Sage swung a powerful right to the Russian's mouth. He heard the man's jaw crack from the blow. In front of his wide-eyed men, the Red Army officer sagged to the ground, out cold.

Sage now ordered the Russian enlisted men to unload the cart and replace the purloined parcels with their unconscious officer. Looking warily back over their shoulders, the soldiers duly wheeled their officer out the gate. Sage stormed back to the White House. As he told the two Russian sergeants of the camp detachment what had taken place, he noticed that a piece of tooth from the Russian officer's mouth was embedded in his knuckle.

Having launched US Army hostilities against the Red Army, Sage was thinking he'd better be making tracks, but the sergeants were totally sympathetic. An order banning looting had just been transmitted by the Soviet high command, and the sergeants assured Sage that they would sort out the matter. The sergeants' colonel subsequently passed on a message for Sage to lie low for a few days. The looters had been from a unit that was passing through Schubin, and they moved on before long.[5]

THE FIRST SCHUBIN ESCAPEE HOME RUNS

By February 2, at Wegheim, Ernest Gruenberg and Frank Colley had itchy feet. Thirty escaped American POWs, including Craig Campbell from Schokken, had limped into the Wegheim hospital by that time via the Rosen estate and Schubin and were in need of medical attention. In addition to tending to them, Gruenberg noted down all their names.

Gruenberg now received permission from Colonel Millett at Schubin for Frank Colley, his new escape partner, John Dimling, who'd turned up at Wegheim after staying at the Rosen estate, and himself to attempt to reach Moscow. Millett was by now planning to shortly make his own run east and would set off within days. Armed with Millett's approval, Gruenberg asked the friendly female Russian major running the Wegheim field hospital to help Colley, Dimling and himself get to Moscow under their own steam.

Late on February 2, the major produced a rail pass from the local Polish authorities that would allow the trio to make the first leg east to Kutno in the Łódź district. The following morning, Saturday, February 3, the convivial major and Exin Poles treated the American trio to a hearty farewell breakfast in the town. As they waited at Exin station through the day, Gruenberg, Colley and Dimling were joined by twenty-six other Schubin escapees.

One of these fellow travelers waiting on the platform at Exin was First Lieutenant Herbert L. "Herb" Garris from North Carolina. He'd been captured not long after parachuting into Normandy with the 101st Airborne on D-Day. Handsome, personable Garris had tunneled into the hay in a Rosen barn with two others on the first night of the march. The following day, he'd charmed his way into a bed in the house of Stanisław Mankowski, the estate's Polish manager, who had several unmarried daughters, including the attractive Urszula. But even Garris had tired of the young woman's attentions. He was ready to go home, one way or another.

At 10:00 that night, a crowded train with the twenty-nine Americans among its passengers pulled out of Exin, heading a hundred miles south to Września, after which it would turn east for Kutno. As the train steamed through the night, Ernest Gruenberg got into conversation with some of the Poles aboard, including children of school age. To his horror, he found that ten-year-old Poles could neither read nor write. Fifteen-year-olds had only a basic education and were working ten-hour days in factories. Since 1939, the Nazis had banned Polish children from attending school. Considering all Poles subhuman, they had even prevented them from marrying until they were in their mid-twenties, to keep the Polish birthrate down.

At Kutno, the twenty-nine Americans split into three groups. Herb Garris was in a party that would end up in Warsaw and then at the displaced persons camp at Rembertów outside Warsaw. Administered by the Russian NKVD (the People's Commissariat for Internal Affairs), the camp was in a former Polish military school. Gruenberg, Colley and Dimling had heard bad things about that camp and chose to avoid it. With their goal still Moscow, the trio hitchhiked east into the western Soviet Union, finding rides on empty Red Army supply trucks, wagons, horse-drawn sleds, and sometimes on trains, with no officials ever asking to see passes or tickets. At each stopping place, locals gave them food and a bed.

Altogether the journey took the Gruenberg trio two weeks after they left Exin, with the last leg aboard a troop train that took them to a station in the central northwest part of Moscow. After they stepped down from the train on February 17 and emerged from the sprawling station looking lost, they were approached by a Red Army soldier who spoke basic English and asked where they wanted to go. When the Americans said they were looking for the United States embassy, the young Russian said that it was not far away and volunteered to lead them there.

Through the peaceful streets of central Moscow tramped the American trio with their Russian guide. Around them, the city was cloaked in winter gray, and no smiles creased the faces of the passing Muscovites as they hurried to and from their jobs. Yet, to John Dimling, after all the destruction and despair they had seen in Poland, Moscow was a paradise.[1] The helpful Russian soldier led them to Novinsky Boulevard and an ornate nine-story building that had been the US embassy since the United States recognized the Soviet Union in 1933. Pointing to the door, the soldier grinned.

"You're a true boy scout," said one of the Americans.

"Yes, boy scout," the Russian agreed.[2]

Thanking him sincerely, the trio proceeded inside. American embassy staff looked at them in horror. In nondescript uniforms, they had neither shaved nor washed since leaving Schubin more than three weeks earlier. With beards and long hair, they looked, and smelled, like hobos. But once they spoke and identified themselves as US Army officers who had escaped the Nazis, they were embraced by embassy staff.

General Deane, the chief of the American Military Mission, did not meet Gruenberg, Colley and Dimling until that night. By that time, the trio had bathed and shaved, had been given haircuts, and had been allocated clean uniforms with insignia of rank. They once more looked, and felt, like US Army officers. By the time Deane saw them, the staff of the American Military Mission had fed the trio a veritable feast and opened more than one bottle of whisky. They were partying hard.

Three days earlier, Deane had received advice from the de facto Polish ambassador in Moscow that 1,000 escaped American POWs were in various Polish cities liberated by Soviet troops, although no names or details were given. This news had excited Deane, who readied the American POW recovery plan he had prepared six months earlier. Yet his Russian counterpart, Lieutenant General K. D. Golubev, had not notified him that any Americans were in Russian hands.

This didn't surprise Deane. His relations with Golubev had become strained. The previous year, the Russians had agreed that USAAF bombers of Eastern Command (ESCOM) would be permitted to operate out of three airfields in Soviet territory. In June, the Luftwaffe had caught American B-17s on the ground at Poltava in central Ukraine, destroying fifty and damaging nineteen. The Soviets had undertaken to provide ESCOM with fighter and antiaircraft protection, but few Russian fighters or AA guns had been sent to Poltava. ESCOM had subsequently pulled its bombers out of bases in Soviet territory.

So as Deane spoke with Gruenberg, Colley and Dimling at their liberation party, he was keen to learn from them just how many Americans were genuinely on the loose in Soviet-occupied Poland and the western Soviet Union. Gruenberg estimated that, at most, 200 American servicemen were at that stage under Russian control. He based that figure on the number he knew to have been with Colonel Drury, the small number of escapees with Colonel Millett back at Oflag 64, and the thirty escapees he'd seen at the Russian field hospital at Wegheim.

Gruenberg, Colley and Dimling mentioned that they had bumped into other small parties of American Oflag 64 escapees roaming free in eastern Poland. All had told the trio of unpleasant experiences with Russian troops who had stolen their watches and sometimes roughed them up. Those Americans were actively avoiding Russians and ignoring Red Army signs they had seen in various Polish towns that directed escaped Allied servicemen to Russian assembly camps at Rembertów, Września, Lublin, and Łódź.

At this point, Gruenberg handed over to General Deane the list of names he'd compiled of the hospitalized Americans at Wegheim. Deane had those names transmitted to Washington that night, so that families in the United States could be notified that their loved ones had escaped from the Germans. The three escapees also told Deane that, as far as they knew, the general's old friend Colonel Goode was still leading the Schubin column west into Germany under German guard, accompanied by Lieutenant Colonel Waters. Deane made sure that G-2 promptly received that information.

Deane waited until the next day, February 18, to debrief the Gruenberg trio in detail, after which he met with General Golubev and demanded to know why he had not been notified that Gruenberg, Colley and Dimling had been liberated by the Red Army and authorized to travel to Moscow. This was news to Golubev, who said he'd never heard of the trio. And he was privately furious that they'd slipped through to the US embassy unnoticed. The NKVD had orders to intercept and corral all Americans on the loose, and would now prove even more diligent in that respect. Very few additional escaped American POWs would succeed in reaching Moscow's US embassy after this.

In this meeting with Deane, Golubev did admit to knowing that 450 American POWs were now in Red Army hands. Deane didn't trust this figure, relying on the Polish ambassador's estimate of 1,000 Americans on the loose. Golubev's figure was actually reasonably accurate, taking into account the Drury, Gans and Millett groups from Oflag 64, the men from Oflag 64-Z, the men in the Red Army hospital at Wegheim, and escapees from the Schubin column now in Russian hands.

Golubev told Deane that it was his government's intention to send all these Americans, and any others who fell into Russian hands, by rail to a large transit camp for former Allied POWs at the Ukrainian port of Odessa on the Black Sea: from there the Allies could ship them home. Should the need arise, said Golubev, a second transit camp would also be opened at Murmansk, north of the Arctic Circle on the Barents Sea. Deane immediately sought Russian permission to dispatch contact teams of three to five US military personnel to a number of centers behind Russian lines. Under Deane's plan, the USAAF would fly emergency supplies into these centers from the ESCOM base at Poltava and fly out seriously ill escaped kriegies.

The Russian general responded that one American contact team could be sent to Odessa to receive Americans funneled there by the Red Army, and another could be sent to Lublin in Poland to make sure all Americans went to Odessa. Lublin was the location of the Communist "provisional" government of Poland being supported by the Soviets—in opposition to the Polish government in exile that had been based in London since 1939.

This was the extent of Russian concessions. General Golubev also specified that Deane's American contact teams would have to be flown in Soviet aircraft while inside Soviet territory. Months before this, Deane had negotiated what he believed a hard-and-fast agreement with the Russian Foreign Office over American access to, and repatriation of, their liberated POWs. On February 11, the Yalta Conference in the Crimea between Roosevelt, Stalin and Churchill had wrapped up, and the leaders' agreement spelled out how Returned Allied Military Personnel (RAMPs) would be treated by the United States, the USSR and Britain, in much more liberal terms than Golubev was now offering.

Deane was extremely unhappy with Golubev's limited concessions. "I felt it to be a serious violation of our agreement," he would say.[3] Returning to the US Military Mission, he chose the personnel who would make up the Odessa and Lublin contact teams. Then, that afternoon, he chaired a press conference in his office, a press conference apparently called, at least in part, to embarrass the Russians into being more helpful regarding escaped American POWs. The star attractions of the press conference were Gruenberg, Colley and Dimling, who would soon be dubbed the Moscow Trio by the American media.

As these were the first Americans to have escaped from German custody and passed through Russian hands to reach US government hands, Allied pressmen, including Eddy Gilmore of the Associated

Press, eagerly plied them with questions. Having been briefed by the general to be circumspect when it came to the Russians, the trio was careful not to say anything bad about them. Instead, they spoke at length about their capture and treatment by the Germans, reserving special mention for one German transit camp at Chalons in France, which they referred to as "Starvation Manor."

It was the trio's forced march from Schubin and their escape from the column that most interested the reporters. Gruenberg told the pressmen about the road outside Oflag 64 being choked with fleeing German civilians for days before the POWs joined that exodus west.

"It was some scene," added Colley. "And, mind you, this wasn't a main road, but a secondary road."

"How many refugees would you estimate there were?" asked one reporter.

"I would say there were thousands upon thousands of them," Gruenberg answered, unable to relay the fear, distress and despair they had seen on that road day after day.

"Did the German civilians mind you being mixed up in their refugee column?"

"Oh, a couple of women cursed us," Gruenberg replied. "But the Poles let us hitch our sleds and carts to their wagons. They gave us a wink."[4]

Gruenberg also mentioned that other Schubin escapees were on the loose in Poland, Germany and Russia, although he couldn't put a figure on the number involved. He mentioned several stories he'd heard from Americans and Poles en route to Moscow of Schubin escapees, including Captain George H. Dunkelberg of the 101st Airborne, who joined up with Soviet troops going into Germany and fought the Germans with borrowed Russian weapons. Gruenberg said that, to overcome the language barrier, Dunkelberg used a "grunt and point" system of communication with the Russians.[5]

The wires hummed with the pressmen's reports, and the day after the Moscow press conference, the story of the Moscow Trio's escape from the Germans, and of the plight of American POWs still marching in Nazi custody ahead of the Red Army's advance, appeared in newspapers large and small across the United States. For the first time, Americans at home would appreciate the desperate straits in which thousands of American prisoners found themselves even as the Allies were closing in on Berlin and the end of the war in Europe was in sight.

The Moscow Trio was soon on a USAAF transport aircraft flying out of Moscow and heading for the United States. Within days, they would be the first Schubin escapees to set foot back on home soil. The press was subsequently kept away from them, as it would be from all returning POWs, for US Military Intelligence now put a blanket ban on former kriegies talking publicly about their experiences. Too much had already been said by the Moscow Trio. When debriefed by G-2's Captured Personnel and Materiel (CPM) Branch, American RAMPs would be required to sign an acknowledgment that, under the Espionage Act, they could not reveal anything about their captivity or their liberation. This was to ensure that morale at home was not affected, that war crimes proceedings following the war were not compromised, and that the Russians weren't offended.

* * *

SCHUBIN TUNNEL KINGS Bill Cory and Spud Murphy had traveled with Colonel Drury's Oflag 64 hospital party to Rembertów. Their traveling companions, Bill Fabian and Hervey Robinson, had been hospitalized, and Cory and Murphy quickly became disenchanted with Rembertów's conditions and the NKVD guards, so they decided to escape Russian custody and head for Moscow and the US embassy. They were joined by Peter Gaish, who'd hidden in the hay at Baron von Rosen's estate before returning to Schubin in time for the exodus with Colonel Drury. Gaish had Serbo-Croat heritage and could speak a little Polish and Russian.

In early February, about the same time that Gruenberg, Colley and Dimling had set off on their push to Moscow, the Cory trio slipped by inattentive Russian guards at the Rembertów camp. For days, they walked and rode sleds, hay wagons and trucks, heading steadily east through southeast Poland, until they reached the city called Lvov by the occupying Soviets (Polish Lwów). As soon as Russian troops in

Lvov saw the disheveled, unshaven Americans in nondescript uniforms, they accused them of being German infiltrators and handed them over to the NKVD, who tossed them into the local jail.

Vladimir Belayev, an inquisitive Russian journalist, found the trio there. After covering Allied naval operations into Murmansk, he'd developed a liking for Americans and Britons. Bringing a Jewish woman to act as his translator—she'd taught English at Kraków University before the war—Belayev questioned the trio and became convinced that Cory and his companions were genuine US Army officers. He in turn convinced the NKVD lieutenant in charge to parole the trio into the care of the senior Red Army general in Lvov. That general had been a prewar Soviet military attaché in Washington, and he, too, loved Americans.

The genial general took the three Americans under his wing, installing them in the best hotel in town, the George, and organizing hot baths and a feast for them. While Cory, Murphy and Gaish were being entertained by the general, word arrived that another five Americans were in the hotel lobby. The Cory trio rushed out to greet who they expected would be more escaped kriegies but found that the Americans were USAAF personnel from ESCOM at Poltava. Led by a Major Nicholson, the airmen said they were in Lvov to locate aircrew and bombsights from American bombers shot down in the area.

The ESCOM men spent the next few days haggling with the general and the NKVD over the fate of the Cory trio before finally convincing the Russians to hand them over. Cory, Murphy and Gaish were flown the 1,500 miles from Lvov to Poltava. From Poltava, the USAAF flew them to Tehran in Iran, where they were spruced up in new uniforms before being flown in stages across the Atlantic to Miami. Cory, Murphy and Gaish landed on American soil on February 28, becoming the second group of Schubin escapees to reach home, close behind the Moscow Trio. On G-2 orders, they arrived without the media's knowledge or any fanfare.[6]

For the many hundreds of other Schubin inmates both on the run in Poland and still in German custody, getting home was not going to be anywhere as easy as it had been for the Moscow and Cory trios.

12

KRIEGIES ON THE RUN

At Oflag 64, Jerry Sage learned on February 4 that Colonel Millett had left Schubin and headed east. Sage and Charlie Kouns decided to follow the colonel's example, and, gaining a place on a four-seat, horse-drawn Polish sleigh heading northeast for Bromberg (Polish Bydgoszcz), they departed from Schubin on Monday, February 5, in heavy snow.

As they slid along, they came upon a lone, fresh-faced Russian soldier on the roadside out in the middle of nowhere. The short, stocky figure in a thick coat and fur Chapka cap was trying to hitch a ride. The Americans urged the driver to stop, and the sleigh drew to a halt beside the solitary figure.

"*Spasibo*," said the soldier in thanks, stepping up onto a runner and holding onto the back of a seat as the sleigh moved off again.

Sage noticed that the weapon slung over the soldier's back was fitted with a sniper's scope. Pointing to the soldier and the rifle, Sage tried his limited Russian. "You kill many Germans?"

"*Da, da,*" the soldier responded with a grin, using fingers to count out thirty plus.

"Over thirty Krauts dead," said a nodding Sage, impressed.

The soldier's bulky overcoat was now unbuttoned to reveal the military decoration of the Order of the Red Star for the defense of Stalingrad. The act also revealed that the soldier had ample breasts. The decorated sniper was a woman. And an attractive one. When both Sage and Kouns let out exclamations of surprise, the sniper laughed, removed her cap and shook her head. Fair hair tumbled down over her shoulders. Sage would describe her as looking like Norwegian Olympic skater and movie star Sonja Henie. Sometime later, the femme fatale was dropped off to join her unit, after which Sage and Kouns alighted in Bromberg and found a room in another local hotel run by the Red Cross.[1]

• • •

Pessimist Billy Bingham and his escape partner, Bob Kroll, had made it to the displaced persons camp at Rembertów, where they joined Colonel Drury and the kriegies from Oflag 64's hospital, including Wright Bryan and Jonel Hill. The American party at Rembertów continued to grow as Holder, Durgin, Diggs, Tacy and other Schubin escapees also arrived after briefly returning to Schubin and being rounded up by the NKVD.

Bingham and Kroll found this place to be worse than any German POW camp. American kriegies were thrown in with 1,500 civilians from across eastern Europe, all living in a single two-story building. There was no running water or heat. It was bitterly cold, and at night, sleeping on straw on the floor, the Americans could only huddle together for warmth. For food, all the Red Army gave them was barley.

After a while, a Russian major came through the camp, and Bingham and Kroll confronted him. Declaring they were US Army officers, they demanded transport to Moscow. The major looked them up and down with disgust. Neither had bathed or shaved in months.

Bingham was wearing a worn US Army shirt, Ukrainian breeches, a legging wrapped around just one leg, and a Polish greatcoat.

"You do not look like officers," said the skeptical Russian.[2]

The duo was eventually able to convince the major they were the real McCoy, and he gave them a slip of paper containing written approval to use any available transport to travel into the Soviet Union. That was fine except that few of the Russian enlisted men they would show the piece of paper to could read. In the camp, Bingham and Kroll had befriended a pair of attractive young Ukrainian women who admitted to having been the girlfriends of German soldiers who had dumped them in Poland when the Wehrmacht retreated. Like Bingham, the girls could speak some German. And they were keen to get home to the Ukraine.

"We will take you to Moscow to see Stalin," said one of the girls with a grin.

"No," Bingham responded, "we'll take you back to the United States and make you movie stars."[3]

So Bingham, Kroll and the cheeky Ukrainian girls teamed up. Armed with the major's written authorization, the quartet slipped from the Rembertów camp and boarded an eastbound train, taking places in a crowded boxcar. Fifty miles east of Rembertów, the train pulled into a station in a small town. The door to the Americans' boxcar was thrown open. Russian soldiers barged in, grabbed the two protesting Ukrainian women, dragged them out and flung them to the ground on the platform.

As Bingham and Kroll watched helplessly from inside the boxcar, the Russians proceeded to batter the two women to death with rifle butts for being German collaborators. It was over in seconds. The Russians had obviously been tipped off by someone on the train who recognized the women and knew their history. The stunned and sickened Bingham and Kroll were left untouched. The boxcar door rolled shut, and the train resumed its eastward journey. The pair didn't reach Moscow. Directed by the NKVD, they eventually arrived at Odessa in the first RAMPs party to arrive at the port city for evacuation. General Deane's contact team had arrived from Moscow just the day before and was there to greet them.

Through the rest of February, all the American kriegies who had been collected by the NKVD at Rembertów and elsewhere in Poland arrived at Odessa. Jerry Sage was among them. In Lublin, he'd tried to return to his OSS role, pursuing information about the provisional government, but he, too, had been rounded up by the Soviet spy agency. With Turkey entering the war on the Allied side in February, Istanbul and the Dardanelles opened up as transit points, and on March 5 the British steamer *Moreton Bay*, the first Allied troopship carrying freed Schubinites away from the Soviet Union, sailed from Odessa on the initial leg of the kriegies' homeward journey.

Alas, for the majority of Schubinites who were still in German hands, tough times still lay ahead.

13

THE HAMMELBURG SCHUBINITES

In the early hours of Friday, March 9, having been on the move for more than six weeks since leaving Oflag 64 in Poland, Pop Goode arrived by rail at Hammelburg in Bavaria's Bad Kissingen district in southern Germany. Reaching the town a little ahead of the bulk of his remaining men, Goode was accompanied by Johnny Waters and his "shadow staff," including officers appointed to replace those who had been left behind with sick parties or who had escaped. Goode was still toting the bagpipes he had carried all the way from Schubin.

Of the 1,470 men who had left Schubin with Goode, just 490 would reach Hammelburg, site of the POW camp Oflag XIII-B. Of the remainder, Goode would calculate that 241 had escaped during the early days of the march from Schubin. Four men, including Gentleman Jim Alger, had been left by Goode at a German navy base at Swinemünde (Polish Świnoujście) because they could walk no farther. Another one hundred ill men had been left at a camp at Flatow (Polish Złotów). The balance of 635 men had remained at Stalag III-A, a vast camp at Luckenwalde, thirty miles south of Berlin, that was filled to overflowing with tens of thousands of Allied POWs.[1]

On February 15, the Schubin column, then still comprising 1,100 men, had arrived at Luckenwalde with Goode. By that time, the column had been moving through Germany via cities, towns and villages filled with German troops, police and civilians, all of whom were on the alert for escaped POWs, forced laborers, deserters and downed Allied airmen. Not only had opportunities for escape dried up, there were no Polish residents to feed and shelter escapees and pass them on to the underground as there had been during the first week of the column's march through Polish territory.

The Schubin party had remained intact at Luckenwalde for three weeks. During this period, the hated Hauptmann Zimmermann had departed after volunteering for combat. Shortly afterward, he'd been killed in an American air raid. With the Russian advance nearing Berlin, in early March the Wehrmacht withdrew Oberst Schneider and his grenadier company from Luckenwalde to join the desperate defense of the German capital. It was also decided to send as many of the American prisoners as possible south to Bavaria, which was still controlled by the Germans. Colonel Goode and close to 500 Schubin kriegies considered fit to travel were chosen to be sent to Oflag XIII-B at Hammelburg. Among the Schubinites who remained behind the wire at Luckenwalde when Goode's party went south were diarist Thornton Sigler, Schubin tunneler Robert J. Rose, and serial escaper Jack Van Vliet.

When Goode and his Schubin boys reached Hammelburg by train from Luckenwalde, Oflag XIII-B, once a German army cavalry school, was already occupied by 1,000 American officers and 4,000 Serbian officers of the Royal Yugoslavian Army in two adjoining compounds. These Americans had been captured only recently. Most were "Bulgies," taken during the Battle of the Bulge. To Goode's astonishment, these recently captured American officers had an unkempt and surly appearance. He went directly to the camp infirmary to look it over. Next paying a visit to the SAO's office next door, he summoned the four American colonels already in the camp, including the SAO.

When they arrived, Goode established that he had seniority, then announced that he was taking over as SAO of Oflag XIII-B.

As Goode now learned, discipline had quickly broken down here. Ignoring the previous SAO and other senior officers, a couple of captains had been running the American compound as if it were their own little fiefdom. That was not going to continue. Appointing Johnny Waters as his XO, Goode gave him the task of getting the camp's American population back into military order, fast.

At 6:45 that morning, a train pulled into Hammelburg station carrying the rest of Goode's Schubin party. Even though they were suffering from the poor kriegie diet and unsanitary POW camp conditions experienced by all Schubinites, these men tramped the considerable distance from the railroad station on the west of Hammelburg to Oflag XIII-B on the southern outskirts of the town in fine fettle, marching into the camp in step and with heads high.

Among the US Army officers already in the camp, and admiring Colonel Goode's Schubin contingent as they marched through the gates, was a handsome, fair-haired first lieutenant—John Hadley Nicanor "Jack" Hemingway, the eldest son of the famed novelist Ernest Hemingway. The life of Jack Hemingway, nicknamed "Bumby" by his father, had been colorful right from the start. His second middle name came from a Spanish matador his dad admired. His godparents were the author Gertrude Stein and her lover, Alice B. Toklas. Born in Canada, Jack had grown up in Paris and the Austrian Alps.

Jack had enlisted in the US Army in 1943, attended officer candidate school, and become a green second lieutenant in the military police. Before long, pulling a few strings by using his name and connections, Jack was transferred to the OSS. This, he thought, should impress his notoriously gung-ho father. Of 4,000 OSS candidates, only fifty, including young Hemingway and Jerry Sage, were chosen for active service. As it turned out, Jack Hemingway's time in Europe prior to the war, and the fact that he spoke fluent French, qualified him admirably for OSS work. As did his good-natured, even-tempered approach to life.

Jack had undertaken several OSS missions in German-occupied

France before the mission in late October 1944 that had resulted in his capture. He hadn't been long attached to the 3rd Infantry Division in the Vosges Mountains of Alsace-Lorraine as OSS liaison when the division began encountering stiffening German resistance. The OSS's Captain Justin Greene arrived on the scene with a French "Joe," a civilian secret agent who was to be infiltrated behind enemy lines. Jack escorted Greene and his Joe through heavy forest beyond the 3rd Infantry's most forward positions. They'd been about to send the Joe across a clearing when German troops from an alpine unit spotted them and opened up. In the fusillade, the Joe was killed, Greene took a bullet in the foot, and Jack was hit in the right arm. Another burst from the German squad sent into the trees to mop up caught Hemingway in the shoulder.

Hemingway and Greene were captured and evacuated via a German field hospital to a hospital in the German city of Stuttgart. The German doctors had wanted to amputate Jack's arm, but, even though he was a prisoner, he was able to exercise freedom of will in this one thing, refusing to let them take his arm. As an alternative, he downed sulfonamide antibacterial tablets and gallons of water, which he credited with saving his arm. In the first days of 1945, Hemingway and Greene had been discharged from the Stuttgart hospital with two other American officer patients who had also been captured in France, Lieutenants Dewey Stuart and Ray Saigh.

With an escort, the quartet had traveled in a regular railroad car to Hammelburg. Hemingway had befriended Stuart and Saigh en route, and at Hammelburg the three of them became tight. Like Hemingway, Stuart and Saigh were determined to escape. Throughout this period, emulating Jerry Sage at Schubin, Hemingway had succeeded in keeping his OSS role secret. As far as fellow kriegies and his captors were concerned, Jack had been merely a junior infantry officer with the 3rd Division.

Appalled by the collapse in military discipline at Oflag XIII-B, Hemingway was delighted to see Colonel Goode take charge and shake up the kriegie population. That population was about to be shaken up even more by a bold US Army rescue bid.

14

PATTON WANTS THEM LIBERATED

Following his debrief of the Moscow Trio at the US embassy in Moscow during the third week of February, General Deane had cabled Washington with the news that Paul Goode and Johnny Waters were being transferred by the Wehrmacht deep into Germany at the head of evacuated US personnel from Oflag 64. Deane also made a point of contacting General George Patton's headquarters with the same intelligence.

"One story they (Gruenberg, Colley and Dimling) told, which was of considerable interest to me," Deane would say later, "concerned a lifelong friend, Colonel Paul R. Goode." Via the trio of escapers, Deane learned that Goode had remained with the Schubin kriegies to look after the men under him, ignoring opportunities to personally escape. From the trio, too, Deane ascertained that Johnny Waters had remained with the party. "We were also able to let General Patton know that his son-in-law, Colonel J. K. Waters, was in the best of health but was still in German custody, being moved to a camp in the interior," Deane would reveal.[1]

Clearly, Deane was hopeful that his close friend Paul Goode would be liberated by General Patton's advancing US Third Army. And he sagely alerted Patton to the fact that his son-in-law was in Goode's party, a fact that might be expected to win Patton's attention and interest. It did. Patton sought information from US Military Intelligence on the precise whereabouts of Waters and Goode's Schubin group. On Sunday, March 25, General Patton was informed that Waters was one of 300 Schubin inmates who were now in the Oflag XIII-B POW camp at Hammelburg.

At Patton's headquarters, the general's staff began poring over maps of Bavaria to pinpoint the exact location of this Hammelburg camp. Twenty-five miles west of the city of Schweinfurt, the center of German ball-bearing manufacture, Hammelburg was a sleepy town of 6,000 residents just sixty miles from the advancing Third Army's current position. To date, the town had been hardly touched by the war.

The source of US intelligence about the presence of Waters and the other Schubin POWs at Hammelburg has never been revealed. To have been so close to the truth, even if the number of Schubinites said to be at Hammelburg was understated by some 200, that source was possibly a clandestine radio transmitter in the possession of the Serbs within XIII-B. But at this point, US Military Intelligence and Patton's HQ were totally unaware that another 1,000 US officers had already been imprisoned at Hammelburg for some weeks when the men from Schubin arrived.

Late that same evening of March 25, an order was flashed from Patton's HQ to the 4th Armored Division ordering the creation of an armored task force that would race to Hammelburg through enemy-held territory to liberate the Schubinites at Oflag XIII-B. Patton's personal motto, as he'd told GIs in England just prior to D-Day, consisted of three words: "Audacity! Audacity! Audacity!" And that was what he expected the 4th Armored to apply to this mission, catching "Jerry" off guard and pulling off a stunning rescue.

The order was received by the 4th Armored's commander, Brigadier General William M. Hoge. He resisted, complaining that his troops were exhausted and he couldn't spare the men required for such a special operation. Not to be denied, Patton rang Hoge personally. Half-bullying, half-cajoling Hoge into agreeing to execute the order, Patton promised to make up any losses incurred during the mission, man for man, tank for tank.

For the job, the unhappy Hoge selected his Combat Command B. When informed of the task force requirements early on the morning of March 26, Combat Command B's CO, thirty-year-old Lieutenant Colonel Creighton Abrams, also resisted the order until informed that General Patton was flying down to see him personally about the mission. And that mission must commence at 5:00 that afternoon!

At 10:00 a.m., Patton duly arrived at Abrams' HQ, complete with his famed varnished helmet displaying his general's stars, his riding breeches, his tankers' boots, and his holstered, pearl-handled revolver. When Patton demanded to know who would be leading the mission, Abrams nominated himself. But Patton said he wanted a small, fast task force under a less senior officer. Abrams had already ordered Lieutenant Colonel Hal Cohen to withdraw his 10th Armored Infantry Battalion from combat at Aschaffenburg on the River Main to act as his second-in-command on the mission. So Abrams now named Cohen to lead—depending on the condition of his piles.

"Piles!" exclaimed Patton. A student of military history, Patton knew that the emperor Napoleon had suffered from severe piles at the time of the Battle of Waterloo and had been forced to command his army from a chair rather than from the back of his horse for much of the battle. Patton sent for a medical officer.

Patton, his aides, Abrams, and the battalion surgeon descended on Lieutenant Colonel Cohen's headquarters, where Cohen and his deputies were discussing the makeup of the required task force. Patton promptly asked Cohen to step into the next room with the surgeon and himself.

"Drop your pants, and grab your ankles," Patton then ordered.

When Cohen complied, the surgeon whistled, partly in surprise, partly out of sympathy, before declaring that half a dozen of Cohen's hemorrhoids were the size of birds' eggs.

"That is some sorry ass," Patton declared.[2]

The ugly sight convinced Patton that someone else would have to lead this mission. Cohen chose his S3, his operations officer, Captain Abraham Baum. Just three days shy of his twenty-fourth birthday, the six-foot-two-inch, long-nosed Baum was a New Yorker, a native of the Bronx. Enlisting as a private in 1941, he'd been quickly commissioned and promoted. Baum would later say that, when invited in for a meeting with General Patton, he was thinking, "What the hell am I doing here?"[3]

Patton, apprised of Baum's impressive combat record, immediately approved his appointment to lead the task force, which, from this point forward, would be known as Task Force Baum. Taking the young captain aside, Patton told him that, if he pulled off this mission, he would be up for a Medal of Honor. But what was the mission? Patton had yet to pass on that information. When he departed the 10th Armored Battalion HQ, the general left behind Major Alexander Stiller. Stiller had served with Patton during the First World War and had been his trusted aide all through this war. Major Stiller, said Patton as he went out the door, would fill everyone in on the details of the mission. Only now, from Stiller, would the armored division officers learn their precise objective.

Why, Cohen wanted to know, was the task force being sent to Hammelburg?

Stiller replied that there was a POW camp in the town that contained 300 US Army officers who had previously been imprisoned at Schubin.

"And . . . ?" Cohen asked.

"Patton wants them liberated," Stiller advised matter-of-factly.[4]

Not only were the Schubin boys to be liberated, Stiller revealed, the task force would have to bring them back to American lines. The plan was to race through the night to Hammelburg, arriving there by dawn and surprising its defenders. Stiller startled the gathering even further by announcing that he would be going along on the mission, but merely as an observer.

At the time, no one in that room could figure out why Stiller would be tagging along. Only later did they put two and two together: Stiller would be only man in the task force who knew John K. Waters by sight. Stiller actually admitted to Abe Baum before the task force set off that his mission was to rescue Waters, but, until his dying day, General Patton would declare that this mission was not about rescuing his son-in-law. Many others would think otherwise.

The task force was quickly put together by Baum and his superior, Lieutenant Colonel Cohen. Patton had specified that no more than 300 men be involved. Cohen felt that something more like 3,000 men should be sent on a mission like this, but orders were orders. The task force's main element would be C Company, 37th Tank Battalion, made up of ten M4 Sherman medium tanks. With a crew of five and a 75 mm main gun, the iconic thirty-ton Sherman was a match for almost anything the Wehrmacht possessed.

The Shermans, commanded by Second Lieutenant William J. "Bill" Nutto, would be complemented by a platoon of five sparsely armored four-man M3 light tanks equipped with 37 mm guns. From the 37th Tank Battalion's D Company, the M3s would be commanded by Second Lieutenant William Weaver. The M3 had the advantage of being able to turn easily and quickly in tight spaces, which the Sherman was not able to do. Further fire support would be provided by a platoon of three self-propelled 105 mm guns commanded by Technical Sergeant Charles O. Graham from Thurmond, West Virginia. Essentially, the SPGs (self-propelled guns) were Shermans with a fixed heavy gun in place of a turret. There would also be an M29C Weasel amphibious tank in the column.[5]

To bring out the 300 POWS, twenty-seven halftracks were included. They were manned by the 10th Armored Infantry's Company A, commanded by Captain Robert Lange. Open trucks with normal wheels up front and rubber tracks on the rear, halftracks had a driver and radio operator who rode in the cab plus a machine gunner in the back and could also carry ten infantrymen comfortably. In Task Force Baum, one halftrack would serve as a maintenance vehicle for the tanks while another, equipped with a long-range radio, would be the column's command vehicle. Some of the halftracks were loaded with jerry cans filled with enough gasoline to fuel the entire task force's return from Hammelburg. Baum also had orders to use any German vehicles he captured to carry POWs should he lose half-tracks en route to Oflag XIII-B.

There would also be eight jeeps in the column. An infantry reconnaissance detachment of nine men under Second Lieutenant Norman Hoffner occupied three jeeps. The other jeeps would be those of Captain Baum and his aide, Sergeant Ellis Wise, a medics' jeep, a maintenance jeep, and one carrying Patton's tag-along aide, Major Stiller. Altogether, Task Force Baum would consist of 54 vehicles and 312 men.[6]

Cohen and Baum decided to send the task force through the red-roofed German village of Schweinheim. Less than a mile south of Aschaffenburg, it was still held by German forces. After passing through Schweinheim, the task force would have just eight miles to travel before reaching Reichsstrasse (Highway) 26, the main east-west route to Hammelburg. Cohen and Baum figured that, once on that highway, everything should be plain sailing for the armored column.

To prepare the way for Task Force Baum, it would be necessary to blast a way through Schweinheim's narrow streets. For this job, Cohen's superior, Lieutenant Colonel Abrams, selected the Shermans of B Company, 37th Tank Battalion, under Captain Richard Pancake, and the foot soldiers of Captain Adrian Tessier's B Company, 10th Armored Infantry. Pancake and Tessier worked together so regularly, and so well, that they had adopted novel radio code names: "Chicken" and "Shit."

By 5:00 p.m., Task Force Baum and Pancake and Tessier's units had assembled on a low hill within sight of Schweinheim. At 8:30, an artillery barrage raked the village. Thirty minutes later, Chicken and Shit ordered their units forward. Two hundred yards into Schweinheim, the lead American tank was knocked out by a handheld *Panzerfaust*. The German equivalent of the bazooka, the Panzerfaust was more effective than the two-man American weapon. Forerunner of today's rocket-propelled grenade launcher, or RPG, and packing a warhead at the end of a rocket, this throwaway, one-time anti-armor weapon could be used by a single untrained operator to destroy even the heaviest tank if he could get close enough. Millions of low-cost Panzerfausts were produced, and there were plenty of them in Schweinheim.

Pancake's second tank platoon peeled off into side streets, only for defenders to attack them from cellars in their rear and from rooftops. Those defenders were a combination of women and old men of the Volkssturm home guard and cadets from the Waffen-SS officer school that had until recently operated in Aschaffenburg. After a second Sherman was abandoned by its crew when it was rocked by a grenade blast, a German jumped into it, started it up, and turned one of its machine guns on the advancing Americans.

With Pancake's armor stalled, Tessier's infantry had to fight their way along the village's main street, house by house, sustaining casualties all the way. An accurate German mortar proved particularly mettlesome, and Tessier personally led six GIs at the run in an out-flanking move that caught the four-man mortar team by surprise. As one of his men kicked the mortar over, Tessier grabbed the German lieutenant in charge and shoved him up against a wall, knocking the man's coal scuttle helmet off in the brief scuffle.

"Amerikanisches Schwein!" cursed the lieutenant.[7]

Perhaps it was the curse. Or the SS tabs on the lieutenant's collar. Or the sneer on his face. Or all three. But Tessier didn't take kindly to this guy. Using his free hand, he quickly reached down to the combat knife he kept sheathed in his boot, straightened, then slit the lieutenant's throat. As the German sagged to the ground, gurgling, the three teenagers on his mortar team were on their knees, begging for their lives. Tessier had them taken to the rear.

Despite this, by 11:00 that night the main street's last ten houses were still in German hands, and Pancake's tanks and Tessier's infantry were bogged down. Meanwhile, on the hillside overlooking the village, Abe Baum had been impatiently pacing back and forth in front of his waiting column. Below, he could see houses burning while exploding shells periodically lit up the moonless night. Pancake and Tessier had estimated it would take thirty minutes to clear Schweinheim. They, and Task Force Baum, were now way behind schedule.

Jumping into his jeep, Baum drove down into the village to find out what the holdup was. Seeing the blockages, Baum told Pancake to get his tanks up onto the sidewalks. Task Force Baum was coming through, no matter what. Back to the hilltop he raced. With sirens on his tanks wailing, Baum pushed his column down into the village and along the main street in single file, M3s leading the way. They took small-arms fire, but the entire column emerged undamaged on the other side of Schweinheim around midnight. With pedals to the metal to make up time, Task Force Baum plowed on through the night, heading for the highway to Hammelburg.

15

FIGHTING THROUGH TO HAMMELBURG

AT 4:15 ON THE MORNING OF TUESDAY, MARCH 27, FOUR HOURS AFTER Task Force Baum broke out of Schweinheim, Hauptmann Walter Eggemann was awakened by a telephone call at Nazi Party district headquarters at Würzburg, a pretty city on the River Main thirty-five miles south of Hammelburg. The thirty-three-year-old captain was the holder of the Ritterkreuz, the Knight's Cross, one of Germany's highest bravery awards, earned in 1943 on the Russian front when he was a junior infantry officer with a grenadier regiment. Now Eggemann had a very different role.

Ever since the July 1944 attempt on Adolf Hitler's life, the SS had assumed increasing power in the Reich, giving Reichsführer Heinrich Himmler control over military affairs that had previously been the sole domain of the army, navy and air force. Hauptmann Eggemann, now attached to the Waffen-SS, had been appointed Himmler's special representative in three military districts. Although only a captain, Eggemann's special appointment gave him the power to overrule generals and to have senior officers removed from their posts and shot for failing to do their duty to the Führer.

This was why Oberleutnant Trenk, who'd been sleeping at the *Rathaus*, or town hall, at Lohr, on the River Main between Würzburg and Aschaffenburg, had telephoned Eggemann before he contacted anyone else. Lohr town hall was being inundated with calls from villages to the southeast saying that an American armored column was moving rapidly along Reichsstrasse 26 toward the city from Schweinheim. At this point, Eggemann had no idea that this column was heading for Hammelburg. However, knowing that the German army operated a military training area, the Lager Hammelburg, outside that town, he instructed Trenk to advise the senior officer there of the approach of the American column. Trenk subsequently called Oberst Richard Hoppe, commander of the Lager Hammelburg, to pass on the information. Hoppe had a tank alert issued to all units in the vicinity, then went back to bed.

Hauptmann Eggemann was considerably more active than the training area colonel. He rang the Wehrmacht's 7th Army HQ at the nearby town of Heigenbrücken, seeking and receiving approval to immediately take command of all forces in the Hammelburg area to resist any American push in the direction of the town. Eggemann then dressed and prepared to monitor the progress of the American column. Captain Eggemann's involvement would prove to have a major influence on the fates of both Task Force Baum and the Schubin boys at Hammelburg.

■ ■ ■

FOR ABE BAUM, everything was taking way too long. After the delay at Schweinheim, Task Force Baum had found Highway 26 and pushed northeast. Speeding along the tree-lined roadway, they'd fired on a German military camp they passed just as its recruits were forming up for dawn parade. Soon afterward, two contingents of German troops on the road had capitulated to the task force with raised hands. This had slowed things down some more as surrendered weapons were mashed beneath tank tracks. The disarmed Germans were told to wait for the next Americans to come along.

In failing to reach Hammelburg before dawn, the task force had lost the element of surprise. And it still had a long way to go, giving the Germans plenty of time to organize resistance in the Americans' path. This all worried the hell out of the young task force commander, and he now put five Shermans at the head of the column to sweep aside opposition.

Just outside Lohr, the task force came upon a roadblock of an overturned truck and telegraph poles. As the lead tanks slowed, a Panzerfaust projectile rocketed from the roadblock with a *whoomp* and blasted the first Sherman. With its driver dead, the American tank slewed to the right and stopped. Surviving crew members scrambled out of hatches. The second tank pushed the roadblock aside, and fleeing Germans were sprayed with machine-gun fire. After the disabled Sherman had been blown up with grenades, the column moved on.

Rounding a bend, the lead tanks ran into several trucks hauling flak guns, coming from the opposite direction. As the German trucks were raked with tank fire, they stopped dead. Their Luftwaffe flak crews were slaughtered where they sat. As the armored column passed the smoking trucks, the Americans in the task force saw, with varying emotions, that the dead flak crew members were all women.

Bypassing Lohr a half mile to the city's north, the column hurried on, its guns wrecking two trains steaming along on rail lines parallel to Highway 26. The highway also ran along the western side of the River Main. Barges and their tugboats moving leisurely along the river were sprayed with accurate tank fire. To modern eyes, it seems that this was all playing out like a video game. But the game was soon to become deadly for Baum's men.

For speed, the M3s were back in the lead as the column approached the city of Gemünden, up the Main from Würzburg. Baum had all his tanks shell Gemünden's extensive railroad marshalling yards where eight trains were lined up, then sent his first radio message back to

Colonel Cohen, reporting their progress and calling for an airstrike on the crowded marshalling yards.

The marshalling yards had in fact been bombed late the previous afternoon. That air raid had found a unit of German tank destroyers sitting on flat cars in the yards. Panzerjägerkompanie 251, known as Danube 1, had been on its way from Linz in Austria to reinforce German forces outside Aschaffenburg. Danube 1's commander, Hauptmann Heinrich Koehl, had sheltered with his crews in the town during the air raid.

Koehl's tank destroyers, sixteen-ton *Jagdpanzer* 38 *Hetzers*, armed with 75 mm guns just like Abe Baum's Shermans, had been delivered to the unit the previous month brand new from the Škoda factory in Czechoslovakia. They were so new that there hadn't been time to give them the usual camouflage paint job. Their stark gunmetal gray hulls were simply emblazoned with German crosses. All nine fighting Hetzers and a *Bergepanzer* 38 recovery version of the Hetzer had escaped the American air raid unscathed. In the early evening, Koehl had followed orders to remove his Hetzers from their train and conceal them in trees on the slopes of the Zollberg, north of the River Saale, for the night.[1]

Three rivers, the Main, the Saale, and the Sinn, join at Gemünden. While Task Force Baum was now north of the Main, to follow Highway 26 north it still had to go through the city and use its road bridge to cross the Saale. As the column reached Gemünden, Baum sent his recon platoon under Lieutenant Norm Hoffner ahead into the downtown area. Hoffner reported back that the streets were deserted. Alerted to approaching American tanks, the terrified citizens of Gemünden were hiding in their cellars. Hoffner found antitank mines lying on the roadside at the Saale bridge, which apparently had been abandoned by defenders.

A company of Wehrmacht engineers from Regensburg had reached Gemünden not long before the Americans with orders to blow up the bridge and mine the approaches. Interrupted in their work by the arrival of Task Force Baum, the German engineers had taken up defensive positions on both sides of the river. The American recon platoon tossed the mines aside, detonating several, before coming under machine-gun fire from two houses on the far side of the Saale. On learning this, Baum decided to send the light tanks forward, supported by infantry, to take the bridge.

As the M3s pushed right up to the bridge, German fire increased. The rattle of machine guns from the other side of the river was joined by the *crump* of an antitank gun firing from ruins on a hill across the water and the *whoomp* of unseen Panzerfausts closer by. Five yards from the bridge, the leading light tank took a direct hit, shuddered and came to a halt before bursting into flames. Crewmen, some badly burned, bailed out.

With the tank blocking the way, the cigar-chomping Lieutenant Bill Nutto, riding in the second M3, jumped down and ran to it, just as Captain Baum arrived on the scene in his jeep. When the lieutenant yelled at the sergeant commanding the lead tank to get his disabled M3 out of the way, the traumatized NCO looked at Nutto, eyes wide.

"I'm quitting! I'm quitting!" bawled the sergeant. Then, seeing Captain Baum running up, he bolted for the rear.[2]

Just as Baum joined Nutto, both saw a Panzerfaust projectile wobbling through the air toward them. They would owe their lives to the fact that the Panzerfaust's effective range was seventy yards. Fired from some distance away, this projectile dipped as it ran out of propulsion and plowed into the roadway only feet from the pair. But it detonated just the same. The blast threw Nutto to the ground, peppering his body with shrapnel. Looking around, Nutto saw Baum beside him, on his knees, his face white.

When Baum pulled himself to his feet, Nutto saw that the captain had been wounded in the right knee and right hand. Having two of the task force's senior officers wounded so early into the mission was far from auspicious. As a medic helped Nutto back to a halftrack, Baum's radio operator bandaged Baum's pain-wracked knee. Looking past the burning lead tank, Baum saw Infantry Lieutenant Elmer Sutton dash across the bridge and reach the river's far side. Two GIs were running across the bridge in the wake of their platoon leader. Another two were about to take off. At that moment there was a

loud boom. The German engineers had had time to plant an explosive charge beneath a bridge span, and now they set it off, right under
the pair of running Americans.

A plume of smoke, fire and shattered stone and concrete rose into
the air. No trace of the two running GIs would ever be found. Sutton, cut off on the far side of the river, would fall into German hands.
As the debris settled, Baum cursed. The bridge had been severed. The
way was blocked. Hobbling back to his jeep, Baum radioed the column: "Back 'em up!"[3]

As the American vehicles reversed away from the bridge, Baum
was joined by Major Stiller. Together they studied a map. With his
bloodied right hand, Baum tapped the map. They would leave Highway 26 and head north, looking for a crossing of the River Sinn to
bypass Gemünden. Sending Sergeant Wise in a jeep to find a road
north, Baum ordered the column to turn around. He then radioed
Colonel Cohen to tell him that he'd lost two tanks and that eighteen
of his officers and men had been killed, captured or wounded. But,
he added, he was still proceeding with the mission.

Around 9:00 a.m., as the American column headed away, a master
sergeant from the German engineer unit, Oberfeldwebel Eugen Zoller,
emerged from cover at the Saale bridge and clambered up and into
the wrecked M3 to see if he could salvage anything useful. Zoller
emerged triumphantly waving an American map left behind by the
tank's commander. The sergeant hurried with it to his company
commander. The officer was equally delighted: on the map was clearly
marked the route of Task Force Baum—from Aschaffenburg to
Hammelburg. The officer promptly advised his superiors.

Now that the Germans knew where Abe Baum and his men were
headed, orders went out to all available units in the Hammelburg area
to report to Oberst Hoppe at his Lager Hammelburg HQ, located
300 yards north of the POW camps. Word was also relayed to the
mayor of Hammelburg, Karl Clement. A fanatical Nazi and the town's
mayor since 1936, Clement immediately broadcast an alert to the
people of Hammelburg via the public address speakers set throughout the town, urging them to evacuate at once.

At 10:00, 1,300 men from three companies of the Wehrmacht's 113th Grenadier Regiment were sitting idly in carriages at the Waigolshausen railroad station, waiting for a locomotive, when orders came through to their most senior officer, a mere first lieutenant, Oberleutnant Demmel, to commandeer road transport and head at once for Hammelburg to support the Hetzers of Danube 1. From now on, this infantry detachment would bear the code name Kampfgruppe Demmel.

At the same time, Hauptmann Franz Gehrig, of Officer Candidate School 17 at Camp Grafenwöhr in eastern Bavaria, was ordered to immediately take his officer cadets to Hammelburg to join the defense. Gehrig promptly armed his one hundred cadets and loaded them into four gray MAN buses powered by ungainly but practical wood gas burners attached to the buses' rear ends. Most of the cadets were NCOs with a year or so of combat experience. The buses set off for Hammelburg via Würzburg.

Thirty minutes later, the tank destroyers of Danube 1 arrived at Hammelburg on a freight train that they'd boarded at Gemünden north of the destroyed Saale bridge. The Hetzers' engines were already running when the train pulled into Hammelburg's station in the western part of the town. Hauptmann Koehl's ten armored vehicles were unloaded from the freight wagons in record time, after which they assembled in a clay pit not far from the station. As Koehl waited at the clay pit, a small Luftwaffe reconnaissance aircraft, a Fieseler Storch, or Stork, flew over.

The Stork had been shadowing Task Force Baum. The Americans had known it was there, opening up with machine-gun and small-arms fire at one point, but the pilot had kept out of range, persistently sticking with the Americans like an annoying mosquito. Circling the clay pit now, the Luftwaffe pilot dropped a note to the tank destroyers, giving the latest position and direction of the American armored column.

Armed with this information, Hauptmann Koehl gave orders for the Hetzers to move out. They proceeded southwest along the north-south highway, Reichsstrasse 27, via Obereschenbach. Short of an intersection where a rough side road jagged off toward the Lager Hammelburg, Koehl halted his Hetzers and lined them up behind a small rise to intercept the approaching American tanks. Believing that a small bridge due west was too weak for heavy vehicles, Koehl expected the American column to approach along the road from the south. As several of Koehl's men patched a field telephone into the local phone line, his gun crews loaded their guns. Now the Hetzers waited for the Americans to come to them.

At 11:00 that morning, as the last of the civilians who had been streaming from the town for the past two hours departed, turning Hammelburg into a virtual ghost town, another train rolled into the station. This one unloaded trainee signalers from a company of the 10th Signal Training and Replacement Battalion led by a Hauptmann Kammerle. Oberst Hoppe ordered Kammerle to combine his signalers with the Volkssturm home guard led by local Volkssturm leader Josef Merkle to defend the town and its POW camps.

With most of the town's defenders being trainee signalers and home guard, there was little apart from the Hetzers to prevent the American task force from reaching Hammelburg. The odds were still in Abe Baum's favor.

■ ■ ■

FOLLOWING BACK ROADS north, Task Force Baum had a stroke of bad luck and several strokes of good luck. The lead Sherman threw a track and had to be destroyed. Its crew joined Baum's infantry. The column then ran into a German paratroop sergeant on a motorcycle who said he was on his way to Hammelburg for a wedding. The Americans suspected that he was a deserter. Under threat of death, the sergeant became the column's guide. Next, a German staff car blundered into the column's path. One of the occupants, the taciturn General Oriel Lotz, was taken prisoner and tied to the hood of a task force halftrack. Looking for a crossing as it followed the winding Sinn River, the column continued north.

With the German paratroop sergeant's guidance, the task force found a small bridge at the hamlet of Burgsinn. Wehrmacht engineers had been ordered to blow up all bridges in the path of the American column, but thinking the Burgsinn bridge too small and too frail to support armored vehicles, they had not bothered with it. Slowly, warily, Task Force Baum successfully crossed the bridge. The column then pressed on southeast for Hammelburg along narrow, winding roads.

In the hilly, forested countryside east of Burgsinn, the column ran into a work detail of Russian POWs whose German guards ran off. General Lotz was handed over to the Russians, and the column continued. There was much speculation among the task force's men as to what the Russians would do to the German general. Only much later would the Americans learn that, after they moved on, the resolute General Lotz had regrouped the German guards and regained control of the Russian POWs.

* * *

To THE SOUTH, at Würzburg, Hauptmann Eggemann had established a temporary HQ at the Galgenberg Barracks, from where he'd been keeping himself apprised of the progress of the American armored column and the disposition of German forces being rallied to counter it. His latest information had the Americans approaching Burgsinn. Assuming the bridge there had been blown up, he felt sure the Americans must be trapped on the western side of the Sinn. He also knew that Danube 1 had arrived in Hammelburg.

Around 1:00 that afternoon, Eggemann placed a call to Hauptmann Koehl, the tank destroyers' commander. Eggemann instructed Koehl to immediately deploy his Hetzers to Burgsinn to intercept the Americans.

Koehl flatly refused to move. "I am only answerable to 7th Army," he responded before hanging up. A priest before the war, Koehl knew all about the hierarchy of command. With no orders from either 7th Army HQ or Oberst Hoppe, Koehl wasn't going anywhere. He kept the Hetzers where they were.[4]

A furious Eggemann subsequently called Generalmajor Christoph von Gersdorff at 7th Army HQ, and requested, in the strongest possible terms, that Koehl's Hetzers and the in-transit men of Kampfgruppe

Demmel be immediately placed under his direct command. General von Gersdorff said he'd get back to him. He didn't. Eggemann was left seething. So, when, an hour later, Hauptmann Gehrig's four gray MAN buses pulled into the Galgenberg Barracks to resupply en route to Hammelburg, Eggemann promptly gave the training school captain new orders.

"Gehrig, you will proceed to Burgsinn, via Gemünden," he commanded, "and destroy the American column."[5]

Gehrig, a short man with chubby cheeks and an easy smile, was impressed by the courtly captain with the Knight's Cross dangling from his neck. He was also much more politically aware than Danube 1's Hauptmann Koehl: Gehrig was not going to disobey an order from Reichsführer Himmler's personal representative. He and his cadets quickly restocked their buses with wood fuel, reboarded, and, now dubbed Kampfgruppe Gehrig, set off to obey Eggemann's instructions.

Twenty minutes later, in Hammelburg, Oberst Hoppe received a telephone call from a Hauptmann Rose, a captain with the Lager's railroad engineering school. On his own initiative, Rose had taken a few of his students southwest from Hammelburg to the Reussenberg, the highest hill in the district, shown as Hill 427 on American maps. Atop the hill stood the weathered stone ruins of a castle destroyed by the Swabian League in 1523 and never rebuilt. High in a tower amid those ruins, Rose had established an observation post, linking it to the local telephone system via field telephone. With his binoculars, Rose was scanning the landscape to the west.

"Twelve enemy tanks on the road from Aschenroth," Rose reported to Hoppe. "Heading toward Obereschenbach."[6]

Oberst Hoppe passed on the news to POW camp commander Generalmajor Günther von Goeckel at Oflag XIII-B that American armor was rapidly closing on Hammelburg.

Only the Hetzers of Danube 1 would now stand between Task Force Baum and the POW camps at Hammelburg—if Hauptmann Koehl had made the right decision about where to ambush the approaching task force.

THE BATTLE FOR THE CAMP

At 3:00 p.m., Danube 1 commander Hauptmann Koehl spotted enemy tanks advancing along the road toward Hammelburg. They were speeding along Reichsstrasse 27, having joined the highway a little east of Aschenroth. Koehl ordered his gunners to acquire targets.

Abe Baum had not been briefed on the precise location of his objective. He only knew that Oflag XIII-B lay a little to the south of Hammelburg. As his column charged along with Hammelburg now due east, Baum saw a track curving off to the right, going east up a rise. Captain Baum now decided to follow that road in the hope of finding the camp. Over his radio, he ordered the column to swing to the right once they reached the intersection.

As the column's lead tanks neared the intersection, Danube 1 opened fire. Seconds later, 75 mm shells came whistling from the north and exploded all around the Shermans. But the column was moving so fast on the flat that not a single German round found its target. The lead American tanks immediately began returning fire, and their crews would feel certain that they had knocked out two of the tank destroyers. In fact, the American shells, hitting the hull-down Hetzers' solid front armor, did little damage. The shelling did have one plus for the Americans: it hit telephone poles beside the road and brought down the local phone lines. At that moment, German staff who had remained at their posts at the Hammelburg post office found that all telephone and telegraph communication into the town from the west had been severed.

• • •

AT OFLAG XIII-B, the commandant, Generalmajor von Goeckel, summoned the senior Serbian and American officers to his office. Oberst Hoppe had informed the commandant of the approach of the American armored column and of his inability to guarantee that the Americans would not get through his ad hoc defenses.

When SAO Colonel Goode arrived at Goeckel's office, the general had his German coal scuttle helmet on the desk and his automatic pistol holstered on his hip. The senior Serbian officer, Colonel General Brastich, had arrived ahead of Goode. Camp liaison officer Hauptmann Hans Fuchs proceeded to translate into English for Goode as the agitated commandant informed the pair that an American column was approaching the oflag with the probable intent of liberating it. As a consequence, Goeckel was intending to speed up the ordered transfer of prisoners from the camp.

The news of the approaching American column cheered Goode, but his Serbian colleague remained stone-faced. Goode proceeded to convince the commandant to stall the transfer of American troops for twenty-four hours, until the picture had cleared, rather than put prisoners in harm's way outside the camp. Goode's real motive was to ensure that he and his men were in the camp when American troops arrived to liberate it. But his argument rang true with the pragmatic German general. Under the Geneva Convention, POW camp commandants were required to take all steps to prevent their prisoners from becoming casualties should hostilities arise. To do otherwise would constitute a war crime.[1]

While agreeing to stall the American transfer, Goeckel warned both Goode and his Serbian counterpart that the camp would be defended by troops answering to Oberst Hoppe, not by the camp guards, and that the attacking Americans could be expected to fire into the camp in response. "I beg you to remember," the commandant added, "that the Americans will be firing in your direction when they fire at us."[2]

Pop Goode could only nod grimly.

Goeckel urged the two senior POW officers to get their men to take cover in either the camp's air raid trenches or their barracks. As Goode and Brastich departed to warn their men, Goeckel ordered his guards to leave their posts and move to the neighboring Stalag VIII-B camp. He had orders from Berlin to march the Russian prisoners from Stalag VIII-B and relocate them to the north. For the march, he planned to combine his hundred guards from XIII-B with the guards at the Russian compound.

Goode left Goeckel's office accompanied by Hauptmann Fuchs. Outside, both heard the sound of heavy guns firing beyond the hills to the west and looked at each other. This was the start of the engagement between Task Force Baum and Danube 1. Both men knew this signaled the approach of the American column, although that knowledge stimulated very different thoughts in each man's mind. As Goode hurried to the American barracks to prepare his men for liberation, Fuchs went to the Serbian compound and sought out the Serbian adjutant, Dragon Yosefovitch.

When Fuchs found the Serb, he gave him the key to the camp armory. Fuchs knew that Yosefovitch was a royalist and opposed to Serbian communists in the camp. He told Yosefovitch to use spare rifles in the armory to arm his fellow royalists against the communists and keep order in their compound. Both men doubted that the US Army would be interested in liberating anyone other than Americans.

At this moment, the camp's guards were coming down from their goon towers around the camp perimeter, bringing their heavy machine guns with them. At the same time, the recently arrived men of Signal Training and Replacement Battalion 10 were being joined by local men of the Volkssturm as they dug trenches outside the camp. The defenders set up machine guns and a 20 mm antiaircraft gun at the trenches and in stone houses nearby. Apart from Panzerfausts, this would be their only defense against the American tanks. What was more, few of these defenders had ever fired a shot in anger. Not in this war anyway.

• • •

FOLLOWING ABE BAUM's orders, his column was turning right and pushing up the hill. But the new route put the American vehicles side-on to the Hetzers of Danube 1, and the gradient slowed them down, making them easier targets. German gunners zeroed in on the lead Sherman. Bracketed with shells, it took a direct hit, erupted in flame and halted. The next Sherman was also hit, but its crew managed to get it off the road before they bailed out. It would later be recovered and taken over by the crew whose Sherman had thrown a track earlier in the day.

Five hundred yards up the slope, the road widened at a prewar tourist lookout, and Baum ordered his three self-propelled guns to position themselves there, off the road, to lay down covering fire as the rest of the column labored up the hill. The lead Sherman, now burning fiercely and blocking the road, had to be shoved aside to allow this to happen. As the SPGs were getting into place at the lookout, another Sherman and a halftrack were hit by shells from the Hetzers.

Apparently there was not enough room at the lookout for all three self-propelled guns, for only two went into action. With other American vehicles struggling by behind them, the SPGs began firing at the Hetzers a thousand yards away, first with smoke shells to mask the American column, then with 105 mm armor-piercing rounds.

Twenty-four-year-old Technical Sergeant Charles Graham had been in command of the SPG troop for only two days. His predecessor, a lieutenant, had lost his life during the battle for Aschaffenburg. As Graham's two 105 mm guns were pounding away at the Hetzers, he spotted movement on Highway 27. Heading toward the

German tank destroyers' position came a small convoy of German Hanomag halftracks. Graham ordered his gunner to alter range and target.

A minute later, a 105 mm round from Graham's SPG plowed into one of the German halftracks. The vehicle exploded in a fireball that billowed into the afternoon sky. Engulfed in flames, it rolled to a halt. The explosion was so fierce that it detonated the loads of the remaining halftracks in the German convoy. All had been carrying gasoline for Hauptmann Koehl's Hetzers. Graham felt the heat from the blazing German trucks all the way up at his lookout position. The exact number of halftracks destroyed is disputed. Graham put the number at six. German records say it was three. Either way, the Hanomags were in flames, and the Hetzers had been deprived of precious fuel.

Meanwhile, Captain Baum was having trouble keeping his column moving. Bumping back down the slope in his jeep, passing burning American vehicles, he found that the German fire had sent a number of his men bailing out of their halftracks to seek cover on the ground. Baum angrily ordered every driver back into his stationary vehicle. He finally got the column moving again, and it eventually cleared the hill and disappeared from the view of Koehl and his gunners, who ceased fire.

Task Force Baum left behind the wreckage of two Shermans, an M3, five halftracks and two jeeps, all chalked up to Koehl's Hetzers. The American halftracks were burning brightly, for, like the incinerated Hanomags 1,500 yards away, they had been carrying fuel— fuel that was intended to get them all back to American lines. Task Force Baum's only fuel supplies now consisted of the gasoline remaining in vehicles' tanks and the fuel being carried in jerry cans on each.

The Hetzers now also pulled out. Hauptmann Koehl shepherded them back into Hammelburg, then northeast toward Euerdorf, a hamlet halfway between Hammelburg and Bad Kissingen. Unlike Baum, Koehl had the capacity to resupply. That night, fuel and ammunition would be sent by train from Schweinfurt to Danube 1 at Euerdorf. Meanwhile, up at his location at the lookout, Sergeant Charlie Graham held his position with two SPGs until the Hetzers had disappeared to the north. Because the SPGs were built on the chassis of Sherman tanks, Koehl would mistakenly report that, when he withdrew at 4:30, two American tanks remained in position, with their guns apparently positioned to cover Hammelburg's Saale River bridge.

Once the tank destroyers disappeared from view, Sergeant Graham ordered his guns to follow the remainder of Task Force Baum.

■ ■ ■

HAD KOEHL FOLLOWED Hauptmann Eggemann's orders and gone to Burgsinn via Gemünden, he would have missed Task Force Baum, as Kampfgruppe Gehrig did. At 4:00 p.m., Hauptmann Gehrig's buses had reached Burgsinn only for the captain to be informed by residents that the American column had passed through the town hours earlier and crossed the Sinn via Burgsinn's still-intact bridge.

Gehrig found Wehrmacht engineers at the bridge, belatedly about to destroy it, but he convinced the officer in charge to hold off. Believing the American column to be the advance guard of General Patton's army, and thinking that more American forces could not be far behind, Gehrig, on his own initiative, began deploying his cadets west of the town in reconnaissance platoons to warn of the approach of more American tanks.

Shortly afterward, a dispatch rider arrived in Burgsinn by motorcycle, bearing new orders from Hauptmann Eggemann. He had by this time learned that the American task force was fighting outside Hammelburg. Eggemann also knew that in dispatching Gehrig to Burgsinn he'd sent the cadets on a wild goose chase. Eggemann now ordered the only combat group that was responding to his orders to tail Task Force Baum to Hammelburg and engage it. Gehrig recalled his recon platoons and again put them aboard the MAN buses. Kampfgruppe Gehrig then set off after the Americans, heading east.

■ ■ ■

FROM A PLATEAU atop the hill that his column had just climbed at great expense, Abe Baum surveyed Oflag XIII-B through binoculars. As he had hoped, by turning up the hill he had put the task force in sight of its objective. The sprawling twin POW camps of Hammelburg lay 1,700 yards below on a gentle slope.

On the plateau, the column reformed and waited for task force members who had earlier abandoned vehicles and now came in on foot, followed by Graham's SPG rearguard. As Baum was briefing his remaining officers and senior NCOs, Bill Nutto came limping to join them. Despite the wounds he received at Gemünden, which had since been bandaged, the lieutenant was determined to again lead his tanks, and Baum was pleased to have him back. Baum now planned the assault on the camp.

The tanks would form a line with fifty to a hundred feet separating them from each other. The remaining M3s would be on the right, the six Shermans on the left. The infantry would be broken up into squads of six or seven men with each squad following close behind a tank in the formation. Major Stiller, the observer from General Patton's HQ, volunteered to lead one of these squads. All other vehicles would remain up on the plateau with the SPGs poking their guns over the crest to provide covering fire for the advancing tanks and infantry.

...

JUST BEFORE 6:00 p.m., the four well-traveled gray MAN buses carrying Hauptmann Gehrig and his hundred officer cadets trundled into the village of Höllrich, five miles southwest of Oflag XIII-B. Minutes earlier, while on the road, Gehrig had heard the sounds of heavy guns firing in the direction of Hammelburg. So, here at Höllrich, Gehrig ordered his men to dismount and set up a roadblock on the northern side of the village.

While his cadets cut down pine trees to create the roadblock, trimming off their branches for use in camouflaging their buses, Gehrig set up a command post in a barn set back from the road. On trying to use a local telephone to contact the HQ at Lager Hammelburg to learn the situation there, Gehrig discovered that phone communication with Hammelburg was out. For the moment, he was totally in the dark about what was going on to the northeast.

Before long, a motorcycle dispatch rider found the cadet detachment. The dispatch, from Oberst Hoppe at Hammelburg, ordered Gehrig to move into the military training area to intercept the American column. But the vague order failed to specify either a route to take or a location to aim for. There were two roads into the training area. Gehrig knew that if he followed one, the Americans might use the other and bypass him. Worse, Gehrig had not been given any idea where the American column was, or where other German forces were in the area.

The order that Gehrig had received from Eggemann, Himmler's representative, required him to destroy the American column. To Gehrig's mind, this broad command allowed a certain amount of latitude. So, deciding to hedge his bets, he opted to remain at the roadblock with half his men and send the other half in two buses to Lager Hammelburg to satisfy Oberst Hoppe's order.

Traveling via the uninhabited infantry training village of Bonnland, the buses would fail to encounter any elements of Task Force Baum en route. As the two MANs trundled away, Gehrig, aware that Höllrich was close to an intersection of the two roads out of the training area, sent a recon patrol on foot down the road south, toward the village of Hessdorf. His decision to stay put, and his choice of Höllrich for his roadblock, would prove key to the fate of Task Force Baum.

■ ■ ■

ON THE HILL outside Oflag XIII-B, it was around 6:00 p.m. when, with a waving arm, Captain Baum gave the signal to advance. At 5 mph, the tanks rolled down the slope, heading for the camp. Walking quickly in their wake with weapons ready, infantrymen bunched behind the tanks.

Graham's SPG fired a 105 mm round over their heads. It hit a hay barn just outside the camp's barbed wire perimeter fences, setting the contents alight. Graham's crew cheered. The smoke from the burning hay soon obscured the field for both sides. There was no answering fire. Only once the line of tanks was 200 yards from the wire did the trainee signalers and pensioner militiamen in the foxholes in front of the camp open up. Spandaus jabbered. The light flak gun barked. Rifles snapped. Panzerfausts whooshed.

In response, the tanks' machine guns raked the trenches, and their 75 mm guns boomed. As the SPGs continued to fire, the camp's water tower was holed and began spewing water. The 20 mm flak gun took a direct hit. Its crew was wiped out. When figures in gray uniforms were spotted in the Serbian compound to the right, task force machine-gunners, mistaking Serbian prisoners for Germans, sent rounds in their direction, too. Serbs dove for cover, and tracer bullets among the rounds started fires in several Serb barracks.

Baum, from his jeep on the hill, saw concentrated fire coming from buildings to the left of his formation, and radioed Nutto to focus on them with his Shermans while the M3s held back. As Nutto complied, the Shermans turned farther to the left, exposing the infantry behind them, who were forced to scuttle around beside the tanks, which were now barely moving. Meanwhile, on the right, the M3s and their supporting infantry came to a halt.

This gave German defenders the impression that they had suppressed the American infantry until they realized that the Shermans were outflanking their men. The order to withdraw from the foxholes was given, and German defenders fell back from the trenches.

■ ■ ■

INSIDE THE CAMP, the American prisoners were hunkered down as the battle raged. At the hospital toward the rear of the compound, American medical personnel had removed all patients from their beds and laid them on the floor.

Accompanied by Johnny Waters, Pop Goode was sheltering in the SAO's office adjacent to the hospital at the rear of the compound when he looked up to see a flushed General von Goeckel standing in his doorway with Hauptmann Fuchs at his side. Reminding Goode that the Geneva Convention prohibited fighting in POW camps, Goeckel called on him to ask the attacking Americans to cease fire. When Goode responded that he had no way of communicating with the American force, Goeckel said that he must do so.

"I am now your prisoner," the general announced dramatically. "It is your responsibility."[3]

Lieutenant Colonel Waters now volunteered to try to make contact with the American attackers and organize an end to the fighting. Goode was happy to let him try, and Goeckel ordered Fuchs to accompany Waters through German lines. The pair hurried away to accomplish the mission. While Waters located a homemade American flag that had been smuggled all the way from Schubin, Fuchs grabbed a bedsheet to use as a white flag. Three kriegie officers also eagerly joined the party—Captain Emil Stutter and Lieutenants Jim Mills and George Meskall. The five men, with Waters and Fuchs in the lead holding American and white flags high, made their way through the camp and out the gate, which had been unlocked on the commandant's orders.

Across the road from the camp gate there stood a range of buildings, including the commandant's residence. Turning left, the party was walking past the commandant's house when a German soldier in camouflage smock, an enlisted man, appeared from around the building's corner. He raised his rifle.[4]

"Amerikaner!" Waters called urgently to the soldier.

As it turned out, this was the worst thing Waters could have said. After all, the German signaler was defending the camp against attacking Americans. The soldier pulled the trigger. His round, fired from close range, hit the American lieutenant colonel below the right hip, and dropped him like a stone.

"Nein, nein, nein!" yelled Hauptmann Fuchs, rushing toward the private, white flag fluttering, just as the soldier was swinging his weapon toward the other members of the flag party, who were raising their hands.

"You son of a bitch!" thought Waters as he lay on the ground, unable to feel anything below the waist. "You've ruined my fishing." Then he saw the German soldier grab his own officer with his free hand and push Fuchs up against a wooden guard box. An incredulous Waters was sure that Fuchs was about to be shot by his own side.[5]

Fuchs was talking fast, telling the soldier that General von Goeckel had authorized the party to make contact with the Americans out-side the camp and secure a ceasefire to prevent casualties inside the camp. The soldier lowered his rifle but would not let the party pro-ceed any farther. He ordered them back into the camp.

Stutter, Meskall and Mills quickly came to Waters' side. They im-mediately realized he was in a bad way. While Meskall remained with Waters, Stutter and Mills dashed inside the commandant's house, emerging with a blanket from Goeckel's own bed. After easing Waters onto the blanket, the trio took hold of it and hurried back through the camp gate with the wounded man. As they set off, one of them thought to pick up the American flag that Waters had dropped when he went down. Fuchs brought up the rear.

Just inside the camp, they were met by Serbian adjutant Yosefo-vitch, who had been watching the party's progress from a barrack window. Yosefovitch, who had befriended Waters after the American arrived in camp, sent for a stretcher. Two Serbian stretcher bearers took over carrying the wounded lieutenant colonel. With the remain-der of the party following close behind, they took him to the com-pound hospital. It was overflowing with sick Americans, and they were waved away by a German doctor who said there was no more room, so they carried Waters to the hospital in the Yugoslavian army com-pound.

This hospital's chief physician was a Serbian, Colonel Radovan Danich. With his assistant, a dentist, Danich removed Waters' trou-sers and inspected the wound as the others crowded around. The doc-tor did not look hopeful. After entering Waters' thigh, the signalman's bullet had deflected off bone and, chipping the coccyx, had exited via his left buttock. Closer inspection later would confirm that, had the bullet entered a fraction higher, Waters might have been dead, or paralyzed for the rest of his days. Even now, without proper medical facilities, the chances of his surviving appeared slim.

But Yosefovitch was determined. "This officer must live!" he com-manded.[6]

17

BUSTING OUT

IN THE FIGHTING OUTSIDE THE WIRE, THE GERMAN DEFENDERS HAD lost several men, both killed and wounded. Apparently alerted by the private who'd shot Johnny Waters that the camp commandant was now seeking a ceasefire, Hauptmann Kammerle ordered all German troops who remained outside the camp to withdraw and regroup in the town to the north. They pulled back in such good order that Baum, watching from the hilltop, assumed the signalers to be hardened combat troops. Once established in the town, Kammerle would send back a small patrol to keep him informed of what was going on at the camp.

With resistance at an end, Baum ordered Lieutenant Weaver's M3s to enter the camp. As the light tanks rolled forward, their infantry squads jumped on their backs. Nearing the wire, Weaver spotted several American POWs at the flagpole by the camp gate. These men hauled down the red, white and black German military flag and sent up Johnny Waters' star-spangled banner in its place.

Weaver now told his driver to hit the wire at speed, near the flag-pole. The M3 crashed through the outer wire, mashed the coils of barbed wire lying between the two fences, then forced its way through the inner fence, whose wire sang as it snapped. As Weaver's tank entered the compound, a second M3 ran along the fence at a right angle, and its crew merrily squashed the wire into the ground.

Barrack doors flew open and, as all the M3s entered the compound, American POWs came rushing out to greet their liberators. Soon the tanks had ground to a halt. Surrounded by ecstatic prisoners, they could go no farther. As tankers threw down spare packs of cigarettes and ration cartons to kriegies, the prisoners acted like excited children on playground equipment, yelling at the tops of their voices as they swarmed all over the tanks. American prisoners shook tankers by the hand, hugged them, and plagued them with questions. Disheveled and undisciplined, they had the appearance of a rabble, not US Army officers.

Something else surprised the tankers. There were many more American prisoners here than they had been led to believe. That was Abe Baum's first impression, too, when he reached the camp in his jeep, leading the remainder of the column. Where had all these American POWs come from? Before he'd set out on this mission, Major Stiller had led Baum to believe they were going after 300 men from Schubin.

Stiller himself had left the column. Pushing through the throng of celebrating POWs, he asked men he passed where he could find Colonel Waters. From one, he learned that Waters had been seriously wounded only minutes before and had been taken to the hospital in the Serbian compound. Locating the hospital, a worried Stiller went inside. Directed to Dragon Yosefovitch, Stiller learned firsthand how the man he'd been sent to rescue had been gunned down while under the protection of a white flag.

Via the Serbian adjutant, the doctors told Stiller about Waters' wound, explaining that he'd been lucky a major artery hadn't been severed. In that case, he would have bled out in minutes. Even so, in the crowded hospital's unsanitary conditions, the doctors were worried about infection setting in. And then the medicos told Stiller something that made his heart sink—under the circumstances, there was no way that Waters could travel with Task Force Baum when it pulled out and headed back to American lines. That would risk his life. Waters would have to stay behind in the camp.

The news meant that the mission, as far as Stiller was concerned, was a failure. So many American lives lost in getting this far, and for what? Putting on a brave face, Stiller went to Waters' bedside. He would remain with him until the column got under way again in the breakout.

Abe Baum was meanwhile trapped in his jeep by the milling mass of kriegies. He was just thinking about punching his way through the mob when a US colonel elbowed his way to him. Holding out his hand, a weary-eyed Pop Goode introduced himself as the camp's SAO. When Baum told him that he'd been led to expect to find only 300 Schubin inmates here, Goode responded that there were five times that many Americans in the camp. Fifteen hundred American POWs? Baum would later confess that he was stunned by this revelation and could have cried, knowing he had no capacity to rescue so many of his countrymen.[1]

Goode was expecting Baum and his men to occupy the compound until stronger US forces arrived, but Baum surprised him by saying that the last he knew, the US Third Army was still sixty miles away, and his orders were to collect as many Americans as he could and get them back behind friendly lines. Both men knew there was no way that Baum's small column would be able to carry 1,500 men.

"You'd better tell them that," said Goode, indicating the elated POWs all around them.

"Me?" Baum retorted. He shook his head. "You tell 'em."

Not only was Goode the senior officer present, these American prisoners all came under his command. As far as Baum was concerned, it would be up to Goode to decide who stayed and who went.[2] Leaving Goode, Baum pushed his way through the crowd, rounded up his subordinates, and ordered them to reorganize the column in preparation for moving out, with tanks front and back. Returning to his jeep, he found Colonel Goode precisely where he'd left him.

Goode told Baum that no decision had yet been taken on what to do with his men. The look on the white-haired colonel's face told Baum the SAO didn't want to have to choose who among his men stayed, and who went. With a sigh, Baum climbed onto the hood of his jeep, then shouted for quiet. Gradually, the men around him shut up, and all eyes turned his way. Baum spelled it out: the column was going to have to make a fighting withdrawal to American lines sixty miles away at the River Main, and there were not enough vehicles to take everyone.

As groans and looks of dismay spread throughout the crowd, Goode, beside Baum, observed pragmatically, "You men fall into three groups. Those who can't physically make it and will have to stay behind. Those who can walk out. And those who ride with the column in the knowledge they'll probably have to fight their way out."[3]

Baum nodded. A long, silent pause followed until Baum finally asked those who wanted to accompany the task force to raise their hands. Hundreds did. Without waiting any longer, many men ran to the column's tanks, halftracks and jeeps, and piled aboard as the vehicles were backing up and maneuvering to form up for the pullout. Schubin kriegie Captain Donald Stewart, who'd been to the Katyn Massacre site with Jack Van Vliet in 1943, was watching the activity when he realized that one tank driver had failed to see a wounded GI from the column lying on the ground in his path. Stewart yelled a warning, but it was too late. The tank rolled over the soldier, and one of its tracks separated his head from his body.

Another Schubin kriegie, Lieutenant Robert "Bob" Thompson from the 36th Infantry Division, who'd been captured in France the previous September, had been in the compound hospital suffering from malaria. Ignoring a high temperature, Thompson found the strength to leave his bed. Staggering outside, he was intent on hitching a ride with the column. By this time, the vehicles were overflowing with men. Some clung like limpets to the backs of tanks. Hundreds of others had piled into halftracks along with Baum's infantry.

Thompson reckoned he had no chance of finding a place, so, instead, he hid in bushes outside the fence to wait and see what transpired.

Baum, meantime, again called his officers and senior NCOs into conference. By this time, the sun had well and truly set, and stars were sparkling in the heavens above. Spreading a map on the hood of his jeep, the captain ordered Lieutenant Nutto to take a detachment of Shermans and halftracks and move quickly west to find Reichsstrasse 27, the highway that would take the column back to the Main, and ensure that the road was clear. Baum tapped the map at the village of Bonnland. Once Nutto reached that, he was to probe west along the road in the direction of Höllrich, beyond Hill 427. The rest of the column would follow in that direction once Nutto radioed the "all clear."

As Baum was giving his instructions, Major Stiller came up and informed him that Lieutenant Colonel Waters was too badly wounded to accompany them. Frankly, Baum didn't give a damn. He had too many other American lives to worry about. Stiller now argued with Baum over the direction he intended to take. The major plugged for heading north through Hammelburg, to link up with Highway 27 that way, but Baum reminded him that the painfully effective German tank destroyers were somewhere to the north, and he had no desire to tangle with them again, especially when his vehicles were laden with kriegies. As Stiller continued to argue with Baum in front of the task force commander's subordinates, Baum lost his temper and told him to butt out.

"I'm still running this show!" Baum snapped, silencing the major. He then ordered Nutto to move out with his detachment and undertake his assignment.[4]

All stood watching as Nutto, cigar in mouth, led six Shermans and five halftracks that rolled away, spewing smoke from their exhausts. At that moment, there was a loud explosion from the rear of the main column, and the M3 light tank stationed at the column's back end went up in flames. While the Americans had been consumed with their movement plans, no one had been posted on lookout.

The German patrol from Hauptmann Kammerle's company of

trainee signalers had been able to creep to within less than 200 feet of the tank at the rear of the column. A Gefreiter (Private) Pelzer had brought a Panzerfaust to bear and blasted the M3 in its most vulnerable spot, the lightly armored rear. The detonation lit up the night. Shocked crewmen scrambled from the flaming wreckage. As the M3 burned, the German patrol slithered back into the darkness.

The tank's destruction shook up everyone in the column. An exasperated Baum ordered his vehicles to spread out fast and take up defensive positions until he learned from Nutto that the road out was clear. As the vehicles were re-maneuvering, kriegie Bob Thompson jumped up from his hiding place and ran to the nearest crowded half-track as it rolled by. A hand reached down, and someone hauled him aboard to join the crush in the back.

Watching all this, Schubin kriegie Clarence Meltesen was disgusted by the chaos. Meltesen had stayed with Colonel Goode all through the evacuation from Schubin and the march to Hammelburg, but now he was ready to take his chances at escape. But not with Task Force Baum. Meltesen decided to put his Ranger training to good use and live off the land while making his way independently toward the US Third Army, hoping the Germans would be occupied trying to stop the task force. Teaming up with fellow lieutenants Daniel R. Lewandowski and John J. Kent, Jr., Meltesen now departed the camp and lit out through the darkness on foot, heading west, leaving the stationary task force in their wake.

■ ■ ■

As HIS HENSCHEL truck drove into the village of Fuchsstadt, a mile east of Hammelburg, Luftwaffe Leutnant Hans Bartmeier saw the bulky shapes of Wehrmacht Hetzer tank destroyers lined up at the roadside. Ordering his driver to stop, Bartmeier reported to the Hetzers' CO, Hauptmann Koehl. After refueling and rearming at Euerdorf, Koehl had brought his Hetzers back to within striking distance of Hammelburg.

In appearance, the two men were very unalike. Koehl was a chubby, beady-eyed man. Young Bartmeier was a tall blond with a fierce look in his eye, a veritable Viking. Bartmeier told Koehl that, earlier in the evening, he and his twenty-man flak detachment had been ordered from outside Schweinfurt, to join the resistance against the American column at Hammelburg. Koehl, unsure of the situation in Hammelburg, said he was planning to sit tight and await orders in the morning. The proactive Bartmeier had no intention of waiting for orders, or for morning. Keen for action, the Luftwaffe lieutenant divided his detachment into three squads armed with heavy machine guns and Panzerfausts and led them south on foot toward the POW camps. He would discover the situation there for himself.

■ ■ ■

As Nutto's SPEARHEAD column warily inched its way south through the military training area toward Bonnland, its tanks and halftracks laden with POWs from Hammelburg, the vehicles stopped every now and then and turned off their engines so that Nutto could listen for sounds of German vehicles or troops. Ultracautious, he had no intention of blundering into an ambush.

At one of these halts, Nutto heard men singing as they tramped along on the other side of a rise. Assuming these were German troops, the Americans waited in silence until the singers had passed. In fact, these men were French and Russian POWs returning from a woodcutting assignment. The only German troops in the vicinity were the men of Gehrig's patrol toward Hessdorf, farther south, and they certainly weren't singing. They, too, were listening—for the approach of the Americans.

Nutto moved on, but his lead tank ran into a roadblock of logs stacked neatly across the road. Who had built this roadblock, no one knows—probably the party that Nutto heard marching away in such good voice. When Nutto radioed back to Baum at the camp and reported the roadblock, Baum told him to wait there. Driving at breakneck speed in his jeep, Baum soon joined the probe vehicles, arriving at 9:30.

When Nutto pointed out the roadblock, Baum ordered him to back up to a small side road he'd passed a little way to the rear of their position. Nutto's vehicles did so, and they were soon on a narrow dirt road that led them northwest toward Hill 340, known to the Germans as the Michelsberg, with Baum accompanying Nutto's vehicles.

A jeep sent forward to reconnoiter came upon a roadblock and took small-arms fire from the slopes of Hill 340, where trainee railroad engineers from Hauptmann Rose's detachment were picketed, and fled back to the task force. As Baum was receiving a report from recon officer Hoffner, the jeep's driver burst into tears. Hoffner replaced his traumatized driver behind the wheel.

Aware now of a roadblock to the northwest, Baum ordered Nutto to swing his column southwest to avoid it, heading for Höllrich and Reichsstrasse 27 on the road that ran along the base of Hill 340 and the neighboring Hill 427, the Reussenberg. Meanwhile, the Germans above the roadblock withdrew to report to Hauptmann Rose up in the ruins on the Reussenberg. As Nutto pushed on, Baum set off back to the camp to rejoin the main column. Missing an intersection, Nutto's tanks and halftracks proceeded toward Hessdorf, backtracked yet again, then finally turned north toward Höllrich.

At one point, as the column waited on the road to Höllrich while Nutto scouted ahead, the French and Russian POWs appeared from behind high stone walls on either side of the thoroughfare. They asked the column's surprised GIs if they were Americans and had come to liberate them. The men of the column angrily told the foreign POWs to beat it before they drew German attention to them and got them all killed.

■ ■ ■

When Abe Baum returned to the main column outside the oflag, he noted that many of the American POWs who had previously crowded onto and around its vehicles had left the column and returned to the camp's barracks. He couldn't blame them. He was even more frustrated and exhausted than they were. And then his radio operator received a message from Bill Nutto.

"We're in Höllrich, and we found the highway!"[5]

With relief, Baum ordered the main column to move out and follow

Nutto's detachment. When the column pulled out from the camp, Colonel Goode was among the POWs riding with it. By one estimation, there were 600 American POWs on the vehicles of Nutto and Baum's two divided columns, but at least half of Goode's men, both Schubin boys and original Hammelburg inmates, were staying put in the camp.[6]

18

ONE HELLUVA NIGHT

Not long after Nutto sent Baum the message that he'd found Highway 27, two Panzerfausts were fired at his tank from close range. Before getting this far, Nutto had scouted ahead on foot and entered Höllrich. Finding the entrance to the village clear, and with all quiet in the main street, Nutto had returned to his tank and led the column all the way to the northern end of Höllrich. A roadblock of fallen trees lay in their path. On either side of the column, the main street was lined with confining stone houses linked by stone walls. The street itself was too narrow for the armored vehicles to turn around. They could either go forward or back up.

It was a classic ambush, and Nutto and his men had been sucked right into it. Hauptmann Gehrig's officer cadets were ready and waiting for them. The patrol sent by Gehrig toward Hessdorf had heard the Shermans approach and came scuttling back to warn the captain at his Höllrich command post, from where he'd carefully organized the disposition of his fifty remaining cadets.

Nutto, sitting in his open hatch in the lead Sherman, saw the two

Panzerfausts let go from just feet away. At such close range, they were inevitably direct hits. After the impact of the multiple blasts, Nutto found a crewman below him shoving him up and out through his hatch in the turret. Nutto fell down the side of his Sherman and landed on the body of one of the kriegies who, moments before, had been riding on his tank. Dazed and crawling for cover, Nutto saw the second Sherman in line barrel into his own machine. Unarmed kriegies were being felled by German machine-gun fire. And, Nutto swore, in the flash of battle, he saw a German Tiger tank fire its 88 mm gun at the column.

Several kriegies on following tanks would also declare they saw a Tiger that night, camouflaged with tree branches and firing on Nutto's Shermans as American tank drivers desperately tried to reverse out of the ambush. Yet, according to Wehrmacht records and German personal accounts, there were no Tiger tanks anywhere near Höllrich, or in the Hammelburg area, that night. What the Americans may have seen was the gray bulk of the butt end of a MAN bus, covered with tree branches, with officer cadets firing Panzerfausts out its rear windows.

One American account even had a 75 mm shell from a Sherman bounce off the "Tiger." Schubin kriegie Lieutenant Brooks Kleber, riding in the first halftrack in line, didn't see a Tiger, but he did see Panzerfausts slamming into the lead tanks. Kleber was frozen with fear, dreading a projectile coming his way—he was sitting on top of a pile of ammunition in the back of the halftrack.

A German officer cadet popped up, Panzerfaust on his shoulder. Machine-gun rounds from a Sherman cut him down, but not before he got off his shot. A passenger in another halftrack, Schubinite Harry B. Long, saw the second Sherman, which was trying to bypass Nutto's tank, take the Panzerfaust hit. In the explosion that followed, kriegies riding on the tank's back were flung into the air like rag dolls. The four remaining tanks and five halftracks backed up frantically, hitting houses and stone walls. A side street provided a place to reverse into and then turn and head back the way the column had come.

Within minutes, all nine surviving American vehicles were speeding from Höllrich and heading back the way they'd come. Not all the kriegies who had been traveling with the probe column returned with it. Several had been killed in the ambush. Another six kriegies— a lieutenant colonel, three majors, and two junior officers who had been blown off the column's two lead tanks and survived—had found cover behind stone walls until the firing ceased and the column had pulled back. These men subsequently scurried across open country through the darkness. In two groups, they headed west for American lines on foot.

Back in Höllrich, Bill Nutto was lying in the village street with dead Americans sprawled nearby. The second Sherman was burning, but Nutto's lead tank wasn't. To his surprise, Nutto heard German soldiers climb inside his tank and start it up. After the officer cadets drove the Sherman off the street and into the garden of one of the village houses, Nutto felt his foot being kicked. Looking up, he saw a German officer standing over him with an automatic pistol pointed at his head.

"Are you a Negro?" the German asked.

Realizing that his face must be caked with dirt and grease, Nutto replied that he wasn't black and tried to drag up his sleeve to reveal the white of his arm.[1]

The officer grunted and walked to the next American lying on the cobblestones, who proved to be dead. Nutto would now become a prisoner. Whether the officer encountered by the lieutenant was Gehrig or a subordinate is unclear. What is clear is that Gehrig now issued orders to two of his cadets. Each of them strapped a Panzerfaust on his back, then, using bicycles found in the village, they set off after the retreating American column.

• • •

IT WAS TEN minutes after midnight on the morning of Wednesday, March 28, by the time Leutnant Bartmeier and his small flak detachment reached Oflag XIII-B after tramping overland from Fuchsstadt. They found the M3 light tank blasted earlier by Hauptmann Kammerle's signalers still burning outside the camp gate, and the remains of the hay barn glowing. Four dead Americans lay near the knocked-out tank. Several of them wore US Army tanker gear, so Bartmeier assumed they were all the tank's crewmen. Bartmeier's men arrived at the same time as the first bus containing the officer cadets, under a Leutnant Daudelt, sent from Höllrich by Hauptmann Gehrig. The second bus would labor up to the camp thirty-five minutes later.

On learning that the American column had departed the camp only ten minutes earlier, Bartmeier dispatched one of his squads, led by a twenty-four-year-old corporal, Unteroffizier Heinrich Grosse-Berkenbusch, to trail the Americans on foot with machine guns and Panzerfausts. Bartmeier then combined the rest of his men with Leutnant Daudelt's twenty-five cadets, and together they set out to regain control of the oflag.

In the Serbian compound, Bartmeier's troops came under fire from fifty royalists armed by Dragon Yosefovitch after Hauptmann Fuchs had given him the key to the weapons store. Following a short, sharp engagement, the outgunned Serbs threw down their aged French and Belgian rifles. By 1:30 a.m., the camp was back in German hands, and the hundreds of American kriegies who had remained in their compound were no longer free men. It was as if Task Force Baum had never been there.

Out in the military training area, Unteroffizier Grosse-Berkenbusch and his squad followed a pair of American armored vehicles overland for two hours. In the darkness, the corporal identified them as Shermans, but they were almost certainly two of the task force's SPGs that were either lost or acting as rearguard to the column. Several times, the flak men almost crept close enough to let off a Panzerfaust, but each time they had to fall back when they saw what they thought were screening American infantry close by.

Like men of Task Force Baum, the Germans were confused by things they saw—or thought they saw—that dark night. These American infantrymen seen by the Panzerfaust squad were almost certainly kriegies, unarmed men who had left Task Force Baum and were trying to escape through the training area. In the end, the two

American armored vehicles reached a road and sped away. Grosse-Berkenbusch and his men returned to the oflag.

· · ·

ABE BAUM, SPEEDING ahead of the main column in his jeep, ran into the remnants of Nutto's retreating column as it backtracked from Hauptmann Gehrig's roadblock at Höllrich. In disbelief, Baum learned that two Shermans had been knocked out and Lieutenant Nutto was missing. Baum, considering Nutto one of his best officers, was shattered by the loss.

Baum now instructed two remaining Shermans to scout south down the road to Hessdorf to see if the task force could exit the area that way. Before the tanks set off, Baum ordered the kriegies riding on them to get off. He also radioed the main column to pull off the road at the base of Hill 427. At a place where forest had been cleared to create farmland on the lower slopes, he'd spotted a stone building as he passed. The column was to assemble there and await further orders once Baum knew that the way via Hessdorf was clear.

The two Shermans started off down the road to the south with Baum following close behind in his jeep. At around 2:30 a.m., Baum thought he spotted movement to the right of the road ahead of the pair of tanks. Moments later, he saw the flash of a Panzerfaust. The two officer cadets on bicycles had managed to get ahead of the tanks, and one of them let off his Panzerfaust at close range. The lead Sherman took a direct hit. Surviving crewmen tumbled out and ran to leap into Baum's jeep as it turned around. The jeep sped back toward Hill 427, with the second Sherman following as fast as it could, withdrawing out of range of the second Panzerfaust-armed cadet.

Baum subsequently led the surviving vehicles from Nutto's probe force back to the cleared ground at the foot of Hill 427, where they rejoined the rest of the column. To the kriegies who were waiting at the stone building—an old farmhouse now used as a barn—the sight of just one Sherman returning was devastating. The rumor would quickly spread among the kriegies that there was a Tiger tank down the road at Höllrich. If Shermans couldn't get through, thought the POWs, how the hell could they?

Colonel Goode would later say that the situation on the Reussenberg by this time smelled bad to him. Climbing up onto an M3, he addressed his men. Those who wished to remain with the task force and fight their way out, he said, were free to do so. As for the remaining men, Goode announced he would lead them back to the oflag, which, he estimated, would involve a hike of six miles.[2]

Abe Baum would recall that only a dozen POWs opted to remain with the task force, although escaper Clarence Meltesen would put the number at fifty. Schubin kriegie Bob Thompson was one of them. As for Baum, he wasn't making anyone go anywhere. All he wanted to do now was get back to the Third Army with as many of his men as he could. At sunup, he told Goode,[3] the column would move off and attempt to break out to the south. At the same time, Goode and his kriegies could commence the march back to Hammelburg. Meanwhile, kriegies and task force members attempted to get some sleep.[4]

■ ■ ■

AT 2:00 THAT Wednesday morning, a convoy of trucks bringing the 1,300 men of the 113th Grenadier Regiment under Oberleutnant Demmel finally rolled through Hammelburg and halted outside Oflag XIII-B. At 3:30, Oberst Hoppe transferred his command post to the oflag to take control of the now substantial force at the camp.

During the early hours of the morning, the damaged telephone lines into Hammelburg west of the town were repaired, and at 4:00 Hoppe received a call from Hauptmann Rose in the castle ruins atop the Reussenberg, Hill 427. Rose, although silenced for hours by the downed phone lines, had been watching and listening all night for signs of the American column on the roads below the hill. Now he was able to report the sounds of tanks passing the Reussenberg.

Rose subsequently sent a party of his engineering students down the hill, and after watching the exhausted Americans from the trees, they snuck back up to report to their captain that the enemy column had occupied a clearing 300 meters (320 yards) below Rose's observation post, near a barn on the Reussenberg farm. This permitted Rose, at 5:00, to again ring Hoppe, reporting in a low voice what his scouts had just told him about the strength of the American force on the cleared ground close by.

"Ten tanks and twenty armored vehicles," Rose advised. "Infantry guards the Reussenberg farm. Estimated strength, 120 men."[5]

At 7:00, Danube 1 commander Hauptmann Koehl arrived at Hoppe's camp HQ and reported for duty. Hoppe briefed Koehl on the Reussenberg location of the American column, but apart from instructing him to be ready to move his Hetzers, he sent Koehl back to Fuchsstadt without orders to transfer Danube 1 to the Reussenberg area.

Twenty minutes later, a staff car arrived at the camp, and out stepped Generalmajor Helmut Hipp. He had driven through the night from the 7th Army headquarters with orders to take command at Hammelburg. Hoppe now briefed General Hipp on the situation. Both men were uncertain as to what to do next. Ten minutes after Hipp's arrival, another staff car arrived at the camp gate. This time it was Hauptmann Eggemann, Himmler's man, who emerged, having driven up from Würzburg. With his Knight's Cross prominent at his throat, Eggemann stomped into Hoppe's HQ trailed by two aides and demanded a briefing.

Eggemann was soon infuriated by the lack of initiative displayed by both Hoppe and Hipp. And he couldn't believe that Koehl had waited through the night at Fuchsstadt before reporting for orders. Declaring that Generalmajor von Gersdorff, the 7th Army's chief of staff, had the previous day agreed to his taking over command of Danube 1 and Oberleutnant Demmel's grenadiers, he told Hoppe and Hipp to step aside. Picking up the phone, Eggemann called Hauptmann Rose at his Reussenberg observation post.

"Are the enemy still at the farm?" Eggemann demanded.

Rose whispered that Americans were still there and informed Eggemann that the latest information he had from his scouts in the improving light was that the American column actually consisted of six tanks and twenty-five other armored vehicles.[6]

Eggemann then called Koehl, who had just arrived back at Fuchsstadt, and ordered him to return to the oflag at once. When Koehl arrived, Eggemann ordered both him and Oberleutnant Demmel to take part in an assault at the Reussenberg, an assault that Eggemann would personally lead. Koehl's Hetzers and Demmel's infantry were to link up at Bonnland in the military training area, then swing west to assemble behind the Michelsberg, where the infantry would dismount. They would then make a combined attack toward the Americans across the hillside farmland, from the Michelsberg to the foot of the Reussenberg.

Eggemann sent the pair away to get their units under way. For the moment, he had the Americans where he wanted them, and he was determined not to let them get away.

BLOOD AND FIRE ON THE REUSSENBERG

AT THE BASE OF THE REUSSENBERG, ABE BAUM HAD ALL THE wounded removed from the column's vehicles and carried to the stone barn, where they were made as comfortable as possible. Hoping that the Germans would take care of them, Baum intended to leave the wounded behind when the column pulled out in daylight. The most senior man among the wounded was Baum's deputy, Captain Lang, who was delirious and in a bad way. Two kriegies injured during the Höllrich ambush had made it back to Hill 427, but they died from their wounds during the night, in the barn.

Baum told the rest of his men and the POWs who were staying with them to get as much rest as they could and urged the kriegie officers to arm themselves and prepare to take charge of squads of his men if they got caught up in a fight with the Germans. Should the task force run into more roadblocks, or even Tiger tanks, Baum said, they would fight their way through, come hell or high water. If they needed to cross a river, he added, they would put a halftrack in the water and drive over the top of it.

Baum also gave orders for gasoline to be siphoned from some of the halftracks to refill the gas tanks of his fighting vehicles. Armor was what he needed for the breakout. With not enough fuel to go around, Baum would be leaving some of the halftracks behind. The sun would rise around 7:30, and Baum set 8:30 for the task force's departure time.

When the sun emerged at 7:30, weary task force members ate the last of their rations and then set about transferring fuel to the tanks. At the same time, Colonel Goode came to Baum and shook his hand. The kriegies returning to camp with Goode had formed up in ranks. Upward of 400 POWs were going back with Goode, who had fashioned a white flag for the march. Each commander sadly wished the other good luck before Goode led his kriegies away, heading back east to Hammelburg and captivity.

Some of the kriegies were neither going back nor staying with the task force. A minority had decided that, now they'd had a taste of freedom, they liked it. Some waited for first light, but others had already slipped away in the darkness—among them the Americans seen by Corporal Grosse-Berkenbusch. Separating from Goode's party of 400, as many as 150 POWs headed away in groups of three and four.[1] Some made their way west through the trees on the slope above the task force's overnight location. Others crossed the road and walked southeast toward the military training area. Still others went north over the Reussenberg.

One of these breakaway groups was led by Jack Hemingway, who was planning to put his OSS training and experience to good use on the run behind enemy lines. He was accompanied by his new pals, Lieutenants Ray Saigh and Dewey Stuart. Now it was all for one and one for all as the trio tried to put as much distance between themselves and the task force as humanly possible. Logic told them that Task Force Baum was about to attract German troops like bears to honey.

A little while after leaving the task force, Colonel Goode's large party of returning kriegies was trudging silently and disconsolately along the road that led northeast, passing Hill 340, the Michelsberg. Men in Goode's party distinctly heard the rumble of heavy engines ticking over beyond the slope of Hill 340. This could only indicate the presence of German vehicles. But Goode did not send any of his men back to Hill 427 to warn Baum, apparently thinking the task force was already under way and leaving the area.

Brooks Kleber was one of the kriegies marching back to camp with the colonel. When Goode's exhausted group tramped despondently back through the Oflag XIII-B gate, now manned by the officer cadets who'd helped retake the camp overnight, Kleber saw a German soldier smile, almost sympathetically, at the passing Americans.

"Get some sleep, fellows," said the German. "You've had a tough night."[2]

As Goode's party was segregated from the rest of the camp population, Colonel Goode was approached by General von Goeckel, who had resumed command in the camp.

"Fortunes change," said the commandant philosophically with a shrug after the pair exchanged salutes. He told Goode that the planned relocation of the American prisoners to another camp would commence later in the morning, when Goode and his returnees would be marched to Hammelburg railroad station for the journey southeast to Nuremberg. In the meantime, he said, Goode's men should try to rest.[3]

Brooks Kleber didn't care where they were being sent. Like many men in the party, the physically and emotionally drained Kleber curled up and promptly fell fast asleep on the spot.

■ ■ ■

CONTRARY TO POP Goode's belief, the task force was still at the Reussenberg farm. It was taking much too long to siphon and transfer fuel, and Baum's set departure time had passed. To speed things up, tank crews crawled beneath several halftracks, cut their fuel lines, and let gasoline gush out and splash into jerry cans held underneath. Fuel ended up leaking on the ground, but eventually the tanks, SPGs and selected halftracks were gassed up and ready to roll.

Abe Baum walked alongside the vehicles that would soon be departing the Reussenberg. Feeling upbeat, he encouraged his men as they mounted up, telling them that, whatever happened, they would fight their way out of this. The task force members and the kriegies accompanying them responded to Baum's mood and were in good spirits. Baum hauled himself into his jeep, which then bumped forward as his tanks began to creep down the slope to form the agreed-on lineup. Halftracks were also on the move.

At that moment, the ground to the northeast became a sheet of flame. The 75 mm guns of nine Hetzers opened fire, and the tank destroyers came rolling over Hill 340 and down the grassy slope toward Task Force Baum at the base of Hill 427. After the Hetzers had moved into position just 1,600 yards from the task force without being seen, Hauptman Eggemann had divided the tank destroyers into two groups, spread in a line across the reverse slope of the Michelsberg—five Hetzers to one side, and four Hetzers and the Bergepanzer recovery vehicle on the other, with a gap between the two. Eggemann had also divided Oberleutnant Demmel's grenadiers into two groups that were placed behind each tank destroyer formation.

Eager young Leutnant Bartmeier had also arrived at the Michelsberg, bringing his flak detachment to join the attack. His Henschel truck ran out of fuel just as it reached the assembly point. These Luftwaffe men were also in the infantry force that trotted along behind the slow-moving line of tank destroyers bearing down on Task Force Baum. The Hetzers' big guns were swiftly firing one shell after another, and their machine guns were chattering.

Abe Baum stared in disbelief at the line of armor bearing down on him. Where the hell had they come from? The Germans were firing more rapidly than he had ever imagined possible. He correctly identified one group of armored vehicles as tank destroyers, but in his shock he was convinced that the other group was made up of five Tiger tanks firing 88 mm guns. Several other Americans in the column would later say the same. Yet, according to German records and military historians, there were no Tigers anywhere near the Reussenberg that day.

Once again, the 75 mm guns on Koehl's Hetzers were deadly accurate. All around Abe Baum, his column seemed to be going up in flames as leaked fuel beneath abandoned halftracks turned them into fireballs. Several tanks and the SPGs managed to swing to face the onslaught and get off a shot or two but without finding targets. Now, from behind them, up in the trees, Panzerfausts were being loosed off, fired by railroad engineer cadets from Hauptmann Rose's group who had come down from his hilltop observation post to join the fight.

Within three minutes of the commencement of the German attack, Task Force Baum no longer existed as a fighting force. In the command halftrack, radio operator Private John Sidles was tapping out the task force's last radio message on his Morse key, informing HQ that the task force was surrounded and taking heavy fire and begging for air support.

With carnage all around him on the hillside, Baum knew that it was all over. "Every man for himself!" he yelled, abandoning his jeep and making for the trees, the pain from his wounded knee forcing him to limp.[4]

Close behind the captain came radio operator Sidles, interpreter Irving Solotoff, and Major Stiller, Patton's aide. Once in the trees, Baum yelled to the scores of his men who were soon congregating there to head west in groups of two and three to avoid detection. Few took any notice of him now. In often large, easy-to-spot groups, they took off in all directions.

SPG commander Technical Sergeant Graham kept his gun firing even as the SPG next to his went up in flame. GIs hugging the ground nearby cursed him and yelled for him to stop firing—he was drawing enemy fire their way. Graham ignored them. Only when machine-gun bullets clattered on his vehicle's armor, and he saw German infantry closing in for the kill with gun and grenade, did Graham give the order to bail out. He and his crew scrambled from the SPG and, keeping low, ran for the trees.

Near the stone barn, Schubinite Lieutenant Bob Thompson had been climbing up into the halftrack he'd adopted when a 75 mm shell slammed into it. The explosion threw him to the ground. Picking himself up, and still holding the M1 carbine with which he'd earlier armed himself, he ran toward the shelter provided by the barn. Before he reached it, the barn was hit by German shells. It erupted in smoke and flame, and before Thompson's eyes the roof and several walls collapsed. Thompson took cover at a corner of the wrecked building, just in time to see a GI jumping from a halftrack lose his leg in an explosion.

Another twenty men, infantrymen from the task force, huddled behind the rubble of the barn with Thompson. After German machine-gun rounds sprayed the open ground nearby, one of the enlisted men suggested they surrender. No one argued. Thompson, realizing he was the only officer in the bunch, stripped off his jacket and shirt. He was wearing two grimy white T-shirts underneath. Removing one, he tied it to the barrel of his M1. Holding the carbine aloft, he waved the makeshift white flag back and forth.

The response was a volley of shots that knocked the weapon from his hands. Then the firing stopped. A German grenadier approached. Around Thompson, GIs were quickly disposing of pistols and compasses they'd acquired as souvenirs from dead Germans as the GIs battled their way from Normandy. Motioning with his rifle, the German ordered the group to its feet.

Thompson rose slowly. The enlisted men followed, hands clasped atop their helmets. Unsure what the Geneva Convention said about kriegies who took up arms against their captors, and worried that he might be executed, Thompson remained with these men to give the impression he was a task force officer. More German troops came up and shepherded the prisoners into the middle of what had been the American armored column.

On the battleground, five tanks and SPGs and several halftracks were burning fiercely, and American dead and wounded lay all around. Under orders from a German officer, Thompson's party collected all the American wounded and loaded them into their own halftracks, which the Germans had by this time commandeered. When one of the M3s, named *Conquering Hero* by its American crew, was found to still be in running order, one of its captured crew members was forced by his captors to drive it to Hammelburg.

All the American vehicles were put to use by the Germans. If a

tank or halftrack was severely damaged, they cannibalized it to repair others. The Luftwaffe's Leutnant Bartmeier took charge of an
American jeep and used it to tow his truck to Hammelburg. Task force
halftracks were used to ferry Thompson and other American prisoners back to Oflag XIII-B. The remains of several American tanks
and SPGs would sit on the lower slopes of the Reussenberg for
decades and be used for target practice by the West German army
and the later modern German army. In 2003, the hull of one of Task
Force Baum's SPGs that was still on the Reussenberg would be removed to a Bavarian museum.

With German grenadiers spreading out in regimented lines to
hunt down men from the task force who'd scattered in all directions,
the battleground was soon all but deserted. At Höllrich, Hauptmann
Gehrig vacated the barn that had been serving as his HQ and prepared it to receive captives as they were brought in.

Hauptmann Eggemann, who had led the successful German assault, remained at the Reussenberg until he was satisfied that the task
force had been satisfactorily dealt with. At midday, he arrived back at
Oflag XIII-B and informed Generalmajor Hipp that the American
force had been eliminated. Throughout the afternoon, Americans
from the task force were brought back to the oflag. All were lodged
in the old horse-training ring in the southern part of the camp.

At 4:00 p.m. Eggemann telephoned Generalmajor von Gersdorff
at 7th Army HQ at Heigenbruecken to report mission accomplished.
But Himmler's man did not stop there. "Generalmajor Hipp, Oberst
Hoppe, and Hauptmann Koehl lacked determination in dealing with
the American force," he declared critically.[5]

The following day, aware of Eggemann's scathing assessment of
his performance, Oberst Hoppe lodged his own report, in which he
praised Eggemann for "forceful and sweeping employment of the battalion and leading the attack." Hoppe also praised Hauptmann Rose
for maintaining his observation post on the Reussenberg just 300 meters from the American column's assembly area. The colonel declared that Hauptmann Kammerle had forcefully and bravely kept his
signalers in the town despite the attack by American armor. And

Hoppe commended Gefreiter Pelzer of Kammerle's company for boldly destroying the American M3 with a Panzerfaust outside the camp gate. Hoppe listed German casualties at and near Hammelburg during the operation as four killed and seven wounded on the night of March 27, and one wounded the following day.[6]

Hoppe made no mention of Gehrig, Koehl or Demmel. All of them had been instrumental in the defeat of the American column but had come under Eggemann's command. To explain the fact that Eggemann had taken command of these officers' units from him, Hoppe wrote that Eggemann and he had received differing orders from 7th Army HQ. Three days later, Eggemann would be promoted to major for his efforts at Hammelburg, and it was recommended that Oak Leaves be added to his Knight's Cross—the second-highest German military decoration and the equivalent of the US Army's Silver Star.[7]

*   *   *

ABE BAUM LIMPED along the forested slopes, accompanied now by Stiller and Sidles. They were heading due west. At one point, the trio decided to come down off the Reussenberg. Just as they were about to break cover, they saw six men from the task force do the same. Almost at once, a line of German infantry materialized from the undergrowth in front of the GIs, and the six were captured. Unseen, Baum and his companions backed up into the trees and hunkered down, intending to wait for nightfall before moving again.

They had been there for a time when a lone German soldier came toward them through the trees. Sidles scuttled away in time to hide behind a tree without being spotted. But the German had seen Baum and Stiller. As he came up, he paused to lay his rifle aside, drawing a pistol. Baum, lying on the ground, was fumbling inside his jacket to draw his own .45 automatic, but his bandaged hand got caught in his clothes. The German fired. His pistol round entered Baum's trousers at the groin area, grazed his scrotum, and passed through the flesh of his inner thigh.

"Son of a bitch, you shot my ball off!" Baum exclaimed in shock.[8]

The German moved closer. Announcing in English, with an American accent, that he'd lived in Bridgeport, Connecticut, until he'd returned home to fight for the Fatherland in 1939, the enemy soldier ordered Baum and Stiller to their feet. Private Sidles, meanwhile, had gotten a bead on the German with his M1. But, knowing that all around him there were hundreds of Germans who had already been summoned by the first shot, Sidles decided that discretion was the better part of valor. Tossing away the carbine, he emerged from cover with his hands in the air.

Soon, Sidles and Stiller had Baum's arms around their shoulders as they helped him back to the battleground. There they joined more American prisoners standing with hands on helmets. With all operative vehicles removed from the site by this stage, this group of prisoners was made to march along the road toward Lager Hammelburg. When they reached a roadside farmhouse, Baum could go no farther. After ordering the others to leave him there, he lapsed into unconsciousness.

Escaped kriegies were also being quickly recaptured. Jack Hemingway was one of them. Hemingway, Saigh and Stuart estimated they'd gone half a mile from the task force that morning when they heard the Hetzer barrage begin behind them. As they kept bumping into other small parties of kriegies on the run, Hemingway realized that no amount of OSS training was going to help him. This was like a fox hunt where there were dozens of foxes. The hounds would have no trouble tracking them down.

Some of the hunters were mere children. During the morning, Hemingway's group blundered into a party of boys wearing shorts and carrying daggers in their belts. They were nervy Hitler Youth from local villages, and their young leader was armed with a Schmeisser that he waved airily in the Americans' direction. As the trio raised their hands, Hemingway politely asked the boy leader to send for his commander. Soon, a Wehrmacht *Feldwebel* arrived on the scene, and he marched the prisoners into Hammelburg township and to the railroad station, where they were loaded aboard a train.

This train's boxcars, each with its roof painted with POW in white and a white US star, were full of 500 American POWs being sent to Nuremberg as part of the resumed relocation of inmates that had been interrupted by the arrival of Task Force Baum. Over several days, the camp would be emptied of all American prisoners except those who were hospitalized. This evacuation would include the hundreds of Task Force Baum members captured before, during and after the Reussenberg battle. Five American POW parties would be sent from Hammelburg by rail. Another four would have to walk all the way.

This first rail party that Hemingway joined was made up of the men Colonel Goode had led back to XIII-B from the Reussenberg, plus the first runaways who, like Hemingway's group, had been caught shortly after the brief battle on the hillside. Hemingway was put in the same boxcar as Goode, and their train sat in Hammelburg's marshalling yard until after dark. With the USAAF now owning the daylight skies over southern Germany, it was too dangerous for the German train to move before nightfall. After dark, the train got under way.

Most of the men who had been with the task force and had been on the run, both kriegies and Baum's men, were rounded up that first day, March 28, or the next. Harry Long was one of them. He was marched back into camp after Colonel Goode's party had departed. When Oberst Hoppe sent in his report on March 29, he wrote that six officers and 300 enlisted men from the task force had been captured by that time. This included several kriegies, among them Bob Thompson, who were lodged in the horse ring with the genuine task force members and mistakenly counted with them by their guards.

■ ■ ■

AFTER LEAVING OFLAG XIII-B, Ranger Clarence Meltesen and his two kriegie companions had followed a trail through the countryside. Avoiding passing German troops, they hid in trees near the village of Obereschenbach during the day. When night fell, they had moved off again, still heading west. Crossing a plowed field, they spotted searching German infantry and hugged the earth. Nearby, the Germans came upon other escapees from the task force hiding in a ditch. Congratulating themselves, the Germans hustled their prisoners away.

The Meltesen trio, remaining unseen, continued on, reaching a river. It was flowing too swiftly to cross, so they backtracked to the trees to hide overnight, only to find the place infested with Task Force Baum refugees. A dawn sweep by German troops the next day netted them all, including the Meltesen group. After joining more prisoners in a barn, they were marched back to the camp.

Another Schubin kriegie, Lieutenant Vic Kanners, had stayed with the task force after the departure of Colonel Goode's party and had helped transfer fuel to nine tanks and halftracks before the Hetzers opened fire. As the shells rained down, Kanners ran to an abandoned halftrack with a tanker, and they succeeded in getting its engine started. The pair had traveled no more than thirty feet in the halftrack when a 75 mm shell slammed into the back of it. The vehicle was kaput, but Kanners and the tanker, unhurt, took off into the trees together. Meeting up with three more tank crewmen, Kanners and his companion teamed up with them. Deciding to head northwest, the quintet walked through the trees all day, putting fifteen miles between themselves and the battleground.

Kanners' exhausted group slept in thick forest that night. In the morning, they crossed a small river, the Franconian Saale, in the vicinity of the village of Gräfendorf. The five men were soon walking along the road on the outskirts of the village, thinking about stealing something to eat. By this stage the tankers had ditched their helmets, and, heads down and hands in pockets, the party passed for foreign forced laborers when a German soldier bicycled by, ignoring them. But one of the young tankers couldn't resist the temptation to give the German the finger behind his back. A civilian close by spotted this and whistled a warning. A squad of German soldiers came trotting from Gräfendorf, and the game was up for Kanners and his four task force colleagues.

In the end, just one Task Force Baum member is known to have walked back to American lines in the wake of the operation—the

212 THE BIG BREAK

column's SPG commander, Sergeant Charles Graham. Six days after jumping out of his SPG and bolting into the trees on the Reussenberg with shells and bullets whizzing all around him, Graham was being chased along a road by German troops when a mortar barrage separated him from them. A little farther along, he walked into a skirmish line of US Army troops from the advancing 45th Division. But Graham wasn't safe yet.

Believing there couldn't possibly be any US troops in front of them, these GIs accused Graham of being a German in American uniform and wanted to shoot him. Eventually talking his way through, he was sent to a hospital behind the lines, where a captain informed him he was being charged with desertion. Graham exploded and demanded that Third Army HQ be contacted and advised that he was the only survivor from Task Force Baum.

Three days later, cleaned up and in a fresh uniform, Graham reported to General Hoge, and then to Lieutenant Colonel Abrams. Via Graham's report, General Patton learned that his son-in-law was in the POW camp hospital at Hammelburg, badly wounded. He also learned that, apart from Graham, the men of the task force he'd sent to rescue Johnny Waters and his Schubin colleagues, including his own aide Alexander Stiller, were now either dead or also POWs.

At war's end, the official US Army casualty figures for Task Force Baum would be nine killed in action, sixteen missing and believed killed, and thirty-two wounded. The identities and number of Schubin and Hammelburg kriegies killed and wounded during the operation were never recorded. At a conservative estimate, at least ten died in or as a result of the Höllrich ambush and the battle on the Reussenberg.

There were, however, several good news stories. As a result of Task Force Baum, two parties of Schubin kriegies and one group of Hammelburg POWs did escape to American lines. Three Schubin majors, Robert Christensen, George Williams, and Harry Rock, had been riding on Lieutenant Nutto's lead tank when it was ambushed at Höllrich. After being blown off the Sherman, the trio had thrown themselves over a stone wall and escaped overland. For seven days, they evaded capture by moving only in darkness, all the while heading steadily toward US forces. On the night of April 2–3, they reached advance elements of the 14th Armored Division and were promptly evacuated to a hospital in Paris.

Another Schubinite, Lieutenant Colonel James W. Lockett, formerly XO of the 112th Infantry, 28th Infantry Division, was riding on the second Sherman knocked out in the Höllrich ambush, right behind the Christensen group. He and two other kriegies blasted from the back of that second tank similarly escaped overland. Independent of the Christensen group, this trio also traveled at night and reached American forces at Aschaffenburg—as fate would have it, Task Force Baum's jumping-off point.

Within days, Lockett was aboard a USAAF aircraft, Stateside bound. One of his stopping points en route to New York City was the airbase at Gander, Newfoundland. There, as his aircraft refueled, Lockett was ushered into a mess for a mouthwatering dinner of roast beef. And who should already be sitting at the table but Christensen, Williams and Rock. It was a memorable reunion dinner for the Schubin boys.

Meanwhile, along with four other Hammelburg kriegies, First Lieutenant Thomas O. Morton of the 90th Infantry Division also escaped from the Nutto column after the ambush at Höllrich. The quintet had reached the Main River by their fourth night on the run. After crossing the river in a stolen boat, they pushed toward the sounds of gunfire, which indicated that advancing US forces were not far away. They proceeded to walk right into a German outpost and were recaptured and lodged in a jail at Karlstadt.

Almost immediately, Morton's group again escaped by outsmarting their war-weary guards. Heading overland toward Bamberg, they came upon advancing elements of the 45th Infantry Division and were welcomed back into friendly hands. Morton was ill by that stage and was admitted to a US military evacuation hospital, where he was diagnosed with hepatitis.

So Task Force Baum was not a total failure. It did result in some Schubin and Hammelburg kriegies escaping and reaching American lines, with most of them getting home before war's end. In the wake of the Moscow Trio and the Cory Trio, who were flown back to the United States in February, the two groups of Schubinites who escaped Hammelburg through the agency of Task Force Baum were the next Oflag 64 prisoners to reach the States. Ironically, apart from the Gruenberg and Cory trios, this Schubin group from Hammelburg beat home the more than 200 men who'd escaped from the Germans during the evacuation of Oflag 64 eight weeks earlier. They were still in Russian hands.

■ ■ ■

HAPLESS TASK FORCE commander Abe Baum was one of the American wounded taken to the hospital at Oflag XIII-B. Found at the roadside by German troops on March 28, he was conveyed back to the Hammelburg camp on a horse-drawn wagon and lodged in a hospital bed beside Johnny Waters. The Germans assumed that Major Stiller had led the task force, and this allowed camp medical staff to cover up Baum's true identity as well as the fact that he was Jewish. They claimed he'd been one of the kriegies with the column. Baum was to subsequently witness the fate of the wounded POWs at Hammelburg. And the fate of Johnny Waters.

20

FREEDOM SO CLOSE

As the first of several trains carrying kriegies from Hammelburg rattled east on the night of March 28, Jack Hemingway was one of thirty-six men in the same boxcar as SAO Colonel Goode. These boxcars were designed to take eight horses or forty men, so this one wasn't as crowded as some. But the last occupants had been four-legged, and the stink of horse manure stayed with them throughout the three-day journey.

Like most of the men in the rocking, rolling boxcar, Colonel Goode nodded off to sleep. After a time, a young lieutenant began to complain that there was no leadership or organization being displayed in the car. He didn't direct his complaints at the colonel, but it was obvious they were meant for him, and other officers in the group tried to get the lieutenant back in line. The raised voices woke Pop Goode, who spoke for himself.

"Lieutenant, you are absolutely right," said the colonel, fixing the lieutenant with his weary gaze. "I have been so depressed and exhausted I have failed in my duty. I am appointing you the quartering officer for this boxcar, and I will give you five minutes to come up with rules and plans to make this a military organization."[1]

All eyes turned to the lieutenant, who paled and went silent. Five minutes later, when the colonel asked him for his rules and plans, the lieutenant came up with several reasonable suggestions, which everybody agreed should be adopted. With the mood in the car elevated, several men asked Jack Hemingway to share stories about his famous father. Jack would have much preferred to talk about fly fishing, but in the end the men in the boxcar were entertained all the way to Nuremberg with a string of personal anecdotes about Ernest Hemingway by his son.[2]

■ ■ ■

ON APRIL 5, as the American advance pushed closer to Hammelburg, Oberst Richard Hoppe transferred his command from Lager Hammelburg to Camp Grafenwöhr. Camp commander General von Goeckel remained at Oflag XIII-B, still in command of a small guard watching over the Americans in the camp hospital.

That night, Abe Baum and the other Americans in the hospital heard the rumble of heavy guns firing in the distance. When the sun rose, the sound of gunfire was much closer. By the gate, German guards lowered the swastika flag, raising a white one in its place, and stacked their weapons. GIs who could get to hospital windows whooped with joy at the sight. Before long, American tanks crunched over the wire and into the camp. Hanging out hospital windows, Americans cheered. By midday, all resistance in Hammelburg had ended, and the POW camp was surrounded by US Army tanks. In the middle of the camp, General von Goeckel stood with his staff, waiting for a senior American officer to arrive so they could formally surrender.

At 1:00 p.m., an American armored car drove into the camp. Kriegies in the hospital saw a major emerge from it and speak briefly with Goeckel, who pointed to the hospital. The clean-shaven, smartly dressed major hurriedly set off in that direction. A heavily bandaged Abe Baum, meeting the major at the entrance to his ward, asked who had liberated the camp and was told it was the 14th Armored, 7th Army. The major identified himself as Charles Odom, chief surgeon, Third Army. He was General Patton's personal physician. And he was on a mission.

"Where's Colonel Waters?" the major asked.

Baum directed him to Johnny Waters' bed down the ward, and Major Odom hurried to Waters' side.

"Funny meeting you here, Charles," Waters said with a wry smile.[3]

After Odom gave Waters a thorough examination, he commended the doctors who had operated on him for doing a fine job. But, he said, he wanted to get Waters to a fully equipped and staffed facility without delay. Hurrying away, he spoke on the armored car's radio. Thirty minutes later, a pair of USAAF Piper Cub light reconnaissance aircraft appeared from the west and touched down on the Lager Hammelburg grass. Two of Odom's men gently placed Waters on a stretcher and carried him out to one of the two waiting Pipers. Odom informed Baum that Waters was being taken to the 34th US Army Evacuation Hospital at Gotha. The aircraft then took off, the first carrying Waters, the second with Odom aboard.

In the ward, where Waters had been until just minutes before, lay Private Robert Zawada, who was minus a leg. A Task Force Baum platoon radio operator, he was the GI whom Schubin kriegie Bob Thompson had seen lose his limb in the short, sharp battle on the Reussenberg the previous week. Looking at Baum, Zawada asked what the brass had against men with one leg. Why leave him behind and take Johnny Waters? Baum had no answer. He had also been left behind. He was bitter, and so were other Americans in the hospital.[4]

Most would be left there in the now liberated POW camp for another three days before being evacuated. But Baum was not planning to hang around. Despite his wounds, he was determined to get to General Patton and find out whether his mission had truly been all about liberating Johnny Waters. Within days, Baum hitchhiked to Gotha and the 34th Evac Hospital.

21

LIBERATION

AFTER THE FIRST GROUP OF HAMMELBURG EVACUEES WAS TRANS-
ported by rail via Nuremberg, Pop Goode led them into Stalag VII-A
at Moosburg in Bavaria at the beginning of April. This massive
camp was overflowing with as many as 100,000 Allied POWs, at least
30,000 of them American. When his group marched through the
camp gate, Goode was still toting the bagpipes he'd carried all the
way from Schubin over the past harrowing weeks. In the last few
days of the journey to Moosburg, Goode had come across a Scottish
piper in a party of British enlisted men who were also being sent to
Moosburg, and the Scot had given him a few lessons.

The USAAF's Colonel Bub Clark, the original North Compound
Big S in the Great Escape and later Big X in Sagan's South Compound, had led an American air force contingent from Stalag Luft 3
that had reached Moosburg several days ahead of Goode's group,
and he was among the first to greet Goode. When Clark commented
that he was surprised that he had brought bagpipes all the way from
Schubin, Goode smiled and assured him that they played a very

pretty tune. Not even Clark was let into the secret that the bagpipes contained an illicit radio receiver.

Over the weeks until April 20, the other four rail groups and four marching groups would be brought to Moosburg until 1,650 American POWs, including Goode's remaining Schubinites and Task Force Baum captives, had been transferred from Hammelburg.

■ ■ ■

UPON REACHING THE US Army's 34th Evacuation Hospital at Gotha, Abe Baum was checked out by the doctors, who found that, although his wounds were healing well, he was still very weak. Consigned to a two-bed ward at the hospital, Baum was soon visited by two officers from G-2, who debriefed him on the task force's operation and then told him that General Patton had classified Task Force Baum "top secret." Baum was instructed not to talk to anyone about it.[1]

Several days later, General Patton himself, accompanied by two aides, visited Johnny Waters in the hospital. After speaking privately with Waters, Patton presented him with the Distinguished Service Cross (DSC) for action in North Africa prior to his capture. Lying in a bed in a ward not far from Johnny Waters when General Patton visited was another kriegie. As chance would have it, this was former Hammelburg inmate Lieutenant Thomas Morton, who'd escaped the Nutto column following the Höllrich ambush and walked back to US lines.

Reaching out a hand to General Patton as he passed, Morton asked weakly how Colonel Waters was doing.

Patton said his son-in-law's wound was nothing, adding, "I had much the same in the last war."

Morton then said, "Thanks, General, for setting up the liberation."

Patton, knowing that the lieutenant was talking about Task Force Baum, responded dismissively, "It was a feint to the east, son, while the main force was turning to the north and then east for the next push."[2]

Patton would continue to maintain this line, but Abe Baum and a lot of others would think differently. A few days later, Patton came to visit Baum himself. As the captain lay in his bed, the general also presented him with the DSC. In Baum's case, it was for leading Task Force Baum. Baum would also soon be promoted to major, just like Eggemann, the German responsible for ending his mission.

⬛ ⬛ ⬛

EARLY ON THE morning of April 22, Russian tanks of the Soviet Fourth Tank Army reached the sprawling POW camp at Luckenwalde. That day, Schubin kriegie Thornton Sigler devoted a whole page in his diary to a single word: FREEDOM. His celebration proved premature. The Schubinites at Luckenwalde discovered that German guards were replaced by Russian guards. The NKVD would not let the Americans leave the camp.

By May 5, inveterate Schubin escaper Jack Van Vliet had had his fill of captivity. Sneaking by the Russian sentries at the Luckenwalde camp, he headed off on a stolen bicycle.[3] He would reach US forces at Duben, on the Mulde River. V.V.'s last break would start a flood of escapes from Luckenwalde by Schubinites, also aiming to link up with US forces. For those who remained behind at Luckenwalde under Russian guard, repatriation would not come until June.

⬛ ⬛ ⬛

ON APRIL 23, at Camp Grafenwöhr, Oberst Hoppe, formerly commander of the Lager Hammelburg training area, knew that the end of the war was only a matter of weeks away. He was also aware that Walter Eggemann's damning report of his conduct during Task Force Baum's Hammelburg raid had ruined his military reputation.

There was even the possibility that Hoppe would be executed as a warning to other Wehrmacht officers in these dark dying days of the Third Reich, with his lack of fortitude held up, in comparison to Eggemann's fanatical determination, to exemplify how not to react in the defense of the Fatherland. At 11:30 that the night, in his quarters, Hoppe took his pistol from its holster, put it to his head and shot and killed himself.

The war would end before Major Eggemann could be awarded his new medal for stopping Task Force Baum.

■ ■ ■

FOR THE SCHUBINITES and tens of thousands of other Allied POWs at Moosburg, liberation came through the agency of the US 14th Armored Division, on April 29. That same afternoon, at 2:30, General Patton himself drove into the camp in a jeep. His aide, Major Stiller, who had been captured at the Reussenberg and became a POW alongside the Schubinites, was located by Patton's aides, and he rejoined the general before Patton spoke to American POWs gathered outside the camp kitchens.

Clarence Meltesen was in that gathering. He would remember Patton spouting a brief speech that lacked any warmth. Meltesen wondered whether the general even realized he was talking to Americans as he declared he was going to get POWs to their home countries as soon as possible and urged them to stay in the camp for the time being.[4]

The Schubinites at Moosburg were eventually sent to Camp Lucky Strike outside Le Havre in France, from where they would be repatriated by sea to the United States. Apart from a small number remaining in US Army hospitals in France and Germany, the last Schubinites finally arrived home on America's shores in July 1945.

WELCOME HOME, KRIEGIE

LIEUTENANT BROOKS KLEBER SAT IN A TAXI ACROSS THE STREET from his uncle's home in Trenton, New Jersey. As the motor ticked over and his hand rested on the door handle, Kleber looked across the street to the house that held so many prewar memories for him and hesitated.

Compared to some of his fellow kriegies, Kleber hadn't spent long in captivity. Captured in June 1944, he'd arrived at Oflag 64 with Pop Goode that October. He'd marched with Goode all the way to Hammelburg. He'd gone through the high hopes and shattered expectations of the failed Task Force Baum rescue bid. He'd marched again with Colonel Goode, this time to Moosburg. And he'd sat in Camp Lucky Strike in France with 300,000 other RAMPs waiting to be sent home. He'd crossed the Atlantic back to the United States aboard the first convoy to sail without an escort since the war began. He'd taken a taxi from Fort Dix to his uncle's door.

But, like many fellow soldiers, Kleber had been damaged by the war. Anxiety was his new comrade in arms. All the time his troopship, *Mariposa*, had been bucking across the gray Atlantic, Kleber had been watching for torpedo tracks as he worried that some U-boat commander who had yet to surrender might want to sink one last ship for the Führer. Ever since his liberation from German custody, whenever he saw a tethered dog, Kleber wondered what sort of life it led. Until recently, Kleber had led the life of a tethered dog. When he saw people who didn't have enough to eat, he worried about them. He would never forget his own starvation diet in captivity.

To Kleber, the experience of liberation, and of freedom, was proving just as traumatic as his capture and dehumanization at the hands of the Germans. All Kleber had to do to reclaim his old life was cross that street to his uncle's house. A street that seemed as wide as the ocean. Gathering all his strength, Brooks Kleber opened the taxi door, stepped out, and put one foot in front of another.

"The crossing of that street was my last psychological obstacle," Kleber would later say. "I had made it home."[1]

Other kriegies also had memorable homecomings. Soon after freed POW Captain William D. Robbins arrived back in the States, he made a point of telephoning a colonel whose son had not made it back. Robbins had been clambering into a halftrack on the Reussenberg on the morning of March 28 when the Hetzers opened fire. Like many others, Robbins had fled into the woods when the German assault began, only to be caught by Eggemann's infantry sweep following the fusillade. Robbins had spent the night as a prisoner in the barn at Höllrich, after which Hauptmann Gehrig's cadets had marched him back to the Reussenberg to take charge of the burial detail for American dead from the battle.

One of the kriegies Robbins had buried that morning was the colonel's son. Robbins wanted to tell the colonel the circumstances of his boy's captivity, about his brave escape attempt, and about his death. But the colonel didn't want to know. To the colonel, capture by the enemy was a disgrace. He hung up on Robbins.

Private Jonel C. Hill, who'd been in the Oflag 64 hospital at the time of the camp's January evacuation, had survived the journeys to Rembertów in February and to Odessa in March. At Odessa he'd had his first bath in months. Via Istanbul and Port Said, Jones had sailed with fellow Schubinites to Naples and the welcoming arms of the US Army. In April, he'd arrived back in the United States, landing at Boston. When he came ashore, reporters were everywhere, trying to get stories from this first shipload of returned American POWs. But the kriegies had been warned not to talk about their experiences, a warning reiterated by US Military Intelligence's CPM section when it debriefed Jones at Fort Devens outside Boston.

Granted a ninety-day furlough, Jones first went home to Wyoming. There, the serenity of the plains overwhelmed him, bringing him to tears. After reuniting with his family, Jones visited a beautiful girl, his future bride. He'd brought home a photo of her that he'd been carrying when he arrived at Schubin. The photo bore a German stamp on the back: "Inspected, Oflag 64." From there he went to Oregon to visit family and then on to San Francisco. In the City by the Bay, relatives took Jones to the historic Mark Hopkins Hotel on Nob Hill and up to Top of the Mark, the hotel's penthouse bar and restaurant, which boasted a 360-degree view of the city. Jones was resplendent in a US Army uniform he'd had custom-made in Naples, complete with an Eisenhower jacket. He'd polished his boots so hard he could see his face in them.

Excitedly, Jones and his family members sat down by the window and drank in the stunning San Francisco vistas. A waiter came by and took their drinks order. And then the manager came over and introduced himself. This was some homecoming for a soldier, thought Jones, and when the manager asked him how old he was, the young man proudly volunteered that he was nineteen.

"Then I'm going to have to ask you all to leave," said the manager.[2]

Jones was old enough to have fought and died for his country. But he was two years shy of the legal drinking age. Welcome home, kriegie.

■ ■ ■

WHEN LIEUTENANT COLONEL Jack Van Vliet told G-2 in Germany about the Katyn Massacre, he was quickly flown home to the United

States, where he was debriefed at the Pentagon in Washington by Major General Clayton Bissell, to whom he handed over the photographs the Germans had given him at Katyn in 1943. Van Vliet was ordered by the general to never speak about what he had seen and heard. For many years, the official US government line on the Katyn Massacre mirrored that of the Soviets, that it had been a Nazi war crime. Only after Poland regained democratic government in the 1990s would the truth come out and Van Vliet's suspicions be upheld: the massacre had indeed been carried out by the Soviets.

Van Vliet was one of a number of Schubin kriegies who remained in the US military after World War II, with many serving through the Korean War and the Cold War. Brooks Kleber was another. When stationed at Fort Monroe, Virginia, Kleber was frequently assigned to escort visiting generals of the West German army around the base.

"I was a guest of your government during World War II," Kleber would tell the German generals. This would generate an awkward silence before Kleber broke into a grin, and they would all laugh. Kleber held no bitterness toward the Germans. To his mind, his time in POW camps had been a lesson in human values.[3]

Many Schubin kriegies went on to achieve high US Army rank and responsibility. Jerry "Dagger" Sage served as a special forces colonel until his retirement in 1972. Gentleman Jim Alger, head of Oflag 64's escape committee, retired in 1970 with the rank of lieutenant general. Johnny Waters became commandant of cadets at the US Military Academy, West Point, and, in the 1960s, US Army commander in the Pacific; he also retired as a lieutenant general. Task Force Baum was a sore point with Waters, and he steadfastly held to the line that Patton's raid had been designed to rescue all Schubin kriegies at Hammelburg, not just him.

Equally, Abe Baum never varied from the opposite view. He went into the clothing business following the war, and was deprived of the opportunity of wringing an admission from General Patton that Task Force Baum was all about rescuing Johnny Waters when Patton died after a road accident in Germany in December 1945. Not long before his death, Patton expressed a single regret about Task Force

Baum. In memoirs serialized by the *Saturday Evening Post* in 1945, he said he'd made a mistake in not sending a 3,000-man combat command to liberate Oflag XIII-B instead of a 300-man task force.

After Jack Hemingway was freed at Moosburg, he made his way to Paris, where he celebrated VE Day on May 8, 1945. Returning to the United States shortly afterward, he traveled on to Cuba to reunite with his father and younger half-brothers, who were shocked by what they saw—Jack had lost seventy pounds in captivity. After the war, Jack devoted himself to his first love, fishing, and became a noted Idaho conservationist. He spent the latter part of his life preserving his father's literary legacy.

Craig Campbell ended up being sent to Odessa by rail, where he rejoined fellow Schubinites. As the first RAMPs were being shipped out, both Campbell and escaper Bob Crandall, who'd reached Odessa by a roundabout route under NKVD supervision, succeeded in having themselves assigned to the troop transport *Duke of Bedford*, which was carrying mostly British personnel and heading for Western Europe when it sailed on March 15.

Both Campbell and Crandall disembarked at the French Mediterranean port of Marseilles, with Crandall determined to return to his unit and Campbell planning to make his way back to General Eisenhower's HQ to report for duty. Campbell and Eisenhower had an emotional reunion before the general put the lieutenant aboard an aircraft bound for the United States. Mamie Eisenhower would write to Campbell's mother from Washington, DC, on April 25 to say that Craig had passed through the capital that morning on his way home. "I know you are a happy mama today," said Mrs. Eisenhower.[4] Following VE Day, Campbell returned to Europe to resume duty as Eisenhower's ADC, but by the end of 1945 he had left the military.

Ed Ward didn't remain in the army long after the war, either. In February 1945, two days after the Moscow Trio had set off from Schubin, Ward had done the same, walking in a group of thirteen kriegies to Hohensalza, then taking a train to Kutno. From there, Ward had hitched rides to Warsaw, then to Lublin, where he'd fallen into NKVD custody. He'd arrived in Odessa on February 28 and was astonished to find unblinking female Russian attendants in charge of the men's shower room. On March 7, he, like the vast majority of Schubin escapees, sailed from Odessa aboard the British troopship *Moreton Bay*, which took them to Naples. From there, Ward sailed to Boston aboard the *Mariposa* and on April 9 entered Camp Miles Standish in Massachusetts for ten days of quarantine and debriefing by G-2. Ward left the army that September.

Along with Ward, Kleber, Jones, Bill Shular, Dale Barton, Mays Anderson, Alfred Nelson, Tom Riggs and hundreds of other escaped Schubin kriegies, H. Randolph "Boomer" Holder and his escape partner, George Durgin, sailed from Odessa aboard the *Moreton Bay*. In Naples, Holder fell ill and was hospitalized. He missed the boat when Durgin and most of the other escaped kriegies sailed for the United States at the end of March. Once he recovered, Holder was flown home by the USAAF via Casablanca and Bermuda.

Holder landed at New York City, arriving back in the United States at much the same time as Durgin and the others. It would be another forty-five years before Holder and Durgin saw each other again. Following the war, Holder returned to his first love, radio. By midlife, he owned two radio stations in Athens, in northeast Georgia, for many years doing the breakfast session at one station. In his trademark deep voice, no matter what the weather, Boomer would always start his shift with, "It's a lovely day to be in Athens."[5]

After Frank Diggs got home he never forgot the Dudziak family, who had helped him and Nelson Tacy to escape in Poland. Following the war, Diggs corresponded regularly with the Dudziaks. When he learned that their one and only horse had died, he bought a horse in the United States and shipped it to them. He visited the family in the 1970s.

Not a few kriegies struggled with their wartime memories. Escapee Spud Murphy was among those who committed suicide. Mays Anderson feared a 1985 visit to Schubin would bring back postwar nightmares. Instead, it laid ghosts to rest. Many would never talk about their kriegie experiences. Alfred Nelson only opened up to his family about his Schubin break when he was in his eighties. Some, like Bill Ash, the first American to escape from Schubin, purged themselves of bad memories by writing successful books about their kriegie experiences.

Ash, who was liberated by British troops, settled in London after the war. He reckoned that one of the best things about becoming an author was all the free food at the book's launch, which contrasted so vividly with the bread and water diet he'd experienced on numerous trips to the Cooler—an experience that contributed to the book's creation. Clarence Meltesen, Boomer Holder, Reid Ellsworth, Frank Diggs, Herb Garris, an increasingly optimistic Billy Bingham and a number of other Schubinites also wrote books about their experiences. While they never became big sellers like Ash's book, those works have provided vital resource material for World War II historians.

SAO Paul "Pop" Goode, the Schubin shepherd who cared for his men through months of imprisonment and grueling marching, remained in the US Army for another seven years until he retired, disabled, in 1952. He passed away in 1959 at the age of sixty-seven. "He was a marvelous individual," said Brooks Kleber. "One of the most valiant men I have ever met."[6]

The other player in this story, the town of Schubin, today's Szubin, is even more of a sleepy backwater than it was in the 1940s. The train does not even run there anymore. Immediately after the war, seeming normality returned to the town just as a number of former expelled Polish residents returned. Józef Kapsa came back and reclaimed his home and print shop on Paderewski Street. He ran the printing business successfully again until Poland came under Communist control, after which it was taken over by the state in 1949, without compensation. Kapsa and his son were employed by the Communists to operate their own print shop for the government until it closed in 1970.

The print shop's wartime owner, German printer Willi Kricks, also survived the war. He and his wife rented a print shop in Altmark before fleeing East Germany's Communist regime in 1950 and settling at Worms, West Germany. There, Kricks established his own printing business. His son, and later his grandson, ran it after his death in 1988. A decade ago, Willi Kricks' German granddaughter knocked on the Kapsa family's door in Szubin. She asked to be shown the print-ery run by her grandparents during the war. Today, the Kapsa print shop building is used as a recording studio by Józef Kapsa's great-grandsons.

A well-tended gravestone stands at Szubin commemorating fifty-nine Red Army soldiers, although only twelve are named. It records that they were killed in the liberation from the Nazis of Szubin and surrounding areas, most during February 1945. Local Poles well knew that the Wehrmacht had abandoned the town without a fight that January, and it has been suggested that, in reality, not a few of these deceased Russians passed out after drinking too much vodka, expiring from the combined effects of excess alcohol and exposure to the winter cold.

Brave Stefania Maludzińska resettled in the town of Toruń, east of Szubin, where she befriended Kazimierz Rakoczy, commandant of the local Citizen's Militia. In 1946 the British government presented Stefania with a certificate of commendation in recognition of her efforts to help POWs escape. This attracted the interest of Poland's Communist Secret Political Police, who arrested Stefania for links with a foreign government. She was released after spending two weeks behind bars. Her friend Commandant Rakoczy was fired from his militia post and sent to work in a coal mine for eighteen months. Both subsequently had trouble finding work. Thrown together by their shared adversity, the couple married.

Stefania Rakoczy passed away in 2014. She was interviewed by Polish radio when American former inmates of Oflag 64 visited the site in the 1970s. Those visitors found key parts of the camp, including the White House, hospital, chapel and commandant's house, still in use. Following the war, the site again housed a reform school. Alfons Jachalski resumed teaching there and was the school's principal from 1968 to 1974. The institution continues today as the MOAS, the Home and School for At-Risk Youth, and contains a scale model of the POW camp.

After making pilgrimages to Szubin, several former kriegies reported that nightmares about the war left them for good. The sight of the quiet little town, and the former camp site now minus its barbed wire fences and goon boxes, and with children playing where they'd lined up for Appell twice a day, made the whole idea of war, and prisoner-of-war camps, seem ridiculous. Which it is.

Visits back to Oflag 64 made other Americans remember the desperation and determination that had driven them to escape the Nazis, in the camp and on the forced march from Schubin. No German or Russian records exist covering that last big break. According to Pop Goode's figures, 241 American officers and enlisted men escaped from the column as it was marched away from Schubin.[7] Combined with the six men who hid in the camp when the column moved out, escapees totaled 247. To that number can be added several Schubin men, including Craig Campbell, who bolted east from Schokken at the same time. At 250-plus, this represents by far the single largest recorded Allied escape of World War II. The largest overall POW escape was by Japanese prisoners from a camp at Cowra in Australia in August 1944, in which 234 POWs died and 334 were recaptured.

It is impossible to say with accuracy whether every single one of the Schubin escapees made it home. One or two may have died, unrecorded, in hospitals in Poland or in confrontations with Russian troops, to be listed among the "missing." But it is certain that almost all the escapees made home runs, making the Schubin break by far the most successful mass escape of the war, leaving the Great Escape well in the shade. All because of American stubbornness, pluck, and grit. And a common irrepressible desire to be free.

NOTES

CHAPTER 1: THE FIRST AMERICAN TO ESCAPE FROM SCHUBIN

1. The number of toilets, 36, was given by Smith in *Wings Day*.
2. Ash, *Under the Wire*.
3. Williams, *The Tunnel*.
4. Kee, *A Crowd Is Not Company*.
5. Ash.
6. Ibid.

CHAPTER 2: ON THE LOOSE

1. Williams, *The Tunnel*.
2. Ibid.
3. "From USA to Szubin," Polskie Radio.
4. Ash, *Under the Wire*.
5. Ibid.
6. Kee, *A Crowd Is Not Company*.
7. Great Escaper "Jimmy" James, in *Moonless Night*, named the man as George Laurence "Happy" Hull, another Great Escaper. Ash, however, was intimately involved in the Asselin break and his identification of Gericke is more likely to be accurate. Smith, in *Wings Day*, also identified him as Gericke.
8. Williams, *The Tunnel*.

9. Ibid.
10. Ibid.
11. Ash.

CHAPTER 3: THE YANKS MOVE IN

1. *Post Oflag 64 Item*, December 1994.
2. Holder, *Escape to Russia*.
3. General Eisenhower to Mr. and Mrs. J. B. Campbell, April 12, 1943.
4. Sage, *Sage*.
5. *The Patton Saber*, Winter 2011.
6. Holder.
7. The Weasel's exact identity is unclear, although, in his G-2 debriefing, Colonel Goode recalled an Unteroffizier Knorr as an unpleasant guard who'd reputedly shot British prisoners in the camp's Oflag XXI-B days and treated Oflag 64 prisoners badly.
8. Sage.

CHAPTER 4: UNDER, OVER OR THROUGH THE WIRE

1. Deane, *The Strange Alliance*.
2. Ibid.
3. Ibid.
4. Ibid.
5. Prior to the war, a Jewish cemetery had existed west of the camp. Several Jews were executed there after the Nazis took control in 1939. Others were made to dig up their cemetery before being deported to concentration camps.
6. Diggs, *Americans behind the Barbed Wire*.
7. Between 1824 and 1878 the region was no longer Prussian. It came under Prussian control again, with German the official language, between 1878 and 1920. In World War I reparations it became part of the Second Polish Republic—until the Nazi invasion.
8. Diggs.
9. Holder, *Escape to Russia*.
10. *Fort Worth Star-Telegram*, May 1971.
11. Holder.
12. Van Vliet, "Escape Artists," *World War II Times*. Van Vliet also said that their subsequent sentence was two weeks, not ten days, as some other sources claim.
13. Meltesen, *Roads to Liberation from Oflag 64*.
14. Holder.
15. Ibid.

CHAPTER 5: DEATH SENTENCES

1. Holder, *Escape to Russia.*
2. Ibid.
3. "From USA to Szubin," Polskie Radio.
4. Ed Ward, Jr., to the author, June 24, 2015.
5. Testimony of Maurice Lampe, Nuremberg War Trials, January 25, 1946: Gilbert, Conot and Overy, *Justice at Nuremberg.*
6. American Prisoners of War in Germany, Oflag 64.
7. Fisher, "Behind the Barbed Wire," Oflag 64 Association website.
8. Hall, "*Living Hell.*"
9. *Post Oflag 64 Item*, December 1994.

CHAPTER 6: THE RUSSIANS ARE COMING

1. "Repatriates from Germany," *Prisoners of War Bulletin*, March 1945.
2. Sage, *Sage.*
3. Ibid.
4. Hill, "A Personal Reminiscence."

CHAPTER 7: THE BIG BREAK, DAY ONE

1. Figures from a survey appearing in *Oflag 64 Item*, January 1945.
2. WWII POW journal of Thornton V. Sigler.
3. Ibid.
4. Meltesen, *Roads to Liberation from Oflag 64.*
5. *Port Charlotte Sun*, February 2003.
6. *Galveston Daily News*, February 23, 1945.
7. Sage, *Sage.*
8. The total of ninety-one men remaining in the hospital on January 21 was given by war correspondent Wright Bryan, who was one of them. Captain Gruenberg, when debriefed by General Deane on February 17, estimated that 200 had congregated at Oflag 64's hospital by the time he passed back through Schubin in late January.
9. Sigler.

CHAPTER 8: GAME ON

1. *Atlanta Journal*, February 22, 1945.
2. "From USA to Szubin," Polskie Radio.
3. Holder, *Escape to Russia.*
4. *Galveston Daily News*, February 23, 1945.
5. Sage, *Sage.*

6. Ibid.
7. Mary Shular Hopper to the author, May 28, 2015. Meltesen gives a different version of the first stages of Shular's escape in *Roads to Liberation from
Oflag 64.*
8. Hill, "A Personal Reminiscence."
9. *Atlanta Journal*, February 22, 1945.
10. Holder.
11. Diggs, *Americans behind the Barbed Wire.*

CHAPTER 9: MEETING THE RUSSKIES

1. *Galveston Daily News*, February 23, 1945.
2. Sage, *Sage.*
3. *Galveston Daily News*, February 23, 1945.
4. Ibid.
5. Holder, *Escape to Russia.*
6. Diggs, *Americans behind the Barbed Wire.*
7. The others were Jim Bancker, Gaither Perry, Carlos Burrows, Frank Tripp
and Bill Burghardt.
8. Ellsworth, *The Reid F. Ellsworth Story.*
9. Ibid.
10. Meltesen, in *Roads to Liberation from Oflag 64*, tells a slightly different story,
imparted to him by Munson, in which Nelson and Munson remained together until after crossing the canal and meeting Russian troops. Nelson
told his story to his daughter Linda Krueger, who passed it on to the author, May 1, 2015.
11. Linda Krueger to the author, May 1, 2015.

CHAPTER 10: MOSCOW OR BUST

1. Sage, *Sage.*
2. Ibid.
3. Holder, *Escape to Russia.*
4. Diggs (in *Americans behind the Barbed Wire*) and Holder gave slightly different versions of the same event.
5. Sage.

CHAPTER 11: THE FIRST SCHUBIN ESCAPEE HOME RUNS

1. *Galveston Daily News*, February 20, 1945.
2. Ibid.
3. Deane, *The Strange Alliance.*
4. *Salt Lake Tribune*, February 20, 1945.

5. *Lethbridge Herald*, February 20, 1945.
6. Cory believed that his trio beat the Moscow Trio back to the United States.

CHAPTER 12: KRIEGIES ON THE RUN

1. Sage, *Sage*.
2. Bingham, *Memoirs of World War II*.
3. Ibid.

CHAPTER 13: THE HAMMELBURG SCHUBINITES

1. These are Goode's figures, given to US Military Intelligence during the debriefing following his liberation.

CHAPTER 14: PATTON WANTS THEM LIBERATED

1. Deane, *The Strange Alliance*.
2. Baron, Baum and Goldhurst, *Raid!*
3. *Los Angeles Times*, March 23, 2013.
4. Baron, Baum and Goldhurst.
5. The Weasel was not mentioned by Baron, Baum and Goldhurst, but Oberst Hoppe, in his March 29 report to the Wehrmacht's 7th Army HQ, lists it among Task Force Baum armored vehicles captured or destroyed on March 27–28. The presence of the Weasel in the column was confirmed by Schubin kriegie and later military historian Brooks Kleber, who was on the Reussenberg, in "Trauma of Capture," *Military History*.
6. Baron, Baum and Goldhurst put the number of men in the task force at 294. Other authoritative accounts give a total of 312 men.
7. Baron, Baum and Goldhurst.

CHAPTER 15: FIGHTING THROUGH TO HAMMELBURG

1. Baron, Baum and Goldhurst (in *Raid!*) state that the tank destroyers faced by Task Force Baum were Ferdinands, armed with 88 mm guns. German records show that Hetzers were used in the Hammelburg actions. Germany ceased production of Ferdinands in 1943, remodeling the few remaining vehicles and renaming them "Elefants." The latter name was appropriate: they were 60-ton monsters. Baron, Baum and Goldhurst also state that Ferdinands were built on the chassis of Panther tanks, which was incorrect. Not only were Ferdinands no longer in existence in 1945, all ninety-one Ferdinand/ Elefants ever built were employed on the Eastern Front, in Italy and in Normandy. In contrast, close to 3,000 Hetzers were built. In 2003, Abe Baum revisited Hammelburg, where he was shown a Hetzer in a local museum,

and German military historians explained to him that it was Hetzers he'd faced in 1945.
2. Baron, Baum and Goldhurst.
3. Peter Domes, Task Force Baum website.
4. Ibid.
5. Ibid.
6. Ibid.

CHAPTER 16: THE BATTLE FOR THE CAMP

1. Debriefing of Colonel Paul R. Goode, SAO at Oflag 64 and Oflag XIII-B.
2. Baron, Baum and Goldhurst, *Raid!*
3. Goode; Baron, Baum and Goldhurst.
4. A US War Department Military Intelligence Service report of November 1, 1945, stated that this soldier was a member of the SS. However, no SS troops are known to have been at Hammelburg at this time. He had to have been one of Kammerle's signalers.
5. Baron, Baum and Goldhurst.
6. Ibid.

CHAPTER 17: BUSTING OUT

1. *Los Angeles Times*, March 23, 2013.
2. Baron, Baum and Goldhurst, *Raid!*
3. Debriefing of Colonel Paul R. Goode, SAO at Oflag 64 and Oflag XIII-B.
4. Baron, Baum and Goldhurst.
5. Ibid.
6. Meltesen, *Roads to Liberation from Oflag 64.*

CHAPTER 18: ONE HELLUVA NIGHT

1. Baron, Baum and Goldhurst, *Raid!*
2. Debriefing of Colonel Paul R. Goode, SAO at Oflag 64 and Oflag XIII-B.
3. Ibid.
4. Baron, Baum and Goldhurst; Goode debriefing; and Meltesen, *Roads to Liberation from Oflag 64.*
5. Domes, Task Force Baum website.
6. Ibid.

CHAPTER 19: BLOOD AND FIRE ON THE REUSSENBERG

1. Meltesen, *Roads to Liberation from Oflag 64.*
2. "Trauma of Capture," *Military History.*

3. Debriefing of Colonel Paul R. Goode, SAO at Oflag 64 and Oflag XIII-B.
4. Baron, Baum and Goldhurst, *Raid!*
5. Domes, Task Force Baum website.
6. Ibid.
7. Ibid.
8. Baron, Baum and Goldhurst.

CHAPTER 20: FREEDOM SO CLOSE

1. Meltesen, *Roads to Liberation from Oflag 64.*
2. Ibid.
3. Baron, Baum and Goldhurst, *Raid!*
4. Ibid.

CHAPTER 21: LIBERATION

1. Baron, Baum and Goldhurst, *Raid!*
2. Meltesen, *Roads to Liberation from Oflag 64.*
3. Ibid.
4. Ibid.

CHAPTER 22: WELCOME HOME, KRIEGIE

1. "Trauma of Capture," *Military History.*
2. Hill, "A Personal Reminiscence."
3. "Trauma of Capture."
4. Mamie Eisenhower to Mrs. J. B. Campbell, April 25, 1945.
5. "Remembering NE Ga's Best Known Voice," *Madison County Journal*, May 8, 2002.
6. "Trauma of Capture."
7. Debriefing of Colonel Paul R. Goode, SAO at Oflag 64 and Oflag XIII-B.

BIBLIOGRAPHY

BOOKS

Ash, W., with Brendan Foley. *Under the Wire: The Wartime Memoir of a Spitfire Pilot, Legendary Escape Artist, and "Cooler King."* London: Bantam, 2005.

Baron, Richard, Abe Baum, and Richard Goldhurst. *Raid! The Untold Story of Patton's Secret Mission.* New York: Putnam, 1981.

Bingham, Billy. *Memoirs of World War II.* Manchester, KY: Possum Trot University Press, 1995.

Brickhill, Paul. *Escape or Die: Authentic Stories of the RAF Escaping Society.* London: Evans Brothers, 1952.

Brickhill, Paul. *The Great Escape.* New York: W. W. Norton, 1950.

Brickhill, Paul. *The Great Escape.* Movie tie-in edition. Greenwich, CT: Fawcett, 1963.

Brickhill, Paul. *Reach for the Sky: The Story of Douglas Bader D.S.O., D.F.C.* London: Collins, 1954.

Brickhill, Paul, and Allan Michie. "Tunnel to Freedom." In *Secrets and Stories of the War.* London: Reader's Digest Association, 1963.

Brickhill, Paul, and Conrad Norton. *Escape to Danger.* London: Faber and Faber, 1946.

Calnan, Thomas D. *Free as a Running Fox.* New York: Dial Press, 1970.

Carroll, Tim. *The Dodger: The Extraordinary Story of Churchill's Cousin and the Great Escape.* Edinburgh: Mainstream, 2012.

Dando-Collins, Stephen. *The Hero Maker: A Biography of Paul Brickhill*. Sydney: Random House, 2016.

Deane, John R. *The Strange Alliance*. New York: Viking, 1947.

Diggs, J. Frank. *Americans behind the Barbed Wire*. New York: iBooks, 2003.

Diggs, J. Frank. *The Welcome Swede*. New York: Vantage Press, 1988.

Edy, Don. *Goon in the Block*. London, Ontario: Edy, 1961.

Ellsworth, Reid F. *The Reid F. Ellsworth Story: An Account of War and Divine Interposition*. Phoenix: Ellsworth, 1997.

Ferguson, Clarence. *Kriegsgefangener 3074: Prisoner of War*. Waco, TX: Ferguson, 1983.

Gamon, Victor. *Not All Glory: True Accounts of RAF Airmen Taken Prisoner in Europe, 1939–1945*. London: Arms and Armour Press, 1996.

Garris, Herbert L. *A Grand Tour of Russia to Odessa, Winter 1945*. Pinehurst, NC: Village Printers, 1985.

Gilbert, Gustave M., Robert E. Conot, and Robert Overy. *Justice at Nuremberg*. Norwalk, CT: Easton Press, 2006.

Harsh, George. *Lonesome Road*. New York: W. W. Norton, 1971.

Holder, H. Randolph. *Escape to Russia*. Athens, GA: Iberian, 1994.

James, Albert B. *Moonless Night: One Man's Struggle for Freedom 1940–1945*. Barnsley, UK: Pen and Sword, 2006.

Jason, Sonya N. *Maria Gulovich: OSS Heroine of World War II*. Jefferson, NC: McFarland, 2009.

Kee, Robert. *A Crowd Is Not Company*. London: J. Cape, 1982.

Lovell, Glenn. *Escape Artist: The Life and Films of John Sturges*. Madison: University of Wisconsin Press, 2008.

Mayer, S. L., and Masam Tokoi, eds. *Der Adler, The Luftwaffe Magazine*. London: Arms and Armour Press, 1977.

Meltesen, Clarence R. *Roads to Liberation from Oflag 64*. 3rd ed. San Francisco: Oflag 64 Press, 2003.

Pearson, Simon. *The Great Escaper: The Life and Death of Roger Bushell*. London: Hodder & Stoughton, 2014.

Rubin, Steven Jay. *Combat Films: American Realism, 1945–2010*. 2nd ed. Jefferson, NC: McFarland, 2011.

Sage, Jerry. *Sage*. Wayne, PA: Miles Standish Press, 1985.

Smith, Graham, ed. *Military Small Arms*. London: Salamander, 1994.

Smith, Sydney. *Wings Day: The Man Who Led the RAF's Epic Battle in German Captivity*. London: Collins, 1968.

Stanley, Peter. *Commando to Colditz*. Sydney: Pier 9, 2009.

Taylor, James, and Warren Shaw. *A Dictionary of the Third Reich*. London: Grafton, 1988.

Turner, John Frayn. *Douglas Bader: A Biography of the Legendary World War II Fighter Pilot.* Shrewsbury, UK: Airlife, 1995.

Vance, Jonathan Franklin William. *A Gallant Company: The Men of the Great Escape.* New York: iBooks, 2003.

Walters, Guy. *The Real Great Escape.* London: Bantam, 2013.

Walton, Marilyn, and Michael Eberhardt. *From Commandant to Captive: The Memoirs of Stalag Luft III Commandant Colonel Friedrich Wilhelm von Lindeiner genannt von Wildau.* Raleigh, NC: Lulu, 2015.

Williams, Eric. *The Tunnel.* London: Collins, 1959.

Williams, Eric. *The Wooden Horse.* London: Collins, 1949.

NEWSPAPERS & JOURNALS

American Legion Magazine, December 1957
Atlanta Journal, February 1945
Baltimore Sun, 1981
Ex-POW Bulletin, January 1993
Fort Worth Star-Telegram, May 1971
Galveston Daily News, February 1945
Lethbridge Herald, Alberta, Canada, February 1945
Los Angeles Times, March 2013
Madison County (GA) Journal, May 2002
Military History, vol. 1, no. 4, February 1985
Moorhead (WI) Daily News, February 1945
Oflag 64 Item, 1943–1945
Port Charlotte (FL) Sun, February 2003
Post Oflag 64 Item, 1994
Providence Journal, December 1985
Prisoners of War Bulletin, vol. 3, no. 3, March 1945, American National Red Cross, Washington, DC
Racine (WI) Journal-Times, February 1945
Salt Lake City Tribune, February 1945
Stars and Stripes, Mediterranean Edition, April 1945
World War II Times, 1985

UNPUBLISHED MANUSCRIPTS

Hall, Norley. "Living Hell: The True Story of Mays W. Anderson and His Life as a German POW." Available online at the Oflag 64 website: oflag64.us/escape-to-russia.html.

Hill, Jonel C. "A Personal Reminiscence about My Adventures as a 19-Year-Old Draftee from Southern Minnesota, an Infantry Private in Europe in World War II." Jonel C. Hill, Company F., 26th Infantry Regiment, 1st Infantry Division. Available online at the Oflag 64 website: oflag64.us/escape-to-russia.html.

LETTERS

William R. Cory to Bob Thompson, September 1, 2002. Private Collection.
Colonel Thomas D. Drake to Mr. and Mrs. J. B. Campbell, November 24, 1944. Dwight Eisenhower Archive, 35104, Heritage Auctions, 2009.
General Dwight D. Eisenhower to Mr. and Mrs. J. B. Campbell, April 12, 1943. Dwight Eisenhower Archive, 35104, Heritage Auctions, 2009.
Mrs. Mamie Eisenhower to Lt. Craig Campbell, January 22, 1943. Dwight Eisenhower Archive, 35104, Heritage Auctions, 2009.
Mrs. Mamie Eisenhower to Lt. Craig Campbell, June 22, 1943. Dwight Eisenhower Archive, 35104, Heritage Auctions, 2009.
Mrs. Mamie Eisenhower to Mrs. J. B. Campbell, April 25, 1945. Dwight Eisenhower Archive, 35104, Heritage Auctions, 2009.

TELEGRAMS

War Department to Mr. and Mrs. J. B. Campbell, June 11, 1943. Dwight Eisenhower Archive, 35104, Heritage Auctions, 2009.
General Dwight D. Eisenhower to Mr. and Mrs. J. B. Campbell, April 4, 1945. Dwight Eisenhower Archive, 35104, Heritage Auctions, 2009.
Colonel Ernest Lee to Mr. and Mrs. J. B. Campbell, March 28, 1945. Dwight Eisenhower Archive, 35104, Heritage Auctions, 2009.

OFFICIAL DOCUMENTS

A Debriefing of Colonel Paul R. Goode, SAO at Oflag 64 and Oflag XIII-B, and a Debriefing of Lt. Colonel James W. Lockett, interned at Oflag XIII-B. US Military Intelligence, CPM Branch, EX Report No. 617, May 17, 1945.
American Prisoners of War in Germany. Oflag 64. Military Intelligence Service, War Department. July 15, 1944, and November 1, 1945.

DIARIES

Schubin diary of Ed Ward, courtesy of Ed Ward, Jr.

World War II POW Journal of Thornton V. Sigler. Available online at
    https://archieve.org/details/WwiiPowJournalOfThorntonV.Sigler.

RADIO BROADCAST

"From USA to Szubin," May 13, 1971, Polskie Radio, Poland. English tran-
    script courtesy of Mariusz Winiecki.

WEBSITES

Oflag 64 Association. www.oflag64.us.
Winiecki, Mariusz. *The Oflag 64 Record*, blog. oflag64altburgund.blogspot
    .com.
Taskforce Baum (Germany). www.taskforcebaum.de.
The Patton Saber, Winter 2011. www.generalpatton.org/Patton_Saber/Patton
    Saber_Winter11.htm.

INDEX